# AMERICANS FROM GERMANY:

## A STUDY IN CULTURAL DIVERSITY

MINORITIES IN AMERICAN LIFE SERIES

# AMERICANS FROM GERMANY:

## A STUDY IN CULTURAL DIVERSITY

ROBERT HENRY BILLIGMEIER

UNIVERSITY OF CALIFORNIA, SANTA BARBARA

WADSWORTH PUBLISHING COMPANY, INC.
Belmont, California

General Editor: Alexander DeConde
University of California, Santa Barbara

THE IRISH IN THE UNITED STATES
John B. Duff, Seton Hall University

THE CHALLENGE OF THE AMERICAN DREAM:
THE CHINESE IN THE UNITED STATES
Francis L. K. Hsu, Northwestern University

THE AMERICAN ITALIANS: THEIR HISTORY AND CULTURE
Andrew F. Rolle, Occidental College

AMERICANS FROM GERMANY: A STUDY IN CULTURAL DIVERSITY
Robert Henry Billigmeier, University of California,
Santa Barbara

Designer: Robert Gross

© 1974 by Wadsworth Publishing Company, Inc., Belmont, California 94002. All rights reserved. No part of this book may
be reproduced, stored in a retrieval system or transcribed, in
any form or by any means, electronic, mechanical, photocopying,
recording or otherwise, without the prior written permission of
the publisher.

ISBN 0-534-00355-9

L. C. Cat. Card No. 74-77331

Printed in the United States of America

1 2 3 4 5 6 7 8 9 10—78 77 76 75 74

This book is dedicated to the memory of my parents
Henry and Meta Masüger Billigmeier and to
my grandparents Georg and Johanna Serr Billigmeier
and Christian and Berta Wendorff Masüger
and above all to my wife
Hanny Salvisberg Billigmeier
whose help and counsel were indispensable.

# SERIES PREFACE

The *Minorities in American Life* series is designed to illuminate hitherto-neglected areas of America's cultural diversity. Each author treats problems, areas, groups, or issues that cannot ordinarily be examined in depth in the usual surveys of American history and related subjects. Although all the volumes are connected to each other through the unifying theme of minority cultures, the series is flexible and open to a number of uses. For example, two or more volumes can be used as units in a comparative study. Each will bring out the distinctive features of an ethnic group, but together the books may show the common as well as the unique features and experiences of each minority studied.

In varying degrees every book includes narrative, analysis, and interpretation. Each is written simply, clearly, and intelligently by an authority on its subject, and all reflect the most recent scholarship. Some restate, with fresh insights, what scholars may already know; others present new syntheses, little-known data, or original ideas related to old concepts; and all are intended to stimulate thought, not merely to pass on information. By opening minority studies to young people, the series also meets a social and educational need. By providing short, sound, and readable books on their life and culture, and by accepting them on their own terms, the series accords minorities the justice and appreciation for their heritage that they have seldom received. By dealing with live issues in a historical context, it also makes the role of minority culture in American life meaningful to young people and opens new doors to an understanding of the American past and present.

Alexander DeConde

# PREFACE

In the pages that follow I have sought to delineate in
both general and specific terms the complex social experience
of one of America's most significant cultural and population
components.  The history of German immigration extends back
well into the seventeenth century and the account that follows
is, in some measure, a longitudinal case study of one of the
oldest and largest immigrant populations in the United States.
In another sense it is an account of a constellation of diverse
elements from Germany each of which, while culturally similar
to the others, has nonetheless distinctive qualities of its own.

As a social scientist and historian with strong interests
in social and cultural history, I have tried to impress upon
the reader the sense of the rich complexity of the social experience of the highly differentiated streams of settlers who
came to North America from German-speaking territories: their
uprooting from European soil, the arrival in their New World,
their competition with other social and ethnic groups for a
place in the economy, their modes of accommodation in the new
social milieu as well as their gradual acculturation and
finally assimilation into American society.  It is my hope that
the proposition is abundantly clear from what I have written
here that one cannot fruitfully study an immigrant group or an
ethnic minority by itself as something apart from the dominant
element in society or indeed from other ethnic segments.  All
such groups are involved in a common social system, and what
happens to each of them cannot be fully understood without an
appreciation of this common involvement.

The years I have spent in studying and teaching in the
field of inter-ethnic relations are, I hope, reflected in the
manner in which the experience of German-speaking immigrants
has been described and analyzed.  While acknowledging that
every immigrant group's experience is unique and that the particular social circumstances of the groups in contact are not
likely to be repeated in all the major specificities, there are

nevertheless certain recurrent patterns in the experience of all immigrant groups. Recognition of these similarities of experience provides us with helpful insights that may serve to illuminate the social experience of the individual groups.

At the end of the task of writing the book I remain deeply fascinated by the complexities and intricacies of the processes that transformed German immigrants into Americans. I can only hope, and do so fervently, that the reading of this book will lead others to share this fascination and enthusiasm.

I wish to acknowledge the debt I owe to Albert Faust whose great work, *The German Element in the United States*, first published in 1909, has provided all later students of this field with invaluable historical materials. For the interest and encouragement of friends and colleagues I am grateful. I wish to thank Professor Moses Rischin, California State University at San Francisco, Professor Robert E. Ward, The Society for German-American Studies, and Alexander DeConde, series editor, University of California at Santa Barbara, for their numerous corrections and their many valuable suggestions. Finally I would like to acknowledge the motivation that comes from my Swiss and German family background and from having spent much of my boyhood in a largely German-speaking community in Sheridan County, North Dakota.

# CONTENTS

## INTRODUCTION

# 1

# 3

## THE PENNSYLVANIA GERMANS FROM THE AMERICAN REVOLUTION TO THE FIRST WORLD WAR 110

# 4

## THE EFFECTS OF HYPHENIZATION AND TWO WORLD WARS 120

# CONCLUSION

## THE GERMAN-AMERICANS AND AMERICAN CULTURAL DIVERSITY 171

# INDEX

# INTRODUCTION

## AMERICAN ETHNIC DIVERSITY AND THE GERMAN-AMERICANS

The cultural diversity arising from the complex mingling of the cultures of Europe, Asia, Africa, and that of the American Indians has produced a cultural pluralism that is one of the chief characteristics of American life. The various ethnic components of the population of the United States share a common culture and a common national identity despite their internal differences. Beyond this shared culture there yet remains a diversity that has given depth and color to the character of communities and regions. Ethnic diversity, provided by the Poles, Italians, Swedes, English, Germans, Irish, Africans and Japanese, has been thus far sufficiently preserved to prevent the emergence of a monotonously homogeneous, cultural mass extending from one end of the continent to the other. Assimilation is not so complete that one can say, unequivocally, that these groups are now ethnic components only in a limited, residual, and subjective sense.

If the diversity is associated with a number of unresolved problems in human relationships, to which Americans desperately need to address themselves, it does have a more positive side of vast importance. Ethnic group affiliation may well be a countervailing force to what is often described as the impersonality of modern society where individual identity is blurred into the undifferentiated mass of mankind.

The significance of national origins to individuals varies greatly from one person to another. Some people attach little importance to their ethnic background—they may indeed have a very vague notion of what it is. At any rate, they are not at all conscious of any special relevance that ethnicity may have to their lives.

Ethnic background does have substantial meaning to other individuals because it seems to be reflected in their interests, preferences, attachments, and behavior. It figures significantly in the way they identify themselves, and in the way they think of themselves. Ethnic origin, as Andrew Greeley reminds us in his insightful book, is one of a number of ways in which we may identify ourselves and it may form a significant part of our self-image.[1]   Actually we know surprisingly little about the ways in which ethnicity becomes meaningful in some lives and not in others—for whom it is meaningful, in what context, and under what conditions.

One of the writer's most esteemed professors during his undergraduate and graduate years at a university on the Pacific coast was an historian whose ancestors came from Germany during the colonial period.   Still he identified himself as being of German descent.   It seems fair to assume that the fact that he went to Germany to study and received his Ph.D. from Heidelberg was in some measure influenced by his consciousness of ethnic origin.   The durability of such identification in a family whose life in America extends well over two centuries must have obvious significance.

In a sample survey conducted by the U.S. Census Bureau in November, 1969, Americans were asked to identify their national origin.   Almost half of the people responded that they were simply "American," meaning that their origins were so mixed that no single country of origin could be appropriately named or that their family's arrival occurred so far in the past that the time and place of emigration had been lost to memory.

Thirty-eight percent of the people listed European countries as the place of family origin.   The largest number of people registered in national contingents—twenty million of them—designated Germany as the land of their ancestry.   The next largest group—nineteen million—listed England, while thirteen million gave Ireland as their ancestral homeland. Nine million listed themselves as being of Spanish origin; seven million as Italian; four million as Polish; and so on.[2] In a newspaper article covering the Bureau of the Census release on the data, the news writer explained that more recent immigrant groups retain a strong sense of their origin and that this sentiment diminishes with time.   It was erroneously explained that the reason the largest contingent listed Germany as their ethnic origin was that the German immigrants came largely in the late nineteenth century.   However, inasmuch as none of the three largest national groups is part of "New Immigration" streams that developed into full flow between 1880 and 1914, some other explanation is needed.   German settlers, like the English, Dutch, and Scotch-Irish, already formed a significant part of the population in the eighteenth century.

Settlers from German lands began to establish their communities in colonial America almost a century before the signing of the Declaration of Independence.   As the population of the British colonies expanded in the eighteenth century, German families came in substantial enough numbers to become a significant element in the colonial population along with the

English, Scots, Scotch-Irish, Dutch, French, and Africans.  If
it is true that the most notable characteristic of the United
States is the quality it possesses by virtue of having achieved
the amalgamation of many peoples and the fusion of many cultures, one must acknowledge that this condition was already
apparent in the eighteenth century.  The several peoples, among
them the Germans, who came in significant numbers in the colonial period introduced a diversity that was to be magnified by
the heavier and more heterogeneous streams of immigrants who
came to the United States after 1840 and particularly after the
Civil War.  German immigrants came from a part of western
Europe highly fragmented into a large number of small sovereign
states, varying much in size and population and distinguished
by significant differences in social character and culture.
Germany, before its unification in 1870 under the leadership of
Prussia, was in reality a general geographical designation for
a constellation of sovereign states only loosely associated
with one another.  "Germany is undoubtedly a very fine country," wrote David Hume in 1748, "full of industrious honest
people, and were it united, it would be the greatest power that
ever was in the world."[3]  But unlike France and England, Germany was not unified; it remained a loose confederation of independent states until 1870.  This looseness of the political
structure permitted the widest variability in social life.

    In any study of German immigrants in America, one of the
first tasks is to define what is meant by *German* and to describe specifically who is to be placed in that category and
who is to be excluded.  The U.S. Bureau of the Census normally
has counted as Germans those who have been born within the
boundaries of the German Republic between the two World Wars
or before the wars of the German Empire; and, before 1870, of
the German states excluding Habsburg territories and, of
course, Switzerland and Luxemburg.  The census use of the cri-
terion of national sovereignty over the territory where the
immigrant was born is sensible and practical for general statistical purposes.  It has serious deficiencies, however, in
describing the broader dimensions of the *Deutschtum* from which
America drew its large German immigrant population.  Alsatians,
although predominantly German in language and culture, were
French citizens until Alsace was taken by Bismarck from Napoleon III and were counted as French in American census at least
before 1870.  Alsatian immigrants arriving in the 1880s were
uncertain about how to respond properly to the question of
their nativity.  The same was true of immigrants from Holstein,
which was annexed to Prussia in 1864.  The Germans of Alsace
were very similar in their culture and dialect to the Germans
of Baden across the Rhine, as the Holsteiners resembled in
their social characteristics the population of German territories immediately to their south.

The German colonists who settled in autonomous communities
in Russia in the late eighteenth and nineteenth centuries were
citizens of Russia, and immigrants from Russian-German colonies
have been classified by the Census Bureau as Russians rather
than as Germans.  In language and culture as well as in their
sense of national identity, German immigrants from the Black
Sea and Volga territories were Germans.  The Saxon and Swabian
colonists who lived for centuries in Transylvania, in what is
now Romania, remained German although separated from the German
heartland by great distances.  Transylvania German immigrants
in the United States have generally annexed themselves in the
same way as Bavarians and Pomeranians have to the main body of
American Germans.  On the other hand there were many immigrants
from Germany before the First World War who, despite their
birth in Germany, were culturally non-Germans; among them would
certainly be counted the culturally Polish immigrants from West
Prussia and the Masurian areas of East Prussia.

The Swiss and Austrians have their own separate identity—
distinct and well established.  Yet one has to acknowledge that
the cultural differences between the German-Swiss and the
neighbors of Baden and Württemberg may be substantially less
than between the latter and fellow citizens of Prussia.  Especially in the colonial period, the Rhenish-Swiss and the
Rhenish-Germans were closely associated in their settlements in
Pennsylvania, New York, Georgia, and elsewhere.  It is difficult in many instances to make accurate distinctions among the
Germans, German-Swiss, and Austrians because of their close association in some areas of settlement or because the Americans
among whom they settled often could make no sense of the distinctions.

Any discussion of the meaning of the category Germans
makes one confront the impressive cultural heterogeneity of the
human population bearing this identification.

Broad statements about national and regional social character are always problematic.  Nevertheless there are persistent differences among human groups that make our generalizations possible and even necessary in facilitating relationships
with them.  Such characterizations may provide insights helpful
to an understanding of some of the primary designs in the in-
tricate tapestry of a culture.  The important caveat should be
added that the inevitable limitations of these characterizations must be recognized.  In Germany before unification, there
were differences of a substantial magnitude in the cultural,
religious, economic, and political character of the numerous
and geographically diverse states composing it.

It has been frequently observed that there are two Germanies.  One is the Germany of military virtue; of a mythology
of heroic greatness; general subordination to political authority; preoccupation with form, system, class, and duty (which is

associated largely with Prussia). The other Germany is a Germany of humanism, scholarly pursuits, scientific inquiry; the Germany of Goethe and Schiller, of Humboldt and Einstein. However, there is still yet another Germany—that of able farmers; well-trained artisans; devout, peace-loving, and diligent men and women. It was the latter Germany from which the largest proportion of settlers came in the colonial period and the early nineteenth century. These Germans came mainly from the lands along the upper Rhine: Alsace, Württemberg, Baden, German-speaking Switzerland, and above all the Palatinate. Particularly after the Revolution of 1848 in Germany and with the advent of Hitler, the scholars, scientists, engineers, artists, and humanists figured most conspicuously in immigration to the United States. The military Germany may well have been reflected in immigration but less clearly and with less tangible consequences.

The several ethnic groups that figured significantly in colonial America responded in different ways to the physical circumstances of the frontier. They responded also in different ways to the Indians, Africans, and to other European groups. Professor R. A. Billington points out that the physical environment of the frontier clearly did not recast the new settlers into a common mold.[4] The English clung tenaciously to their customs. The Scotch-Irish were quite different from the English in their response to the American environment. Their characteristic vigor, self-reliance, faith in progress, concern for functionality rather than beauty, and their aggressiveness made them especially notable among the vanguard of settlement and community building. The differences in the cultures that various national groups brought with them caused them to respond differently to the problems imposed upon them by frontier living. Even the well-knit body of customs that the ethnic groups sought to preserve in their new social and physical environment could not be preserved without important and continual modification.

American historians have not always shown sufficient understanding of the significance of difference in values and behavior among ethnic groups, nor have they appreciated the ways in which such differences added new dimensions or new designs to the complex fabric of American culture. Often, the cultural elements that set the Dutch, the Germans, the Huguenots, and the Swedes apart from the prevailing cultural group and from one another have seemed ephemeral and unimportant and, indeed, wholly outside the standard tests of historical significance. This defect has served to impoverish American social history not only in its relation to the colonial period but also to the whole sweep of national history.[5] Social scientists have given only meager help to historians in bringing them to a more sophisticated understanding of the acculturation of immigrant groups and the reciprocal influence that immigrant groups have exerted upon dominant cultural patterns. The contemporary surge of interest in ethnic groups may yield not only a better understanding of their place in American history, but a richer understanding of human behavior in general.

## NOTES

[1] Andrew M. Greeley, *Why Can't They Be Like Us, America's White Ethnic Groups* (New York: E. P. Dutton, 1971) 51.
[2] U.S. Bureau of the Census, *Current Population Report*, Series P-20, No. 221, "Characteristics of the Population by Ethnic Origin: November 1969," U.S. Government Printing Office, Washington, D.C., 1971.
[3] J. Y. T. Greig, ed., *The Letters of David Hume*, Vol. I (Oxford: Clarendon, 1969) 126.
[4] R. A. Billington, *America's Frontier Heritage* (New York: Holt, Rinehart & Winston, 1966) 73.
[5] See Frederick C. Luebke, *Immigrants and Politics* (Lincoln: University Nebraska Press, 1969).

# FROM GERMANTOWN TO MOUNT VERNON

## THE EARLIEST GERMANS IN NORTH AMERICA

The First German to set foot on American soil was probably a man named Tyrkir, the foster father of Leif Ericsson. According to the account of Leif Ericsson's expedition to Vinland as told in the Norse sagas, a crew of thirty-five men, including Tyrkir, sailed from Greenland in the high summer of the year 1001 and landed in New Foundland. The sagas relate that the German had the additional distinction of being the first European to get drunk in America, having discovered before other crew members some wild grape vines in the woods near the settlement they were building.[1]

After the voyages of Columbus to the Western Hemisphere, German scholars and cartographers took part in the activities that the discoveries stimulated. No German state, not even the Hanseatic cities, seriously considered entering the competition among the powerful states of the time for territorial rights in the New World. In the period of earliest European colonization in the Americas, German lands were troubled by political and religious disturbances. The Thirty Years War had had a devastating economic and demographic effect upon the Germanies. The Hanseatic cities of Hamburg and Bremen continued to prosper, but there was little inclination among their leaders to engage in colonial adventures. Their economic life was closely tied to England and the Netherlands, both of whom were already engaged in such colonial enterprises; the Hanseatic cities could only have suffered by entering into colonial competition with them.[2]

The first German settlers in the North American continent were members of groups composed primarily of other nationalities. There were no German expeditions or German settlements. How many such settlers there were, who they were, where they settled, and what eventually happened to them is not known because of poor historical documentation. Even where there are

fragmentary references to early German residents, we have to
bear in mind that national identifications are often uncertain
and contradictory.   There seems evidence enough to establish
the fact that a small group of Germans was included in a band
of Huguenots who settled at Port Royal in 1607, in what is now
South Carolina.   Several Germans are said to have been among
the first settlers who founded the Jamestown colony in 1607.
Even less is known about the identity of the early German settlers who were scattered in small numbers among the French,
English, and Swedish settlements along the Atlantic coast.
There were a number of Germans in the cosmopolitan population
of New Netherland.   Father Jogues estimated in 1643 that eighteen languages were spoken in New Amsterdam.   Living among the
Dutch were Norwegians, Danes, Finnish, and a number of Germans
from areas bordering on Holland.

The first German-born people to emerge into more than
local prominence in the North American colonies were Peter
Minuit and Jacob Leisler.   When the Dutch West India Company
discharged William van der Hulst as commander of New Netherland, Peter Minuit was appointed by the company to be his
successor.[3]   To most Americans the name of Minuit is associated
with the purchase of Manhattan for $24 worth of trinkets.   Un-
fortunately, historians are still uncertain whether Minuit had
actually taken up his duties as director general when the purchase was made, so credit for effecting the purchase cannot be
definitively established.   In any case, Minuit developed Manhattan Island as a trading post and purchased Staten Island
from the Indians in 1630 on behalf of the colony's *patroon* with
payment in the form of "Duffles, Kettles, Axes, Howes, Wampum,
Drilling Awls, Jews Harps, and diverse other small Wares."   By
1638 Peter Minuit had lost favor with the Dutch company and
left their employ.   This was not to end his colonial interest
in North America, however; he negotiated with the Swedish South
Company, which was interested in trade and colonization in the
New World, and helped in its efforts to found a settlement on
Delaware Bay in what is now New Jersey.   Minuit died in 1641,
and the Swedish colonial claims were absorbed into New Netherland in 1655.

One of the most notable of the early German settlers in
America was Jacob Leisler.   Born in Frankfurt-am-Main, he arrived in the province of New York as a young and penniless soldier in the employ of the Dutch West India Company.   He eventually became governor of the province for a short time and
leader of a political party that played a notable role in the
early stages of the evolution of a political party system in
New York.   Despite difficulties and bitter opposition, Leisler
and members of the Leislerian party did contribute in a significant way to the development of democratic tendencies in New
York.   They fought for the rights of the small farmer, trades-

man, urban artisan, and worker against the provincial aristocracy of merchants and large landowners.

Leisler's Rebellion in New York (1689-91) revealed the regional, national, class, and religious strains that had been
accumulating in the province over several decades.  The uprising gave indication that the democratic tendencies appearing
elsewhere in early colonial America were also beginning to appear in New York.  Here craftsmen, shopkeepers, artisans, and
small farmers found a common necessity in fighting to prevent
the emergence of an aristocracy of landed gentry and large mercantile interests.  The interplay of grievances and resentments
added momentum to the forces of rebellion.  The religious and
other discriminatory policies suffered by the Dutch majority;
the objections of New England towns on Long Island to the domi-
nation of New York; the resentment of farmers to discriminatory
laws and tax assessments; the subordination of the interests of
tradesmen and artisans to the economic advantage of the landed
and mercantile elites; public awareness of political graft and
corruption; and the widespread aspiration for a popularly elected assembly—all drew broad support to the Leisler Rebellion.

The Glorious Revolution in England produced confusion and
disorganization of political processes in New York.  The clash
of contending provincial interests became acute.  Leisler assumed leadership of the popular movement more by the demand of
his followers than by his own choice.  He had worked hard to
achieve success in trade as a young immigrant.  His fortunes
were enhanced by his marriage to the widow of a wealthy Dutch
merchant.  By the time of the outbreak of strife in 1689, he
had become a prosperous and respected merchant, justice of the
peace, and captain of the militia.  His principles and his
public behavior had been such that he was the most logical
choice to lead the popular elements.

His time as popular leader and provincial governor was
brief.  During his regime, both commercial and agricultural
monopolies were dissolved.  Tax burdens were more equitably
apportioned.  Most significantly, self-government was furthered
by the convening of a representative assembly.  This assembly
instituted reforms that put an end to many economic and political abuses that had previously caused such widespread dissatisfaction.

Leisler's enemies were able to convince King William II
that the Leisler Rebellion was in reality directed not against
local aristocratic interests but against royal authority itself.  Leisler and his son-in-law were arrested, tried, and
hanged for treason on May 16, 1691.  Later they were publicly
exonerated and restitution was made to their families.

Much of what the Rebellion had achieved was quickly un-
done.  But the struggle of the Leislerian party continued.

The unimpeachable contribution of the Leislerlians
was in keeping alive the rather puny "democratic"
tradition in New York and in laying the foundation
for a political party (in the more modern sense of
the word) when this "democratic" tendency assumed
larger proportions.[4]

## GERMANTOWN, THE FIRST GERMAN SETTLEMENT

The first important German settlement in the American
colonies was established in 1683 on land lying between the
Schuykill and Delaware Rivers in the newly chartered colony of
Pennsylvania.  Shortly after Philadelphia was founded, a group
of German and Dutch settlers selected a site six miles away.
They called their settlement Deutschstadt, which was soon
translated into Germantown.  The new settlers were largely Mennonites and Pietists who had been converted by Quakers in their
homeland along the Rhine in western Germany.  The leader and
most eminent man among the first settlers was Franz Daniel Pastorius, a cultivated young lawyer and theologian who wrote of
his search in the wilderness of Pennsylvania for

New forest-homes beyond the mighty sea,
There undisturbed and free
To live as brothers of one family.[5]

English Quakers, among them William Penn and George Fox,
had been in missionary contact with Mennonites and other Pie-
tist groups in Germany and Holland before the settlement was
established.  They shared an emphasis upon the inner religious
life of man, upon spirituality rather than dogma, and upon
peace.  George Fox had sent followers to these areas to spread
news of his teachings as early as 1655.  In 1671 William Penn
made his first journey to communities in Holland and western
Germany as a religious messenger.  In 1671 he again went to
Germany to speak with receptive religious groups.  It was
mainly from the converts to the Quaker persuasion that the
first German settlers were drawn for the lands William Penn had
secured across the Atlantic.  For years Penn had dreamed of a
refuge for all those seeking to live in peace and religious
harmony.[6]  Like the founder of the Society of Friends, Penn was
deeply involved in the political and religious disputations
that the new religious teachings provoked in England.  But Penn
and Fox were also concerned about the troubles being experienced by those pious men and women in Germany and Holland who
were moved by the same religious spirit as English Quakers
and were seeking Truth in the same way, through the inward experience of God.  When Penn secured the lands in Pennsylvania,

his religious friends were invited to take part in their settlement.

In 1681 Charles II granted William Penn extensive American
territory, lying north of the settlements of Maryland.  In September of the following year, Penn arrived in America with one
hundred Quakers and a constitution or Frame of Government
already formulated.

Shortly after William Penn received the royal charter, a
brief description of the new land was published in London; in
the same year, 1681, a translation of this account appeared in
German as *Eine Nachricht wegen der Landschaft Pennsylvania in
Amerika*.  The land was offered for easy purchase.  Penn combined humanitarianism with business acumen.  Those who took up
settlement were promised popular government, universal suffrage, and equal rights to all persons irrespective of their
race or religion.

The news led to hurried activity among Pietists who had
become acquainted with Penn, particularly during his last journey to Germany.  They organized themselves as a company for the
purpose of buying a tract of land so that they might immediately found a settlement.  Knowledge of negotiations for purchase of land came to the attention of young Franz Daniel
Pastorius (1651-1719/20) who, being drawn to the teachings of
the Quakers, wished to take part in the settlement.  "This be-
gat," he said, "a desire in my soul to continue in their society and with them to lead a quiet, godly, and honest life in
a howling wilderness."[7]

Pastorius became an agent for the Frankfurt Land Company.
Accompanied by a small retinue of men and women to help him
prepare the later arrivals, he sailed for America in June of
1683.  The Frankfurt Company supplied no settlers; but six
weeks later, on October 6, 1863, a company of German Quaker
passengers arrived on the ship *Concord*.  The arrival of the
*Concord*, the German Mayflower, marks the beginning of the history of German immigration in the American colonies.

The sight of Philadelphia, then about two years old, inspired little awe among the new settlers.  Pastorius described
in his diary the "striking impression" that the small, raw
settlement made upon him, "coming from London, Paris, Amsterdam, and Ghent."[8]  In his journal, *Grund und Lagerbuch*, the
young lawyer and theologian confessed that "the hardships and
trials of the early settlers were great, only equalled by their
Christian endurance and indefatigable industry, so that Germantown in the early days could well be called 'Armentown,' 'the
city of the poor'".[9]  The play on words, "Germantown" and "Armentown," was apt.  Pastorius shared the hardships and endured
them as the other settlers did.  With humor he inscribed a mot-
to over the door of the simple shack in which he first lived:
*Parva domus sed amica bonis, procul est prophani* (small is my

house, it welcomes the good man, let the Godless stay away).
Pastorius enjoyed a warm friendship with Penn with whom he
dined twice a week.  He was gratified to note that Penn had
declared to his counsellors "that he loved me and the High
Germans very much and wished them to do so likewise."[10]

The early German settlers were largely tradesmen and
craftsmen who, in addition to their other skills, were profi-
cient farmers.  They were also skilled weavers, tailors, shoemakers, and carpenters.  The Germantown weavers from Krefeld
soon opened a commercial outlet for their wares in neighboring
Philadelphia, which was rapidly growing into a commercial center.  Although the success of the weavers' enterprise was very
slow, it did eventually prosper.  This is also true of some of
their other enterprises.  The first paper mill in the colonies
was opened by William Ruttinghausen (Rittenhouse) in Germantown.  The community quickly won a reputation for the enterprising character of its people and their sundry skills.

Germantown was incorporated as a town in 1689 and Pastorius became its first mayor or *burgermeister* as well as town
clerk and notary.  The early German settlers were characteristically so reluctant to hold office that fines had to be imposed upon those who refused to accept public responsibilities.
Among the Mennonites the proscriptions against involvement in
worldly affairs were particularly strong.  Mennonites were ex-
cused if they refused election to office because of their
particular religious beliefs, but others had to suffer a fine
of three pounds for such refusal.  The political interest not
only of the Mennonites, but of the other Pietists in general,
was exceedingly weak, and Pastorius complained in 1703 to William Penn about the continued unwillingness of the people to
assume their proper responsibility in public affairs.  He expressed the hope that the arrival of new immigrants might rem-
edy this defect in public life.

Pastorius was a truly remarkable man.  More than any other
person, he was responsible for the success of the Germantown
settlement.  He was well educated; he had studied at the Universities of Altdorf, Strassburg, Basel, and Jena.  "Probably
no man among his contemporaries in America," Albert Faust
wrote, "was his equal, certainly not his superior in classical
culture and encyclopedic learning."[11]  Despite the nature of
his own education and his scholarly interests, Pastorius was
fervent in his advocacy of training young people in practical
skills vital to the progress of the community.  "Never," he
said, "have metaphysics and Aristotelian logic made a savage
a Christian, far less earned a loaf of bread."[12]  When a co-
educational school was established in Germantown he became its
first head.  This was indeed a remarkable school for its time;
in addition to the usual daytime classes, it had a night school
for those who had to work during the day or who were too old
to take part in the regular classes.

The German settlers were characteristically law abiding. The problems of law enforcement were simple, and such infractions as occurred were minor. Although the Germans imbibed alcohol regularly, there was little public drunkenness recorded in community records. In 1693 Germantown acquired stocks for the public punishment of lawbreakers but the stocks received little use. Nevertheless, the local records indicate that the citizens of Germantown were not above committing misdemeanors. Peter Keurlis was fined because he had sold beer with only an innkeeper's license.[13] Georg Müller was punished for laying a wager that he could smoke "above one hundred pipes in one day." Caspar Karsten was punished for calling a policeman a rogue. Johannes Pettinger was fined two shillings in December 1694 because he "did push, and evilly handle, Johannes Kaster." This was a mild fine considering the fact that Johannes Pettinger had been in several previous scrapes.[14] In contrast to Germantown, Bradford records in his *History of Plymouth* that four men were hanged for murder in the first eighteen years of the settlement.[15]

The settlers of Germantown were in continual contact with the Indians in the neighboring woodlands. The Mennonite and Quaker settlers saw in their relationships with the Indians an opportunity to practice the principles of love and peace that they professed and to draw the Indians to Christianity by demonstrating its teachings. In letters to Europe and in other accounts Pastorius wrote detailed descriptions of the Indians and their culture. Included in his description is a list of common Indian phrases and greetings to be used in intercourse with them. Pastorius commended the Indians, "*per errorem* called savages," for their honesty, freedom from deceit, love of children, and general moral behavior. Those Indians who had least contact with those Europeans whom Pastorius called "Mouth Christians" seemed to him the most virtuous.[16] One cunning Indian had tried to sell Pastorius an eagle for a turkey, thinking that a recent immigrant from Germany would be unable to tell the difference. In 1702 Daniel Falckner wrote a book devoted in great part to a description of the Indians and their culture. "To secure and keep their confidence," he wrote, "we let them come to our houses, and do not let them go without eating and drinking, and when they come in the evening we give them permission to lie by the fire and so when we go to them they are more kindly and hospitable."[17]

Slavery was repugnant to the German settlers. In 1688 Germantown took a position against slavery that constituted the first formal action taken by any community in the colonies against its spreading system; this was a century and a quarter before the signing of the Emancipation Proclamation. The public action of the Germantown community constituted the shocked response of its inhabitants to the discovery that even some Quakers had begun to acquire slaves and that other Quakers were

sanctioning this practice.  The document, prepared in the hand-
writing of Pastorius, was addressed to the Quaker community
throughout Pennsylvania; but the Quakers did not concur against
the practice of slavery in a formal resolution until seventeen
years later.

Germantown became a magnetic immigration center, drawing
from those German-speaking Europeans who sought new opportunities and cheap land in less settled areas than Philadelphia and
its environs.  They moved to the surrounding counties of Montgomery, Berks, Lebanon, York, Lehigh, and Northampton, and into
more distant areas.

Germantown became a nucleus of cultural activity and influence for the Germans in the colonies.  Germanic cultural
life began to develop and diversify.  German language newspapers were distributed throughout the region of German settlement.  The printing press of Christopher Sauer was responsible
for many publications important to the history of German settlements in the colonies.  Because of the language barrier, few
English settlers had intimate contact with the cultural life of
the German element.  There were, however, some Anglo Americans
who knew the language well and were disposed to enter into German activities.  It is recorded, for example, that William Penn
preached a German sermon in Germantown early in the settlement's history.

Throughout the colonial period, the original character of
Germantown remained intact.  In 1773 George Washington attended
German church services in Germantown where he had taken up residence during an epidemic of yellow fever in Philadelphia.
Although in the nineteenth century Germantown's proximity to
the expanding city of Philadelphia proved fatal to its distinctive German character, the significant fact remains that
throughout the colonial period Germantown remained one of the
major centers of German influence and population dispersion.

One of the earliest and most distinctive groups of German
immigrants to reach Germantown was a religious sect known as
the Mystics.  They made their settlement near Germantown in the
hills along the Wissahichon River.  Their leader, Johann Kel-
pius, found a natural cave among the rocks of the hills and en-
larged it for his dwelling.  The reputation of the mystical
healing powers of the saintly recluse spread throughout Pennsylvania and many came seeking enlightenment and healing.  Kel-
pius and his Mystic followers cast horoscopes for those who
wished to appeal to the stars for favorable influence in their
lives.

The Cloister of Ephrata was founded by a group of Seventh-
Day Baptists led by Conrad Beissel who were seeking to seclude
themselves from the wickedness of the world.  All property of
the Cloister and the religious community was held in common.
The brothers and sisters shared diligently in the work of the

community and the order prospered.  Tonsure and monkish robes
were adopted and gave the Cloister a picturesque quality.  A
school was established and a printing press printed many textbooks.  Ancient languages and mathematics were taught but the
Cloister was best known for its music and the beauty of its
illustrated manuscripts.

Mennonites who had been converted to the teaching of the
Quakers were among the first settlers in Germantown.  Another
small stream of Mennonite settlements began in 1707 when a
number of families who had heard favorable reports from earlier
settlers arrived in Germantown.  They formed the vanguard of
the Mennonite communities that were founded later in the century.  The largest migration of German and German-Swiss Mennonites to America took place between 1717 and 1732 when approximately three thousand went from the Rhenish Palatinate to
Pennsylvania.

## THE PALATINES IN NEW YORK

By the time of the American Revolution, people of German
origin constituted one of the largest ethnic strains in the
colonies.  Pennsylvania was the most popular settlement; approximately one out of every three persons living there was a
German-American.

Although German-speaking people came to the American
colonies from all the principalities that constituted eighteenth-century Germany, most of the German settlers came from
lands along the Rhine, the Palatinate, Baden, Württemberg, and
Switzerland.  So many were from the Palatinate (*Pfalz*) that the
term Palatine was often applied to all Germans.  Thus one might
hear an English colonial speak of a "Palatine from Hamburg."
In order to answer such questions as "what kind of people came
to the colonies?" and "what were their reasons for leaving
their homes and homeland?", one must consider the social milieu
in which they lived.  Although it is not easy to reconstruct
the considerations that led individuals to decide to emigrate
to America, it is possible to elucidate not only some of the
factors that served to push them from Germany but also those
that served to pull them to the New World.

The Thirty Years War left cruel marks on the people of
Germany.  The Rhenish lands in the southwest were devastated.
The area was among the most productive agricultural land in
Germany and its recuperative powers were strong.  Each recovery
was shortlived; each period of prosperity ended abruptly.  In
1668 Louis XIV devastated the Palatinate, partly because of his
religious policies.  The Palatinate and neighboring lands were
repeatedly invaded by contending armies.  In 1674 Louis XIV
sent Marshall Turenne into the area and again a systematic

despoliation brought widespread devastation and poverty.  The
disputes of the small neighboring states of western Germany
added to the misery and destruction.  In 1680, Worms and other
Rhenish cities were reduced to ashes.

During the War of Spanish Succession, southwestern Germany
was again to suffer the ravages of conquest and occupation.[18]
Its position as a borderland between France and the Germanies
made it particularly vulnerable.  French forces under Marshall
Villars crossed the Rhine in 1707 to terrorize once more the
territories of the Palatinate, Württemberg, and Baden.  The
inhabitants, just recovering their prosperity after a few years
of relative peace and well-being, were again rendered miserable.  The extremely cruel winter of 1708-9 increased their
travail and froze the vast Rhenish vineyards and orchards, a
fact which helps explain why so many of the emigrants were vine
dressers and orchardists.

The financial pressures that the rulers of small German
states put upon their subjects were severe in this period.  The
ambition of the petty rulers to imitate the splendor of the
court of the Sun King in France required the heavy flow of
taxes into the state treasuries.  Such ambitions to establish
miniature Versailles in the small German states further threatened the economic stability of the populace.

Religious disputes added to the general dissatisfaction
that fed the impulse to emigrate.  Religious persecution at
certain times and places was serious enough to compel many to
seek relief through emigration.  While some measures of religious stability had by this time been established in Germany
with the official recognition of the Lutheran, Reformed, and
Catholic churches, there was still much religious discontent,
especially among dissenters.  Various sects not recognized and
not officially tolerated had greater difficulty following their
religious beliefs.  The Anabaptists or Mennonites, Quakers,
Schwenkfelders, Amish, and other religious groups were often
persecuted, even systematically.  In the Swiss canton of Bern,
where political and economic circumstances were far more favorable, religious persecution was the main reason for the departure of the Anabaptists; indeed, many of them were expelled
and found refuge in the Palatinate and Holland before coming to
the American colonies.  Apart from the religious climate, the
general social atmosphere provoked in many religious minds the
hope that somewhere like-minded men could gather together in
communities where love and peace could govern their lives.

Popular unrest contributed to the emigration impetus.  But
just as important in determining the direction and the size of
the movement were the encouragements to mobility provided by
the spreading news that the lands across the Atlantic were
promising and being opened to settlement.  William Penn was an
effective publicist on behalf of the colonies, and consequently

Pennsylvania was by far the colonial area best publicized in
Germany.  A number of books and reports on the English colonies
gained wide circulation and fed readers' hopes for a better
life.  The work of Pastorius had become widely known.  The Rev-
erend Joshua Kocherthal's report on Carolina (*Aussführlich und
umständlicher Bericht von . . . Carolina*), published in Frankfurt in 1709, went into its fourth edition in that year.  A
British parliamentary committee investigating the causes of the
immigration reported in 1711 cited the numerous "books and
papers dispersed in the Palatinate with the Queen's picture
. . . to encourage them to come to *England* in order to be sent
to *Carolina* or other of her Majesty's Plantations to be settled
there."[19]

Beginning in the fall and winter of 1708, people in various communities along the Main, Neckar, and Rhine Rivers left
their homes and began to move down the Rhine in small groups
toward Holland.  By April 1709, there were nine hundred Palatines gathered in Rotterdam hoping that they might get to England and from there be provided transportation to the American
colonies.  The English diplomatic representative in Holland,
James Dayrolle, saw them as a "strong and laborious people" who
could contribute much to England if they could be transported
to the wilderness of America.[20]  They were by this time without
even the funds needed to pay for their transportation to England.  Dayrolle asked the great English general, Marlborough,
to secure Queen Anne's permission to use British naval trans-
ports to bring them to England.  Permission was granted to use
the naval ships being using in the War of Spanish Succession
for this peaceful purpose.  By early May there were 1283 persons waiting to be transported and on May 13 they too were
brought to England by naval convoy.

The Elector of the Palatinate was alarmed at the restless
stirring of people in his and neighboring territories.  He published an edict forbidding further emigration.  Two boats of
emigrants were seized on the Rhine by officials and the passengers imprisoned.  But the drift to Holland continued.  By late
May there were two thousand more at Rotterdam and each week
brought another thousand.  Only through strenuous authoritarian
measures along the paths of migration was the number diminished
somewhat in late July.  If there were any encouragement given
to emigration, Dayrolle informed his government, "you may have
half of Germany if you please, for they are all flying away not
only from the Palatinate but from all other countries in the
neighborhood of the Rhine."[21]

Most of the Palatines and others with them arrived in Rotterdam in a state of destitution.  Dutch charities gave them
what help they could.  By early June approximately six thousand
Palatines had been shipped to England at British expense.  Others managed to get to England on their own when the British

government refused to provide transportation.   By midsummer
eleven thousand refugees were gathered in London, housed in
crowded and unhealthy quarters, anxiously expecting to be
transported to America immediately.   While the government and
the proprietor of colonial lands welcomed Germans willing to
settle in the colonies, they were unprepared for the avalanche.
Various plans were advanced to settlement in England.   Many
were sent to Ireland where they were welcomed for their agricultural skills by Protestant landlords.   A larger number went
to Pennsylvania.

The Lord Proprietors of Carolina were among the first to
make proposals for the relocation of Palatines in their territory.   A party of promoters from Switzerland, led by Christopher von Graffenried and Franz Michel, purchased ten thousand
acres between the Neuse and Cape Fear Rivers in North Carolina.
In October 1709, the commissioners in charge of settling the
Palatines permitted Graffenried and Michel to pick out six
hundred Palatines for their settlement.   They chose young,
healthy, and industrious people of various trades useful in
such settlement.   Later more were sent.

The settlers arrived in America after a long journey that
took many lives and left many others weak and ill.   French pri-
vateers captured a ship carrying the best supplies that had
been gathered for the settlement.   To make matters worse, disputes among colonial officials added to the hardships of the
Palatines.   When Graffenried arrived on the Neuse he found
misery and wretchedness that were almost indescribable.   He
assisted the settlers in establishing themselves on the land
and in founding the town that they called New Bern.

Their problems were not ended, however.   In 1711, the
neighboring Tuscarora Indians attacked the settlement.   Houses
were burned, furniture destroyed, cattle slaughtered, and about
seventy settlers murdered or captured.   After the hostilities
ended, the Palatines slowly managed to secure titles to the
land and in time prospered.   Within a generation they were
scattered over a wide area of North Carolina.

A group of Palatines were sent from London to New York in
1710.   For more than a decade before their departure, proposals
had been made to establish communities of settlers in New York,
or elsewhere in the colonies, who could work the pine forests
and produce naval stores.   Tar and pitch were needed by the
British navy now establishing its leadership among the navies
of the world.   At the time England secured most of its naval
stores from Sweden, and the Swedish companies made them pay
dearly for these products.   Aside from the exorbitance of these
transactions, it was clearly dangerous for Britain to be dependent upon another power for products so vital to its naval
vessels.   A plan was formulated by the British government in an
effort to meet obligations it felt it had to the Palatine

refugees in England and at the same time to establish an industry that would solve the problem of naval stores.  This project
had the added merit of establishing a community of hardy Palatine settlers as a bulwark against the Indians on the vulnerable frontier of the New York colony.  The enterprise reflected
the government's desire to develop in the northern colonies a
staple crop or product that could be exchanged by the colonists
for the purchase of English manufactures.

A group of the Palatines sailed with Governor Lovelace and
settled about fifty-five miles north of New York City on the
frontier.  Newburgh was founded as a German community.  During
the governorship of Lovelace, a system of allowances supported
the colonists in the initial efforts to establish the naval
stores industry.  After the death of Lovelace the system of
support broke down.  Efforts were made by political authorities
to place the Palatines into the status of indentured servants
for an unspecified period until profits not only paid the ex-
penses of the enterprise itself but also paid back the Queen
for costs of transportation and settlement.  In April 1710, approximately 2,500 Palatine immigrants arrived in New York City,
weak and ill from the rigors of the voyage.  At a time when the
population of New York City amounted to only 4,846 and 910
slaves (according to a count in 1712), the arrival of so many
aliens, especially in their condition of health, seemed to
threaten the health and welfare of the city's population.  Most
of the German immigrants were sent to the settlements devoted
to the production of naval stores.  The history of the efforts
at governmental operation of the naval stores industry is brief
but otormy.  The enterprise was abandoned in 1711 when a shift
in British government ushered in a new Ministry.  The plans for
the enterprise had been too hastily laid and too much involved
in political rather than economic concerns.

After a difficult transitional period, the German settlers
acquired land and became farmers on their own without the yoke
of indenture that the enterprise had threatened to impose upon
them.  Many of the highly individualistic Palatines pushed the
frontier before them as they moved on to settlements in the Mohawk and Susquehanna Valleys.  Today many of their descendants
still hold the lands their ancestors occupied in the 1720s.

Palatine families became important in colonial New York
City.  One of the most notable of the early Palatines was John
Peter Zenger who arrived in 1710.  He was among the forty-one
children forcibly taken from their families by the colonial
regime and placed in apprenticeships in New York City.  As a
boy of thirteen Zenger was apprenticed to William Bradford who
was then the only printer in the city.  In 1725 Bradford began
the publication of the city's first newspaper and Zenger became
his partner.  In 1733 Zenger left his partnership and began the
publication of the first independent newspaper in New York.

The young Palatine publisher became a principal in a libel
trial that was widely seen by contemporaries as a monumental
triumph of the popular will over the machinery of aristocratic
government.  The trial of Zenger was long interpreted by American historians as a most important victory for freedom of the
press against arbitrary rulers who sought to suppress or control it.  More recently historians have found that Zenger and
those who undertook his legal defense against colonial governmental action were not the selfless democratic reformers they
seemed to be.  Nor was the trial itself quite as monumental in
its consequences for the history of American freedom of the
press as earlier American historians contended.[22]  More recent
studies of the circumstances surrounding Zenger's trial reveal
that the pro-Zenger party and the governmental party may have
been more interested in advancing private political interests
than in establishing important principles of law.  Nevertheless
the Zenger trial serves as a symbolic representation of the
growth of political freedom in America.  The name of the modest
and apparently unheroic printer and publisher remains linked
with the notion that personal freedom can survive only if the
individual's right to criticize men in high public office remains an important principle and an acceptable demonstration
of individuality.  The man Zenger and his trial are chiefly
significant for what they forecast about the evolution of
American conceptions concerning freedom of expression in the
press.

## THE DISPERSION OF GERMAN SETTLERS

From the beginning, Pennsylvania was characterized by
ethnic diversity.  Throughout the colonial period it was the
most heterogeneous of the American colonies.  In addition to
the Indians, the three major groups were the English, the
Scotch-Irish, and the Germans (including German-speaking
Swiss).  Although members of each group were much scattered
throughout the province, the English were largely concentrated
in the east, the Scotch-Irish in the west, and the Germans between the two.[23]  While there was an intermingling of peoples
in this area even in the earliest years of contact, the territorial concentration and the strength of cultural attachments
were sufficient to preserve three distinct traditions.  There
were, in addition to the three groups, a considerable number of
Welsh, Swedish, Huguenots, Dutch, and others who added to the
diversity of Pennsylvania.

The second current of German immigration began about 1710
with the arrival of Anabaptist families who settled in Lancaster County.  By 1717 the movement of Anabaptist groups had
reached significant proportions.  Between 1717 and 1732 thou-

sands of Anabaptists emigrated from the Palatinate and other
Rhenish areas to find homes in the American wilderness.[24]   Some
were Amish, followers of an Anabaptist elder named Jakob Amman;
they had fled to the Palatinate and Holland seeking refuge from
persecution by the government of the Swiss canton of Bern.   Not
finding the hoped for refuge, they moved on to Penn's promised
haven.   A larger Anabaptist group, the Mennonites, began to
arrive in substantial numbers to form the Mennonite congregations whose branches were ultimately to spread across the
United States and Canada.   The persistent conditions of social
and political unrest in German lands along the Rhine continued
to give impetus to movement.   The cordial invitation of the
Penns to the victims of religious persecution to settle in
their lands was potent in directing the flow of migration.   The
favorable reports of friends and relatives who had established
themselves in Pennsylvania added strength to the attraction.
America fever spread so virulently through the Mennonite congregations of the Rhenish territories that these congregations
were soon almost depleted.   Later Mennonite groups, among them
the Bernese Anabaptists who emigrated from the Jura in 1754,
were quickly amalgamated into established Mennonite settlements
in Lancaster County.

Other Anabaptist congregations were attracted by the sympathetic interest of the Penn family.   The Dunkards, or Tun-
kers, were first represented by a group of twenty families who
settled in 1719 in the growing communities of Germantown and
Skippack.   One of the most prominent men among the growing congregations of this sect was the printer, Christoph Sauer who
printed the first German Bible in America.   The Sauer family
published a German language newspaper *Der Hoch-Deutsch Pennsyl-
vanische Geschichts-Schreiber*, which won wide circulation
throughout the region.   The power of his newspaper made Sauer
one of the most influential men in Pennsylvania and enabled him
to serve his faith and spread knowledge of its principles.

The diversity of German Protestantism increased with the
arrival of the Schwenkfelders in the American colonies.   Kasper
Schwenkfeld, a contemporary of Luther, was a leader of the
Reformation in the area of Silesia.   His followers suffered
long persecution.   When the Emperor Charles VI sent a Jesuit
mission to Silesia in 1720 to complete their extermination,
many fled to Saxony where they found refuge on the estate of
Count Zinzendorf.   On September 24, 1734, the families that had
survived the relentless persecution arrived in Philadelphia,
leaving no organized congregations behind them in Europe.

These sects and smaller ones became known in the New World
as the Plain People because the simplicity of their dress and
manner set them apart so obviously.   The Plain People shared
many principles: a belief in the possibility of atonement for
all men rather than just the elect, nonviolence and opposition

to military service, religious freedom and tolerance, resistance to the state's intrusion on religious life, and a democratic church polity.  In order to preserve their way of life, their *Weltanschauung*, they settled largely as congregations rather than as families or individuals.  It made them less mobile and their values and way of life more stable.  They were chiefly characterized by a staunch unwillingness to be so transformed by the world that their religious values would erode and be lost.  If they could not transform the world, they could at least ensure the survival of their beliefs in that portion of it contained in their settlements.  They were successful, both in a religious and a financial sense.  If the cost of religious life in their terms meant cultural isolation, enough of them were prepared to pay that price to ensure the survival of their religious community.  What the surrounding world has seen as strange unworldliness or even fanatical, fantastic, or anachronistic behavior, they have seen as a way of life that appropriately puts religious values first.

In contrast to the Plain People, the Church People were members of the leading Protestant denominations in Germany, the Lutherans and the German Reformed Church.  Smaller in number in the early period of German influx, their representation became larger and larger until by the time of the American Revolution they far outnumbered the sects.  It was in largest part the Lutherans and the Reformed settlers who gave shape to Pennsylvania German (or Pennsylvania Dutch) culture.  Their influx represented a broadening of the streams of immigration as communities in Württemberg, Baden, Alsace, Hesse, Nasau, Hanau, Anhalt, Lippe, Bremen, and other western German lands, as well as the Palatinate and Switzerland, yielded increased numbers of German-speaking settlers to America.  There were also Catholic Germans among the colonial settlers, but they were not numerous.

The Lutheran congregations in America were fortunate in the quality of the pastors sent to minister to them: Pastors Justus Falckner, William Berkenmeyer, and others ministered effectively to their scattered German flocks, but also served Swedes, Danes, Norwegians, and Transylvanians as well as Negroes, both free and slave.[25]  The greatest among these pastors was Heinrich Melchior Mühlenberg who came to Pennsylvania in 1741 to minister unto three congregations.  He had prepared well for his profession at the Universities in Göttingen and Halle.  Fortunately for the German Lutheran congregations, he was a man of great energy whose tactfulness matched his zeal.  He brought the Lutherans into close cooperation with the German Reformed Church as well as with the Episcopal Church.  Michael Schlatter, leader of the Reformed Church, joined forces with Mühlenberg in advancing the interest of the Protestant Churches.  But they countered the views of the state that was still Quaker dominated, as well as the religious principles of the Quakers,

Mennonites, Amish, and the Moravians in Pennsylvania. Mühlenberg's influence was augmented by his marriage. His wife was
the daughter of Conrad Weiser, who more than anyone else served
to stabilize relations between whites and Indians in Pennsylvania.

The third religious tradition represented among the colonial Germans was that of the Moravians (also known as United
Brethren or Herrnhuter). The Moravians (descendants of the
Hussites) settled in Georgia in 1735-36 among the Salzburgers
at Ebenezer. During the war with Spain when they were expected
to bear arms in defense of the colony despite their religious
principles, they left Georgia for Pennsylvania. Count Zinzendorf visited their new Pennsylvania settlement in 1741 and gave
the place its name, Bethlehem. Here, on the first Christmas
Eve, Zinzendorf led the Moravian congregation in the singing of
his own hymns. The Moravian love of singing grew into the tradition of musical cultivation in Bethlehem, which endures to
the present and the community became noted for its Bach Choir
and annual Bach Festival.

The Moravians actively sought unity among the Protestant
groups. Moreover, they were the most effective of all religious groups in missionary work among the Indians, pushing
actively into the remotest areas of various colonies. Devoted
missionaries like Rauch, Heckenwelder, Zeisberger, Jungmann,
Post, and Sensemann gave much of their lives to spreading
Christian teachings among the Indians. An historian has called
the Moravian missionaries an "early American Peace Corps" not
only because of the zeal with which they learned Indian languages and the respect they showed for the Indians and for
their culture, but also because they lived with them and shared
the hardships of their lives.[26] The missionaries customarily
spent part of each day giving instruction in practical skills
and trades that would be useful in providing the Indians with
better dwellings and the simple items needed to furnish them,
as well as in producing more stable sources of food. Tools and
implements were introduced that the Moravians hoped the Indians
would adapt constructively to family and community needs. The
missionaries genuinely loved and respected the Indians, but
were also aware of widespread lying, cheating, theft, and violence and for this reason sought to bring the teachings of
Christ to them. The Moravian missionaries believed that the
Indians whom they served would make more rapid progress both
materially and spiritually if they were set apart from both
erring white settlers and their heathen fellow tribesmen.[27]
The conversion of Indians to Christian pacificism made them
vulnerable to attacks by aggressive whites and Indians; the
consequences were tragic for the Christian Indian communities.

One of the most fascinating men among the colonial Germans
was Conrad Weiser. His immigrant father encouraged him to live

among Indians until he learned their language.  As an adult he
made a remarkable contribution to the American colonies as an
ambassador between the Six Nations Indian League and Pennsylvania.  His sense of justice was so even-handed that a Seneca
leader lauded him after his death in 1761, as "a great man,
. . . one-half a Seven Nation Indian, and one-half an English-
man."

> We, the Seven Nations, and our Cousins are at a
> great loss, and sit in darkness, as well as you, by
> the death of Conrad Weiser, as since his Death we
> cannot so well understand one another; By this Belt
> we cover his Body with Bark.[28]

By midcentury the German population was increasing rapidly.
Philadelphia was the leading American port for immigrants from
German lands.  Pennsylvania was a populous colony with the
tradition of German immigration that continued to attract settlers.  Germans spread from the area of Philadelphia into the
surrounding counties of Montgomery, Lancaster, and Berks, and
then northward into Lehigh, Northampton, and Monroe Counties.
Despite its English name, the town of Lancaster was from its
beginning overwhelmingly German and Swiss.  By 1740 these
groups represented 75 percent of the lot-holders of Lancaster.
The appearance of the town, the language predominantly used,
and the modes of dress made the community resemble a Rhineland
*Dorf*.[29]  The Germans and Swiss moved westward into Lebanon and
Dauphil Counties, crossed the Susquehanna River and settled in
York, Cumberland, and Adams Counties, finally crossing into
western Maryland.
    By 1730 the tidewater area of Maryland had lost its fron-
tier character.  The land was largely held by plantation owners
using slave labor.  The life of the planter class was stable
and refined, patterned much on that of the English gentry.  An-
napolis, which Jonathon Boucher called "the genteelest town in
North America," was the political and social center of the
tidewater.  Only a scattering of German immigrants had settled
in the tidewater region before 1730, being little attracted by
the slave economy.
    In the third and fourth decades of the century, the fron-
tier counties that lay along the Pennsylvania boundary were
settled by farm families attracted by the generous land offers
of Lord Baltimore.  English farmers moved from the tidewater
area into the frontier.  Germans spreading from Pennsylvania
settled in large numbers on the fertile land of northern and
western Maryland.  The concentrated German settlements in Frederick County were extensions of the cultural realm of the Pennsylvania Germans.  The industrious farmers of Maryland's "old
west," in which Frederick County was central, produced abundant

crops of wheat and corn as well as livestock, which were mar-
keted in Philadelphia and Baltimore. Many of the families who
established themselves in the expanding trade and industry of
Baltimore were from Pennsylvania counties. The German settlers
did much to develop Baltimore as a capitol of foreign trade and
shipbuilding as well as of regional commerce and manufacturing.

Between 1748 and 1753 about twenty-eight hundred Palatines
settled in Maryland. German artisans and craftsmen brought
their skills and enterprise. Among them was John Frederick
Amelung, whose wineglasses, decanters, mirrors, and punch bowls
won renown for their quality. George Washington mentioned his
factory in a letter to Thomas Jefferson and received from Amelung two handmade goblets of flint glass.

A number of German communities were founded in New Jersey.
Some of the leading German families, like the Frelinghuysens
and the Rockefellers, were to play important roles in the history of the colony and state.

It is true, as the historian Faust pointed out many years
ago, that the English form a larger proportion of the white
population of Virginia than they do of most other states and
that this predominance is particularly characteristic of tidewater Virginia. In contrast, however, the Piedmont and the
Long Valley of Virginia were largely settled by Germans and
Scotch-Irish spreading southward from their settlements in
Pennsylvania.

During the governorship of Alexander Spotswood (1710-
1720), Virginian settlements moved steadily westward into the
Piedmont. Intensely interested in filling up vacant western
lands, Governor Spotswood laid the basis for the earliest German settlement in Virginia. Wishing to utilize German skill in
mining and engineering he brought, with the cooperation of
Baron von Graffenried, the twelve German families that founded
the settlement of Germanna in 1714. Later immigrants joined
them, but the mining operations did not long continue and disputes with the Governor over land titles forced them to leave
Germanna to found Germantown along the Licking Run.

It was not until the 1730s that the southward trek of the
Pennsylvania Germans and Pennsylvania Scotch-Irish led to significant settlement in the valley of Virginia. The northern
section of the Shenandoah Valley was predominantly occupied by
German farmers although Scotch-Irish and Huguenots settled
among them. The fertile Valley became a garden area whose
populace remained culturally distinct from the older tobacco
aristocracy of the tidewater.

The southern slope of the Valley of Virginia was first
settled largely by Scotch-Irish and only sparsely by Germans
until a new stream began to flow into the area after the Revolution. German and German Swiss settlements were founded at
Newbern in Pulaski County and in Wythe County. As settlements

in the Valley became more dense, migrations moved not only in a
southwesterly direction, but also eastward across mountain
passes: into Loudon, Fauquier, Rappahannock, Madison, Greene,
Albermarle, and other counties.

The Germans were, for the most part, industrious, thrifty
farmers.  They worked their farms and tended their herds with
their own hands, objecting to slave labor on the grounds that
it was both unethical and inefficient.  Members of the planter
class were scorned becaused they regarded their own labor as
demeaning.  Partly because of their religious principles and
the influence of the frontier, the Germans were strongly individualistic, even democratic.  Their resentment of the tidewater aristocracy effected an enduring influence upon the political life of the province.

The earliest settlement in the Carolinas was established
at New Bern in 1710.  Immigrants arriving by sea came to
Charleston, which became a staging area for the spread of German settlements.  In 1730, Governor Johnson secured the adoption of plans to settle Protestant immigrants in certain
frontier areas.  The basic purpose of such colonization plans
was to strengthen the defenses of the colony against such dangers as Indian attacks, slave insurrections, and the threat
posed by Spaniards beyond the frontiers.  Favorable terms attracted Swiss settlers in Purryburg on the Savannah River in
1735.  Numerous German and Swiss groups were attracted to the
Saxe-Gotha area, which later became Orangeburg and Lexington
Counties.  The first groups arrived in 1735, others in 1736
and 1737, and more particularly between 1744 and 1750.  From
Saxe-Gotha German groups spread out into surrounding areas.

Pennsylvanians of German and Scotch-Irish origins continued to fill the Shenandoah Valley and to move on southwestward
into the Carolinas.  The Germans and Scotch-Irish tended to
move in parallel but different paths, with largely separate
destinations, each founding communities in which it was the
predominant population.

The Moravians in 1753 purchased a large tract of land in
the Piedmont area of North Carolina.  From their center in
Bethlehem, Pennsylvania, Moravian families set out for the
Wachovia tract to found first the town of Bethany in 1759 and
later Salem and other settlements.  They brought their traditional love of music, their architecture, and their religion.
The Moravian emphasis upon brotherly love and peace was reflected in their missionary work among the Indians and the
Negro slaves.  Their language was eventually lost and many of
their folk ways and forms of folk art disappeared along with
the peculiarities of their dress.  One of the most enduring
heritages they left was in the traditions of their husbandry:
the careful choice of farm land, the preservation of soil
through crop rotation, use of meadowland, careful exploitation

of woodlands, deep ploughing, and the replenishing of fertility by the careful spreading of animal manure.

In 1731 Archbishop Leopold Anton von Firmian decreed that all people who were not adherents of Catholicism were to be expelled from the Austrian bishopric of Salzburg. More than thirty thousand Protestants were affected. Some Protestant rulers, among them the King of Prussia and King George II of England, welcomed the refugees to their realms.

At this time, George II granted a charter to James Oglethorpe and John Viscount Perceval to establish a colony on the southern territories that England was currently disputing with Spain. In advancing settlement, the British government hoped to build a bulwark against potential enemies on the frontier of the expanding American colonial empire. The purposes of the private trustees of the territory represented a concern to the oppressed and enslaved. They wished to make the colony a community of family farms supporting a stalwart yeomanry capable of defending their lands. For this purpose the persecuted Lutherans of Salzburg were invited to settle in the marshlands. A considerable community of Salzburgers was established along the Savannah River, centering in the town of Ebenezer. The first group arrived in Savannah in 1736. Along on the voyage across the Atlantic was the founder of Methodism, John Wesley, who was much impressed by the German immigrants. Wesley was particularly struck with the Moravian pastor, Peter Boehler, from whom he later declared he had gained more religious understanding than he had from any man.

The colony prospered and grew. German groups came to Ebenezer and spread out into other territories in Georgia. The community life of the Georgian Salzburgers had its own special character. The individual landholdings were not extensive, and the settlement was compact and isolated from other elements of the population. In all aspects of community life, the Salzburgers were strongly interwoven and intimately bound together. The Lutheran pastors, like John Martin Boltzius of New Ebenezer, exercised a strong influence over the lives of the men and women in their congregations.[30] Orphans and widows were always treated charitably, and among the first institutions they established in Georgia was an orphans' home. A traveler, Thomas Jones, wrote from Savannah in 1740 about his observations of their settlement:

> The people live in the greatest harmony with their ministers and with one another, as one family. They have no drunken, idle, or profligate people among them, but are industrious, and many have grown wealthy. Their industry has been blessed with remarkable and uncommon success, to the envy of their neighbors, having great plenty of all the necessary

conveniences for life (except clothing) within themselves; and supply this town (Savannah) with bread-
kind, as also beef, veal, pork, poultry, etc.[31]

Most of the German immigrants, although poor, came neither
from the most impoverished rural classes nor from urban slums.[32]
A large majority of them brought with them the training and
habits of diligence and thrift that served them well in their
new homeland.  But there were, of course, considerable numbers
in each immigrant group who came without any means, and sometimes without much usable training or experience, not to mention stability of habit and disposition.  Archives in German
cities, districts, and provinces yield abundant testimony to
their eagerness to rid themselves of paupers and petty offenders by encouraging or, indeed, forcing them to emigrate to the
American colonies.  Pardons were sometimes granted to offenders
on the condition that they depart immediately for the New
World.  Material aid was sometimes provided by public authorities to speed the impoverished families on their way in the
interest of the long-term financial advantages to the community.
The system of indenture by which immigrants could "travel
now and pay later," was developed in the seventeenth century
and elaborated upon in the eighteenth.  Immigrants secured
passage by contracting their services for a specific number of
years after arrival in America.  The man seeking such indenture
found a ship's captain who would provide him passage across the
Atlantic.  Upon arrival in America, the captain would sell his
passenger to the highest bidder, with the agreement that he
would serve him for a period of (generally) seven years.  Thus
the captain was assured the cost of providing passage and a
handsome profit as well.  This practice spread to Germany in
the eighteenth century with some unpleasant modifications.  The
German emigrant did not have the protection of a written contract of indenture in which the time of service and the conditions of servitude were definitely established.  His contract
with a ship's captain was only verbal and the captain remained
completely free to auction him off to any person prepared to
pay the largest sum for his "redemption."  The so-called re-
demptioners were easy victims of exploitation.  The best contemporary account of the consequent abuses were written by
Mühlenberg, Sauer, and Mittelberger.  The descriptions of suffering, found in journals such as that of Gottlieb Mittelberger,
are shockingly reminiscent of accounts of the slave trade.[33]
The Atlantic crossing was a frightful experience for most
eighteenth and early nineteenth century immigrants.  For those
coming under indenture the conditions were often incredibly
bad.  As Mittelberger noted, children between the ages of one
and seven seldom were able to survive the disease, diet, and
rigors of the ship's Atlantic crossing.  When parents died at

sea and their children survived, the children were required to work off not only their own fares but those of their parents as well. This often meant that they were required to serve until they reached the age of twenty-one. Sometimes family members were sold to different people and suffered permanent separation from one another.

## GERMAN CULTURE IN PENNSYLVANIA
## AND OTHER AMERICAN COLONIES

Christopher Sauer observed that many of the Germans who settled in colonial Pennsylvania were people of substantial means. Gottlieb Mittelberger made observations concerning the variability of class backgrounds and occupations among the early Germans in America, noting that among the immigrants were skilled workers, men of professional training, even members of the aristocracy. However, a majority of the eighteenth century German settlers arrived in North America without much wealth. Much of the resources that they had possessed at home were consumed in transporting themselves down the Rhine and across the Atlantic, and many arrived destitute. In Pennsylvania, and elsewhere in the colonies, the Germans and Swiss were able to acquire enough tillable land to permit them to prosper. Even ordinary men with limited resources shared in the abundant harvest of the New World. Characteristically they showed an indomitable energy and courage in their enterprises. They were willing to work hard; they were frugal, and they were well trained in the kind of agriculture that the soil and climate of the New World permitted. They were not always understood or liked by their neighbors, but they quickly won an enviable reputation for their honesty, skill, and diligence.

Dr. Benjamin Rush, a distinguished physician and perhaps the first psychiatrist in America, was a keen observer of the German people in his native Pennsylvania. He had grown up among them and remained throughout his life in close professional, cultural, and personal association with them. In 1789 he wrote *An Account of the Manners of the German Inhabitants of Pennsylvania*,[34] in which he showed extraordinary perceptiveness as an observer. Although he spoke mainly of the Germans of Pennsylvania and adjacent areas, what he said of their social character was largely true of Germans in other areas of settlement in the colonial and early national period. The German immigrants continued to come largely from those areas of Germany that had most abundantly yielded settlers in colonial times. They shared the same regional culture.

Pennsylvania remained throughout the first half of the nineteenth century the seedbed of German migrations westward. With their characteristically high fertility, the German

families contributed numerous sons and daughters to the westward movement.  The older children frequently inherited the
family farm and the younger children moved westward, often in
groups.  Because it was well known in Germany, Pennsylvania
continued to attract immigrants who were later to seek cheaper
lands farther west.  Where German settlement was dispersed in
the new settlements, the social character of the people soon
became less easily defined; where larger and more cohesive settlements were formed in the expanding frontier, the patterns of
culture and language use remained more stable.

Benjamin Franklin, like Benjamin Rush, noted how often
German farmers took over partly improved land and developed it.
It is striking how frequently the Germans in Pennsylvania and
elsewhere displaced English and Scotch-Irish farmers in areas
where the limestone soils were particularly good.  The Germans
bought out less successful farmers and introduced new crops and
new methods.

The Swiss and German farmers, according to their contemporaries, were more efficient in clearing the land and preparing
for agriculture than their English or Scotch-Irish neighbors.
In clearing fertile woodlands they cut down trees and bushes,
burned the stumps, and grubbed the roots out of the ground so
that the land could be immediately used and more readily plowed,
harrowed, and reaped than land less carefully prepared.  Farmers who used less strenuous methods of preparing fields for
cultivation often had to wait for years for the stumps to rot
out and suffered loss of time and the expense of repairing
ploughs and other implements that were broken by small stumps
concealed in the ground.

J. Hector St. John Crevecoeur wrote in his *Letters from an
American Farmer*: "From whence the difference arises I know not,
but out of twelve families of emigrants of each country, generally seven Scotch will succeed, nine Germans, and four Irish
. . . . The Irish do not prosper so well; . . . they seem . . .
to labor under a greater degree of ignorance of husbandry than
the others; perhaps it is that their industry had less scope,
and was less exercised at home."[35]

The Pennsylvania Germans were characteristically frugal,
but were not disposed to economize where the welfare of their
farm animals was involved.  Rush noted, as did many others, how
carefully and plentifully they fed their horses and cows so
that the animals were known for their size and health as well
as their productivity.  Generally great care was taken to avoid
overworking or abusing horses in any way that would affect
their strength and usefulness.

The milder marine climate of England did not require the
provision of sturdy barns for farm animals as was necessary in
continental Europe.  In many areas of North America, the climate exposed farm animals to severe heat in summer and cold in

winter unless properly sheltered.  Failure on the part of their
neighbors to provide adequate barns seemed both cruel and eco-
nomically foolhardy to the Swiss and German farmers.  The farmer's first enterprise after clearing his fields was to build an
immense and elaborately designed barn, even before any improvements were made in the rude family dwelling that served his
family in the early stages of their settlement.  The great
Swisser barns were built to endure for generations and became
one of the most distinguishing characteristics of the Pennsylvania German area.[36]

The construction of the permanent family dwelling often
took many years to complete; indeed, the first settlers of a
tract of land expected that their sons would begin improving
the dwelling where they left off.

The observations Dr. Rush made concerning the German farmers seemed to him to be generally applicable to German mechanics, craftsmen, and merchants as well.  Their first object was
to own their own house and hence, he noted, few of them live in
rented houses.

The Germans tended to live with deep attachment to their
land.  Generally they dwelt in compact groups in which family,
religious, language, and even economic bonds were mutually re-
enforcing.  This gave German communities much stability.  Children could rely on family and even community aid in establishing themselves on farms of their own when the right time came.
Neighborly assistance in farm work or building was common.  Social cohesion combined with intensive, effective agricultural
husbandry gave an enduring strength to communities that was not
as common among English-speaking farmers.  It was not until
late in the nineteenth century, in the face of urbanization and
spreading industrialization, that this stability began to erode
somewhat.

There appeared to be an almost organic relationship between the farm family and the farm.  Rush believed that this
sentiment prevented "much folly and vice in young people" in
addition to producing improvements in the farm, "for what in-
ducement can be stronger in a parent to plant an orchard, to
preserve forest trees or to build a commodious and durable
house, than the idea, that they will be possessed by a succession of generations, who shall inherit his blood and name."[37]
Klees noted in the middle of the twentieth century that it is
possible to find a farm in Pennsylvania German territory that
has been handed down from father to son from the time the land
was first settled over a span of perhaps eight or nine generations.[38]

Frequently the Pennsylvania Germans carved inscriptions on
the front of their stone houses, usually high up on the gabled
facade.  Sometimes the inscriptions were simply the initials of
the husband and wife who built the home and the date of its

construction.  Often the inscriptions were passages from the
Bible or expressions of religious feelings concerning the sanc-
tity of family and home.  These external marks were symbolic
expressions of the strong personal identification of families
with their dwellings.

Peter Bricker's home in Lancaster County, built in 1759,
bears the inscription:

> Gott gesegne dieses Haus
> Und alle was da gehet ein und aus;
> Gott gesegne alle sampt,
> Und dazu das ganze Land.[39]

> God bless this house
> And all those who go in and out of it
> God bless them one and all
> And the whole country too.

On the home built by Cornelius Frees in 1743 an elaborate
inscription appears:

> Was nicht zu Gottes Ehr'
> Aus Glauben geht ist Sünde;
> Merck auf, O theures Hertz,
> Verliere keine Stunde.
> Die überkluge Welt
> Versteht doch keine Waaren,
> Sie sucht und findet Koth
> Und läst die Perle fahren.[40]

> That which does not honor God is sin
> Mark well, O faithful heart
> Lose not an hour.
> The conceited world does not understand
>   truth
> It searches far and finds rubble
> And lets the pearls slip by.

The interiors were plainly finished in the beginning but
with prosperity and leisure they became less utilitarian and
more attractively designed.  The newcomers brought with them
from Europe the practice of covering themselves in winter with
feather beds instead of blankets and maintained the tradition
in Pennsylvania as a matter both of convenience and economy.
Rush notes that the apparel of the German farmers was generally
purchased.  Their stoves were designed to use wood more eco-
nomically than the fireplaces of their neighbors.  This enabled them to heat their homes more effectively and made them
more comfortable.  The warmth of their homes gave the occupants

greater freedom of movement in winter; Rush observed that
"twice the business is done by every branch of the family, in
knitting, spinning, and mending farming utensils than is done
in houses where every member of the family crowds near to a
common fireplace, or shivers at a distance from it . . . ."[41]

The traditions of the Rhineland relating to the cultivation of vegetables, fruit trees, grape vines, and flowers were
transplanted to the United States.  Dietary preferences were,
of course, reflected in the kinds of planting.  Other considerations existed as well.  Flax was a necessary source of
textiles in times and places where wolves took regular toll of
sheep.  Aesthetic interests were important.  The love of flowers was reflected not only in flower gardens but in designs on
chests, cabinets, dishes, as well as in beautiful embellish-
ments on birth and baptismal certificates.  Pennsylvania Dutch
(that is, Pennsylvania German) art is close to the *Blumen-
schmuck* brought from the Palatinate and Switzerland.

To the Pennsylvania German farmers, poorly constructed or
wobbly fences around houses, gardens, or fields were Irish
fences.  Careless and shallow plowing was Yankee plowing.  The
old adage was accepted without question: *Wie einer den Zaun
hält, hält er auch das Gut* (As one tends his fence, so he also
tends his farm).

The German farmer consistently preferred family-size farm
holdings and intensive agricultural management.  English,
Scotch-Irish, and Scotch farmers more often aspired to larger
holdings and more commercial-type farming.  The Germans sought
self-sufficiency; to be self-sufficient, families had to diversify their farm activities if the members were to be properly fed and clothed.  Family labor was well organized.  Planta-
tion-style agriculture and slavery were particularly condemned.
Later, Germans in the Piedmont area, in Missouri, and in Texas
stood more clearly than other immigrant groups in favor of
family farms run with family labor.  Farming was regarded not
so much as a commercial occupation as a way of life.

Benjamin Rush noted, as many of his contemporaries did,
that the wives and daughters of the Pennsylvania German farmers
"frequently forsake, for a while, their dairy and spinning-
wheel, and join their husbands and brothers in the labour (in)
. . . their fields and orchards."[42]  Noticing the women working
in the fields, English settlers were sometimes tempted to make
uncomplimentary comments on the physical consequences of such
labor to the women themselves and to their feminine appeal.
Then as now Pennsylvania German youngsters are likely to return
from school to do their chores on the farm while other children
run off to play.

Important to their lives were their implements, equipment,
and tools.  They created the Conestoga wagon, that "ship of
inland commerce," which was to play such a large role in the

westward movement.   The running-gear was usually painted red,
the body blue.   It was covered by a stout white linen or hemp
material stretched tightly.   The covered wagons were drawn by
four or five or even six horses and could bring produce to market in Lancaster, Reading, or Philadelphia over the roughest
roads.

The Pennsylvania German almanacs were repositories of all
manner of lore and superstitions concerning the time to plant
the various fruits and vegetables and the time to harvest them,
when hogs should be slaughtered, and when houses should be
thatched or shingled.   Omens of sickness and death abounded.
Innumerable signs of changes in the weather were part of popular lore.   Despite their staunch Protestant beliefs, the use
of amulets and incantations was not uncommon.

In concluding his book, Dr. Rush addressed himself to the
legislators of Pennsylvania, warning them against making language differences the object of their condemnation:

> Do not contend with their prejudice in favour of
> their language.   It will be the channel through which
> the knowledge and discoveries of one of the wisest
> nations in Europe, may be conveyed into our country.
> In proportion as they are instructed and enlightened
> in their own language, they will become acquainted
> with the language of the United States.   Invite them
> to share in the power and offices of government; it
> will be the means of producing a union in principle
> and conduct between them, and those of their en-
> lightened fellow citizens who are descended from
> other nations. [43]

Finally, he reminded his contemporaries of the values represented by the German sectarians in their midst:

> Above all, cherish with peculiar tenderness, those
> sects among them who hold war to be unlawful—Relieve
> them from the oppression of absurd and unnecessary
> militia laws . . . Perhaps those German Sects of
> Christians among us, who refuse to bear arms for the
> purpose of shedding human blood, may be preserved by
> divine providence, as the centre of a circle which
> shall gradually embrace all the nations of the earth
> in a perpetual treaty of friendship and peace. [44]

The conceptions that one social group entertains concerning another are often composed of disparate and contradictory
elements—a combination of more or less accurate observation
and misunderstandings as well as distortions which, taken together, reflect the nature of the contact between the groups

involved.   Paradoxically, while the Germans were in many areas successfully competing with the English-speaking farmers and craftsmen, they were still viewed as "the dumb Dutch."   They were to suffer from the widespread notion that they were stupid, plodding, unimaginative, unprogressive, and without any appealing or redeeming mental adornment of any kind.

Language difference provided a barrier to a more intimate and balanced understanding of one another.   Germans seemed to learn English slowly, insisting instead upon using High German and the Rhenish-German dialect that most immigrants preferred in familiar discourse.   The slowness in shifting to the use of English fed the suspicions of Anglo-Americans that the Germans were dull-witted and stubborn.

In some areas where the Germans were more dispersed than in others, they assimilated quickly, abandoning their language, customs, and social cohesion.   Where German culture remained intact for a long time, Anglo-Americans feared the Germans might become dominant.   Benjamin Franklin believed that either the English would absorb the Germans or be absorbed by them— that a stable cultural pluralism could not exist.   Several generations later Horace Greeley expressed in the *New York Tribune* a similar concern over the presence of the German element and advocated the forced assimilation of all German groups.   In the early nineteenth century this kind of concern prompted state legislatures to institute educational programs designed to Anglicize German children.   Germans in those communities desiring to preserve traditional values came to regard public education facilities with considerable suspicion for that reason.

Few English or Scotch colonials could claim an extensive familiarity with the cultural traditions that German communities in America had created; they knew little of the rich folk art, the legends and stories, proverbs and popular wisdom, hymns and songs—all of which represented a significant folk expression reflecting every aspect of life.   The influence of German cultural traditions brought from the Rhenish provinces and the hybrid culture they created in America were to influence general American life far more profoundly than contemporaries of both groups realized in this period.   The Germans introduced certain traditions that were destined to spread rapidly among the Anglo-Americans and transform the celebration of the two most important events in the Christian calendar.   A profound change in the celebration of Christmas was wrought with the introduction of the Advent wreath and the Christmas tree with its colorful decoration as well as the tradition of Christmas singing, cooking, and baking.   New England Puritans had not celebrated Christmas, and other sections of the country had traditional ways of celebration very different from those of the present.   The Pennsylvania Germans brought with

them the Easter festivities associated with the Easter rabbit
and Easter eggs, and these were enthusiastically adopted by
most Americans.  According to an ancient Teutonic legend, the
goddess Ostara transformed a bird into a rabbit and the grateful rabbit thereafter laid eggs every spring on the feast of
Ostara.  When the German pagans were Christianized, the legend
became associated with the celebration of Easter and the
Easter eggs were transformed into a symbol of regeneration.
The origin of the Easter rabbit and the colored eggs was largely forgotten but their importance to the celebration of Easter
in America has remained undiminished.

## THE AMERICAN REVOLUTION

The American Revolution was primarily an anticolonial
struggle of a people seeking to establish independence from
overseas rule.  But there were additional dimensions to the
revolutionary impulse.  It was a war to establish kinds of
constitutional structures and traditions that seemed impossible
to achieve under colonial status.  All segments of the population in all of the colonies were touched by the issues of the
Revolution.

The repressive acts of 1774, by which the British monarch
and Parliament tried to punish the colonies in America, aroused
a degree of political concern among the German colonials that
had never before been manifested among them.  The closing of
the port of Boston brought a widespread protest in Pennsylvania,
Maryland, and other areas of heavy German settlement.  From the
beginning, the colonial Germans recognized that the struggle
was something more than a New England conspiracy.  The dissolu-
tion of colonial assemblies by the king seemed to be an act of
tyranny to the individualistic and independent Germans.  Up to
the beginning of the Revolution, the political activities of
the Germans had been largely confined to community affairs.
Memories of arbitrary rule in their European homeland were
still painfully alive.  There was a widely shared conviction
among the Germans that they had, with God's guidance, fled the
inequalities of the Old World society and had become part of a
society that allowed them a life freed from ancestral molds.
Such interpretations of their past made them respond all the
more resolutely to those things that they and their Anglo-
American neighbors believed were threatening to the liberty
they found in the New World, imperfect and incomplete though
that liberty might be.

Committees of correspondence were formed in most of the
largely German counties.  The Lutheran, Reformed, and Catholic
Germans supported the Whigs in their conflict with the Tories.
By 1776 these religious groups represented the vast majority of

German people in the colonies, even in Pennsylvania.  Mennonites, Amish, Quakers, Dunkards, and Schwenkfelders could not
take up arms in the struggle because of their religious views
on violence and war.  Worldly political life normally interested members of these religious sects little, but in the epoch
of the Revolution they were widely convinced that the issues of
the conflict touched them vitally.  They were loyal to the
principles of the Revolution.  Food, clothing, and medical help
were extended without any affront to their religious views.

There were Tories among the Germans as there were among
all groups.  It seems clear that proportionately there were
fewer Tories among the German population than there were in the
population as a whole.  A relatively small proportion of the
total German-American population remained loyal to the British
crown.  Where such loyalty was manifested, it tended to reflect
the political dispositions of the general population in these
geographical areas.

The Germans in the colonies, like the numerous Scotch-
Irish, lacked the ties of interest and sentiment that bound the
English colonials to the mother country and the crown.  In
Pennsylvania, the political alliance between the Germans and
the Scotch-Irish proved to be of great importance in determining the favorable vote of that colony on the resolution in the
Continental Congress in 1776 demanding that the colonies support a declaration of independence.  With six of the colonies
for and six against the resolution, Pennsylvania cast the de-
ciding vote in favor of independence and resistance to Great
Britain.  This fact permitted the Pennsylvania Germans the conviction that they had played an important role in the decision
for the Revolution.

German merchants in Philadelphia were quick to add their
signatures to a document binding merchants against the importa-
tion of English goods.  The aggressive support of German patriots to the Revolutionary cause is reflected in the fullness
of their representation in the conventions that took place in
Philadelphia in June and July 1774 and in January 1775.

One of the colonial newspapers that "fanned the flames of
rebellion" was *Der Wöchentliche Philadelphische Staatsbote*,
published by Henry Miller (Heinrich Müller) in Philadelphia.
Miller had been trained as a journeyman printer in Germany and
had practiced his trade in large European cities before coming
to the colonies with Count von Zinzendorf, leader of the Moravians.  For a time Miller worked for Benjamin Franklin before
establishing his own printing business.  Franklin has the distinction of publishing the first German-language newspaper in
the colonies.  Recognizing the potential profits to be made
from publishing a newspaper for the Swiss and German colonials,
Franklin established *Die Philadelphische Zeitung* in 1732.  It
lasted only briefly.  Unfortunately Franklin employed a Hugue-

not language teacher as editor and his curious German presented
difficulties for his readers.  The articles were poorly adapted
to the interests of German families.  Franklin earlier had made
references to the boorishness of the Pennsylvania Germans, and,
remembering these references, they were little inclined to support his newspaper.  Franklin ceased publishing it, but continued to print books in German.  Miller's *Staatsbote* had a wide
circulation throughout Pennsylvania and surrounding areas,
reaching into the Shenandoah Valley.  Early in the controversy
between the colonies and Great Britain, Miller had much to say
about the "unbearable slavery" being imposed by the tyrannical
British government.[45]  As the tempo of conflict quickened, Miller stirred his German readers with his appeals: "Remember that
your forefathers emigrated to America to escape bondage and to
enjoy liberty."[46]  Miller helped rally the Germans to active
support of colonial leaders in the struggle against Great
Britain.  The high point in his journalistic career came on
July 5, 1776, when he printed the news of the signing of the
Declaration of Independence before any other newspaper in the
colonies.[47]

Miller's principal adversary was Christopher Sauer, the
founder of a family of publishers.  He was sectarian and a
pacifist.  Along with his sons, he remained staunchly loyal to
King George.  Christopher Sauer, in August 1739, began the publication of a German newspaper, *Der Hochdeutsch-Pennsylvanishe
Geschicht-Schreiber*.  Sauer used his newspaper to propagate his
religious ideas.  He opposed the formalism and ecclesiastical
organization of the Lutherans.  He viewed an educated clergy as
inimical to true spirituality.  Heinrich Melchior Mühlenberg,
the Lutheran patriarch, regarded Sauer as a dangerous influence.
He addressed appeals to the Pennsylvania Germans to give their
allegiance to the British.  The evacuation of Philadelphia by
the British in 1778 brought disaster to the Sauer interests.

In the Valley of Virginia, in Maryland, and in other areas
of the colonies, Germans gave their support to the swelling
Revolutionary movement.  At Woodstock, Virginia, on June 16,
1774, the Rev. Peter Mühlenberg was chosen moderator of an assembly that resolved "that it is the inherent right of British
subjects to be governed and taxed by representatives chosen by
themselves only, and that every act of the British Parliament
respecting the internal policy of America is a dangerous and
unconstitutional invasion of our rights and privileges."[48]
The Lutheran refugees from Salzburg, Austria, who had settled
in Georgia were strong in their support of the Revolutionary
cause.  Some Germans in the southern colonies suffered from the
hostilities of zealous Tory groups.  One of the Salzburg patriots, John Adam Treutlen, was elected governor of the province.  Later he joined the army of General Wayne, as did many
other Salzburgers.

There were, of course, many dramatic events marking the response of the Germans to the American Revolution.  In January 1776, in an atmosphere of great tension, the Rev. Peter Mühlenberg delivered a sermon based on a text from Ecclesiastes: "To every thing there is a season and a time to every purpose under the heaven," he declared, ". . . a time of war and a time of peace—a time to pray and a time to preach—but those times have passed away; there is time to fight, and the time to fight has come!"[49]  He pronounced the benediction, threw off his ministerial vestments, and stood before his congregation in the uniform of a colonel in the Continental Army.  The congregation rose to sing Luther's great hymn, *Ein' feste Burg ist unser Gott* ("A mighty fortress is our God").  The doors of the church opened and the men of the congregation marched off to the beat of drums to enlist.  In February 1777 the talented young friend of Washington and Patrick Henry was raised to the rank of brigadier general by the Congress in recognition of his services. The First, Fifth, Ninth, and Thirteenth Virginia Regiments were under his command.  As a commander, Mühlenberg won distinction in battles at Charleston, Brandywine, Germantown, Monmouth, Stony Point, and Yorktown.  His forces shared the terrible winter at Valley Forge with Washington.

The German farmers and artisans of Pennsylvania, Maryland, and Virginia responded quickly to the call to arms.  Companies of riflemen from Pennsylvania German communities sang as they marched along:

> Englands Georgel Kaiser König
> Ist für Gott und uns zu wenig.
>
> Old England's Georgie, emp'ror, king
> For God and us is a trivial thing.

Later generations were to take pride in the fact that companies of riflemen from Berks and York Counties in Pennsylvania were among the first to reach Washington at Cambridge.  They were welcomed recruits.  The rifle they used in combat had been introduced into Pennsylvania and later into the southern frontier by Palatines and Swiss.  Their gunsmiths had improved upon the European models brought with them.  The rifle was lighter than the awkward regulation army musket and enabled riflemen to maneuver more readily.  The skill of the common German riflemen was recognized widely; it is no mere coincidence that the first troops to be raised under the authority of the Congress were riflemen.  The distance and accuracy of their fire made them respected soldiers throughout the colonies.

When asked to compare the abilities of the various national groups fighting in the American army, a Captain Morgan pointed to the exceptional stamina of the Germans, the so-called Dutchman: "As for the fighting part of the matter, the men of all races are pretty much alike; they fight as much as they find necessary, and no more. But, sir, for the grand essential in the composition of a good soldier, give me the 'Dutchman'—he starves well."[50]

Some of the popular heroes of the American Revolution were of German origin. Molly Pitcher, born Mary Ludwig to a Pennsylvania German family, was one. So devoted was she to her husband that she insisted in following him into battle, often ministering to the soldiers. At the battle of Monmouth she won a place in American popular history. When her husband was incapacitated, she took his place at the cannon. Her act helped sustain the wavering men around her. Many more tales were related on winters' evenings for generations among the German families: tales of how a farmer went off to Philadelphia and came back with the Liberty Bell in his wagon to hide it from the British in the Church in Allentown; or how Sergeant Everhart, during the battle of Brandywine, brought the wounded Lafayette to safety; or how Johann Christian Schell defended himself and his family in August 1781 when forty-eight Indians and sixteen Tories attacked his house near Fort Dayton, New York.

German soldiers and German families suffered much tragedy in the war. The predominantly German settlements in the Mohawk Valley and the Scholarie region were more vulnerable to Indian attacks than any other frontier area during the Revolutionary War. They were frontier settlements along the periphery of the Six Nations territory. The English provided the warriors of the Six Nations with incentives to fight with them against American colonists. The prosperous farms and fat cattle of the settlers in the Mohawk and Scholarie Valleys were tempting targets for the warriors. The German settlers assumed responsibility for the defense of the region. Four battalions were organized in the summer of 1775 and placed under four officers given the rank of colonel—all of them German. The force as a whole was put under the military command of Nicholas Herkimer (Herckheimer). General Herkimer proved to be a distinguished military leader in the struggle against the Indians, Royalists, and British forces.

In addition to native-born soldiers of German origin and long-term resident immigrants who were raised to positions of military leadership in the war, many German officers came to the New World to offer their services. A considerable number of trained and experienced German officers arrived. Most of them had served in the army of Frederick the Great of Prussia during the Seven Years War. Benjamin Franklin, while serving as America's diplomatic representative in Paris, met European officers whom he encouraged to go to America and present their services to General Washington. Among such officers were Heinrich Lutterloh and Baron von Steuben. Both were given commis-

sions and served with distinction, Colonel Lutterloh as quarter-
master general and Major General Steuben as inspector general
of the army.  Some officers, among them John Kalb, came with
Lafayette.  General Weissenfels, who was a German officer in
the British army in New York, offered his services to General
Washington when the war broke out.  The artillery officer, Johann Paul Schott, also came to America with the intention of
fighting for the British, but joined the Revolutionary forces
as an artillery officer.  He proved to be a versatile and re-
sourceful military man.  Major Barth von Heer, like the others
a veteran of the Seven Years War, became commander of Washington's trusted bodyguard—a troop of 53 men and 14 officers
nearly all of whom were Germans from Berks and Lancaster Counties in Pennsylvania.

The experienced officers who came from Germany with substantial training and offered their services to the new nation
were able to make a valuable contribution to the American
cause.  But German officers and others of various nationalities
who came to fight against the British also brought tribulations
to the commander of the American forces.  As was true of native
officers as well, there were foreign officers who were, as
Washington complained to Gouverneur Morris in 1778, "military
fortune hunters . . . Men of great ambition, who would sacri-
fice everything to promote their own personal glory—or mere
spies . . ."  The foreign officers were even more difficult to
judge as officers and as men, and Washington was sufficiently
provoked to add in his letter to Gouverneur Morris, "I do most
devoutly wish that we had not a single Foreigner among us, except the Marquis de la Fayette . . ."  On other occasions he
was more generously appreciative of the advantages most of the
foreign officers brought to the commander and his armies.[51]

One of the German officers who contributed most to his
adopted country was General Steuben, although there were times
when he was a hard and stubborn man.  He established a system
of military discipline for the new army, organizing patterns of
drills and maneuvers adapted to the American setting.  He prepared the first army manual, known as Steuben's Regulations, as
a guide for the performance of military duties.  This practical
manual contributed much to the regularization of military
training and the improvement of efficiency and military effectiveness.  After the war, Steuben formulated plans for a military academy in which prospective officers would be broadly
educated in history, civil and international law, speech, and
literature.  He became a regent of the University of New York
and remained active in public affairs until his death in 1794.

Perhaps thirty thousand Hessian soldiers fought for the
British in the colonies during the American Revolution.  The
English government contracted with the rulers of several Ger-
man principalities, including Hesse-Kassel, Hesse-Hanau,

Braunschweig, and others, for military contingents.  Men were
recruited by their rulers and assigned to foreign service in
the British cause in America in return for monies the rulers
received from London.  Not all German states followed such
practices, and Frederick the Great refused to allow any contingents of soldiers en route to America to pass through his
territories.

The Hessian soldiers who fought for the British were long
remembered by the colonial population for their ruthlessness
as this verse from an early American ballad attests:

> Bourgoyne sent Baum to Bennington
> with Hessians there he went
> To plunder and to murder
> were fully their intent
> were fully their intent . . .

It took long to heal the wounds caused by their bayonets.

The Hessian soldiers capably discharged their military
obligations to the British, but desertions were nevertheless
frequent.[52]  Captured Hessians, as well as prisoners taken at
Yorktown, fraternized with colonial German troops.  Many Hessians remained after the war and settled permanently in America
(perhaps six thousand, the exact numbers are not known).  The
Hessians scattered among the established German settlements
from New York to South Carolina.  In no place did they form
settlements of their own, consequently they were quickly absorbed into the larger native German population.

On a summer day in 1783, General Washington stood on the
veranda of his home at Mount Vernon and bade farewell to the
mounted guard that had served the commander-in-chief as his
bodyguard during most of the war.  These German soldiers from
Pennsylvania were the last to leave Washington's side at Mount
Vernon, just as the Pennsylvania Germans had been the first to
respond to his call at Cambridge at the beginning of the conflict.

The trials and suffering shared by the various elements of
the population during the years of struggle strengthened common
sentiments of nationality and nationhood.  The blending of the
major ethnic components of the national population began to accelerate.  The vigor of German cultural traditions and social
character was reflected in this blending process.[53]

## NOTES

[1]Samuel Eliot Morison, *The European Discovery of America, The
Northern Voyages A.D. 500-1600* (New York: Oxford University Press, 1941) 40, 51, 62.

[2]Bruno Gebhardt, *Handbuch der Deutschen Geschichte*, vol. II, *Von der Reformation bis zum Ende des Absolutismus* (Stuttgart: Union Verlag, 1955, 1956) 412 ff.

[3]See the full and reliable account of Minuit in C. A. Weslager, in collaboration with A. R. Dunlap, *Dutch Explorers, Traders and Settlers in the Delaware Valley, 1609-1664* (Philadelphia: University of Pennsylvania Press, 1961).

[4]An impressive documented account of Jacob Leisler's career and his enduring influence in New York is Jerome R. Reich, *Leisler's Rebellion, A Study of Democracy in New York, 1664-1720* (Chicago: University of Chicago Press, 1953).

[5]Written by Pastorius in the introduction to Germantown Records, 1688, and translated from the Latin original into English by John Greenleaf Whittier. Quoted in Samuel Whitaker Pennypacker, *The Settlement of Germantown, Pennsylvania and the Beginning of German Emigration to North America* (Philadelphia: W. J. Campbell, 1899) 59.

[6]E. Dingwall and E. A. Heard, *Pennsylvania 1681-1856, The State Without an Army* (London: C. W. Daneil, 1937) 23.

[7]Albert B. Faust, *The German Element in the United States*, vol. I (Boston and New York: Houghton Mifflin, 1909) 33.

[8]*Ibid.*, 36.

[9]*Ibid.*

[10]Quoted in *ibid.*, 35-36.

[11]*Ibid.*, 44.

[12]*Ibid.*, 39.

[13]*Ibid.*, 40.

[14]Pennypacker, *op. cit.*, 256-257.

[15]William Bradford, *Bradford's History of Plymouth Plantation, 1606-1646*, 432.

[16]Quoted in Pennypacker, *op. cit.*, 90, 235.

[17]*Ibid.*, 245-246.

[18]For a general guide to the complex period see Max Braubach, *Diplomatie und geistiges Leben in 17. und 18. Jahrhundert*, vol. XXX of Bonner Historische Forschungen (Bonn: Rorscheid Verlag, 1969).

[19]An excellent treatment of the migration of the refugees from the Palatinate is to be found in Walter Allen Knittle, *The Early Eighteenth Century Palatine Emigration, A British Government Redemptioner Project to Manufacture Naval Stores* (Philadelphia, 1936). See also Faust, *op. cit.*, vol. I, 73-110.

[20]*Ibid.*, 50-51.

[21]*Ibid.*, 56.

[22]See the introduction by Stanley Nider Katz to James Alexander, *A Brief Narrative of the Case and Trial of John Peter Zenger, Printer of the New York Weekly Journal* (Cambridge: Harvard University Press, 1966).

[23]Marcus Lee Hansen, *The Atlantic Migration, 1607-1860*, Torch-light edition with an introduction by Oscar Handlin (New York: Harper and Row, 1961) provides a valuable insight into the history of immigration before 1860.  See also Wayland F. Dunaway, *The Scotch-Irish of Colonial Pennsylvania* (London: Archon Books, 1962) on the emigration of Ulster Scots to America, their settlement and dispersion throughout the English colonies.

[24]Delbert L. Gratz, *Studies in Anabaptist and Mennonite History*, No. 8.  "Bernese Anabaptists and their American Descendants" (Goshen, Indiana, 1953) gives valuable background for these religious movements.

[25]Abdel Ross Wentz, *A Basic History of Lutheranism in America* (Philadelphia: Mühlenberg Press, 1955) 27.

[26]Thomas F. McHugh, "The Moravian Missions to the American Indian: An Early American Peace Corps," *Pennsylvania History* XXXIII (October 1966) 412-431.

[27]Edmund de Schweinitz, *The Life and Times of David Zeisberger* (Philadelphia: J. B. Lippincott, 1870) 89 passim.

[28]Paul A. W. Wallace, *Conrad Weiser 1696-1760, A Friend of Colonist and Mohawk* (Philadelphia, 1945) 574.

[29]Jerome H. Wood, Jr., "The Town Proprietors of Lancaster, 1730-1790," *The Pennsylvanian Magazine of History and Biography* XCVI (July 1972) 354.

[30]Wentz, *op. cit.*, 31.

[31]Faust, *op. cit.*, 241.

[32]Excellent descriptions of German social conditions in the eighteenth century can be found in W. A. Bruford, *Germany in the Eighteenth Century: The Social Background of the Literary Revival* (Cambridge: Cambridge University Press, 1953).  See particularly Part II, chapters 1, 3, and 5.

[33]See Gottlieb Mittelberger, *Journey to Pennsylvania*, edited and translated by Oscar Handlin and John Clive (Cambridge: Harvard University Press, 1961).

[34]Benjamin Rush, *An Account of the Manner of the German Inhabitants of Pennsylvania* (originally published in 1789), Publication XXI, Pennsylvania-German Society (Lancaster, Pennsylvania, 1910).

[35]J. Hector St. John Crevecoeur, *Letters from an American Farmer* (New York: E. P. Dutton, 1912) 62.

[36]Oscar Kuhns, *The German and Swiss Settlements of Colonial Pennsylvania, a Study of the So-Called Pennsylvania Dutch* (New York, 1901) 94.

[37]Rush, *op. cit.*, 71.

[38]Frederic Klees, *The Pennsylvania Dutch* (New York: Macmillan, 1951) 317.

[39]Kuhns, *op. cit.*, 97.

[40]*Ibid.*, 98.

[41]Rush, *op. cit.*, 61.

[42]*Ibid.*, 66.
[43]*Ibid.*, 117–119.
[44]*Ibid.*, 120.
[45]Carl Wittke, *The German-Language Press in America* (Lexington: University of Kentucky Press, 1957) 22.
[46]Faust, *op. cit.*, vol. I, 291.
[47]Ralph Wood, ed., *The Pennsylvania Germans* (Princeton: Princeton University Press, 1942) 133.
[48]Faust, *op. cit.*, vol. I, 292.
[49]Klees, *op. cit.*, 176.
[50]*Ibid.*, 172–173.
[51]Richard B. Morris, *The American Revolution Reconsidered* (New York: Harper & Row, 1967) 101.
[52]See Clifford Neal Smith, "Some British and German Deserters During the American Revolution," *National Geneological Society Quarterly* LX, no. 4 (December 1972) 267–275.
[53]See the account of the Germans in the period of the American Revolution found in Ralph Wood, *op. cit.*

# 2

## NINETEENTH-CENTURY GERMAN-AMERICA

### THE GERMANS AND THE WESTWARD MOVEMENT

After the close of the American Revolution, popular attention became more intensively focused upon the vast unsettled portions of the continent than it had ever been before. The impulse to explore and settle the fertile lands lying to the west was so compelling and so widely manifested that human migrations moved almost explosively into the broadly stretching frontier. A sense of a special mission or "manifest destiny" to settle the rich and "unused" western regions became increasingly apparent in American thought and action. The migratory movements occurred along a whole series of roads and river routes and, later, railroad lines from settled areas and from immigrant ports of entry.

After the initial explorations came the establishment of hunting and trapping and the development of an economy of trade with Indian tribes. Other kinds of people came with the intention of gaining possession of farm-sized tracts, building homes and barns, and working the land. As farms and ranches multiplied the building of community life became important. The complex process of settlement by which the lands of nomadic Indians were transformed by stages into more densely settled communities generally extended over a generation or two in any given locality. The process was basically the same everywhere. Similar stages occurred in more or less the same progression, but the locus of the process of transformation moved continually westward. Somewhere to the west there was always the frontier, and the imminent awareness of this fact, or what some have called the frontier psychology, became manifest in many dimensions of American social and cultural life.

As soon as the hostilities of the Revolutionary period ceased, there was an immediate acceleration of movement from the old frontier areas into the new, raw frontier.[1] Among the vast influx of settlers into Kentucky and Tennessee were many

Germans along with the English, Scotch-Irish, Scotch, Welsh, and Huguenots. The Germans not only followed the westward paths of the Anglo-Americans, but were also represented among the early hunters and trappers by men like Michael Stoner (Steiner) and George Yeager (Jäger). Many of the most devoted teachers and missionaries who concerned themselves with the welfare of the Indians in this period, as in the past, were German Moravians. Some men attached themselves to Indian tribes and were accepted by them as members. Johann Salling lived for years as Menou, The Silent One, among the Cherokees, hunting, fishing, fighting, and courting with his fellow braves until he was captured by the French and taken to Canada.

If German sectarians showed extraordinary concern for the material and spiritual welfare of the Indians, there were yet other Germans who could be counted among the most unrelenting Indian fighters in the Ohio Valley. Ludwig Wetzel and his brothers, Jacob and Martin, won wide regional fame and popular esteem as marksmen and Indian fighters. As children they had witnessed the slaying of members of their family by marauding Indians. Communities troubled by Indians hostile to settlers tended to look upon the fanatical zeal of the Wetzel brothers as a most commendable virtue. American-born officers of German ancestry served in military campaigns against organized Indian resistance. In the campaign of George Rogers Clark in 1778-79 against Kaskasia (Illinois) and Vincennes (Indiana), Virginia-born officers Captain Leonard Helm and Joseph Bowman as well as other German-American officers took part. One of the most notable of such officers on the Indian frontier was General David Ziegler, a native of Heidelberg. As the commander of Fort Washington, Ziegler won the trust and admiration of settlers of the Ohio Valley for the effectiveness of the measures he took to protect their lives and property. When Cincinnati was organized as a city in 1802, Ziegler was elected its first mayor.

A large number of Germans who had fought in the Revolutionary War took advantage of the privilege, extended to veterans, of obtaining grants of lands in the Blue Grass region of Kentucky. Pennsylvania German families yielded a large number of young men and women to the expanding frontiers; older sons took over the management of the home farm and the younger sons moved westward. The same was also true of the German families in New York, Maryland, Virginia and the Carolinas. The birth rates among German families were high and the scarcity of good, inexpensive land in the areas of heavy German settlement encouraged the youths to establish themselves out west. Their numbers were increased by German-born immigrants who came first to Pennsylvania, which was best known to them, but who learned of more extensive opportunities awaiting them in territories more recently opened to settlement and joined the westward

movement.  The native-born and foreign-born Germans moved into
the Ohio Valley along several well-established roads running
through Maryland and West Virginia into Ohio.  Pennsylvania
Germans moving along this road and parallel routes settled Canton, Massilon, Alliance, and Steubenville and later other communities as well farther to the west.

Another migratory stream followed the path of the New England families who settled in northern Ohio.  German families in
the Mohawk Valley and Hudson Valley followed the New Englanders
along the borders of Lake Erie into Ohio.  Unlike the New Englanders, the Germans settled south of the Western Reserve territory in a broad band of concentrated settlements extending
along the watershed westward across the length of the state.
Many place names of towns, townships, and counties reflect the
sentimental attachments of the early German settlers to their
places of origin: Berlin, Hanover, Strassburg, Dresden, Frank-
fort, Potsdam, Freeburg, Saxon, Winesburg, and others.  Many
other place names reflect the characteristic Christian piety
of the German Moravians, Amish, and other sectarians.  They
felt more comfortable living in communities bearing names like
Bethlehem, Nazareth, Goshen, and Canaan.

As the people established new homes, their religious institutions were brought with them or recreated.  Ministers
sometimes followed their congregations.  When new churches were
formed, ministers had to be found; sometimes they were sent to
the frontier by church and missionary organizations in Germany.
Synods admitted newly formed congregations in distant frontier
areas and served them until the church population in that area
was sufficient to justify the creation of a new synod.  Thus
the Lutheran synod of North Carolina tended the congregations
in Tennessee until 1820, when a new synod was organized there.
Where the "crude, turbulent and godless" frontier grew faster
than the ability of religious institutions to expand, new techniques appeared and were elaborated to meet religious needs;
among these were the systems of ministerial circuit riders and
the frontier camp meeting.  A forerunner of the great religious
camp meeting movement is found in the *Grosse Versammlungen* of
German Lutherans and Methodists in eighteenth-century Pennsylvania.  When the congregations grew beyond the capacity of a
cabin or a church, ministers took their congregations into a
barn.  The camp meetings served not only religious needs of the
often sparsely settled families but their social needs as well.
These social needs, indeed, sometimes grew so compelling in the
early nineteenth century that people came from great distances
to attend the camp meetings.  The meetings were highly charged
with emotion and often became undisciplined.  Earnest pastors
were sometimes distressed at the behavior of those attending
and complained that more souls were being created on such occasions than were being saved.[2]  The hardships and anxieties of

life in the wilderness brought tensions and a sense of loneli-
ness that encouraged such periodical surges of religious emo-
tionalism.  Lutheran leaders in the East warned their western
missionaries against participating in the camp meetings because
they feared the consequences of religious practices that differed so much from "our Lutheran ways."  But Lutheran missionaries like Paul Henkel, as their journals and reports show,
could not fail to utilize the chance the camp meetings provided
to reach large numbers of families widely scattered throughout
the region.[3]  The conditions in the newly settled areas presented the various religious groups with common problems and
common opportunities, and in response to these there arose a
surprising amount of interdenominational cooperation.  Pulpits
were shared, sometimes at the same meeting or service, sometimes on a rotating basis.  Church buildings were often used in
common by different denominational groups.

     As settlements grew, towns appeared and regional centers
began to assume the character of cities.  Germans were not only
farmers; they were prominent in the founding of towns and of
cities like Cincinnati.  Settlements to the north in the Miami
Valley began to receive heavy increments of Germans.  A paper
mill, which was important to the regional economy, was established in the Valley by Christian Waldschmidt (Wallsmith) in
1786.  Dayton and Columbus began to receive German migrants.
Along with farmers, craftsmen, laborers, and professionals,
there were also the less successful immigrants, the drifters
and fortune-seekers.  Many men of substance and talent found
their way into trade and industry.  An extraordinary example
was the Alsatian entrepreneur, Martin Baum, who in 1810 established the first iron foundry in the West.  Among other enterprises, he founded a sugar refinery, a textile factory, and a
bank.  Along with another German, Captain Bechtle, he formed a
shipping company that ran a regular schedule of boats on the
Ohio and Mississippi Rivers, especially between Cincinnati and
New Orleans.  His civic contributions included serving for a
time as mayor of the city and contributing to the founding of
Cincinnati College.  In his beautiful home, he entertained many
who contributed to the cultural and intellectual life of the
region as well as numerous visiting scholars from Germany.
Many Germans were eminently practical men who were interested
in contributing to the economic development of the abundant resources at hand, and they wanted the material returns that such
contributions could bring them.  But a number of them were educated men who had a genuine sense of missionary responsibility
to enrich the cultural life of the communities in which they
settled.  If there was some arrogance in their zeal, their
appreciation of the need to develop cultural institutions and
to encourage cultural activities was, indeed, important.  The
educated Germans were not alone in their concern; they joined
educated Anglo-Americans in furthering these purposes.

Each year native migrants and immigrants pushed into vir-
gin lands and rooted themselves.  Western Ohio, from Cincinnati
on the south to Toledo on the north, received a heavy influx of
settlers between 1820 and 1835.  The movement continued into
Indiana in lands along the Ohio River.  Fort Wayne became an
area of particularly concentrated German settlement.

Cincinnati in this period was rapidly becoming a city with
a cosmopolitan character by virtue of its large proportion of
European immigrants.  Among the approximately 150 community
leaders listed in M. Joblin's *Cincinnati Past and Present or
its Industrial History* published in 1872, roughly one-third
were of German origin.  What is especially remarkable is the
number of persons born in Scotland, Wales, North Ireland, England, and Germany arriving as young men in the decades of the
1830s and 40s who were able to take advantage of the economic
opportunities the expanding city offered.  Most began with
modest means; but with Horatio Alger-like thrift and diligence
as well as good fortune, they established their own enterprises.  Not only were they successful as business men, but
they became much involved in political and civic affairs as
aldermen, directors of orphanages and libraries, participants
in religious communities and organizations, and supporters of
volunteer firemen societies.  Their assimilation was amazingly
rapid; yet a number sent their sons or daughters to Germany for
part of their education.  Most German immigrants, of course,
remained in more modest circumstances than the Jacobs, Lackman,
Seasongood, and Weitzel families, but they were generally respected for their skill and hard work.

By the 1820s, Germans were moving into Missouri along sev-
eral routes.  In the decades following, the heavy influx of
Germans considerably altered the early French character of St.
Louis.

Significantly related to the arrival of immigrants was the
large number of books about the American West being published
in Germany in the first half of the nineteenth century by early
travelers and new settlers.[4]  The authors varied extensively in
their portrayal of America and the American people.  Many of
these publications were widely read and undoubtedly did much to
stimulate emigration.  The works of Gottfried Duden, a graduate
in law and medicine and a skillful writer, were among the most
influential.  He landed in Baltimore in 1824 and made his way
to St. Louis.  Staying overnight in the home of a Pennsylvania
German, he was informed that there was some vacant land in the
area, and decided to buy 275 acres near the confluence of the
Missouri and Mississippi Rivers.  Duden was a wealthy man who
could free himself from the rigors of frontier life.  He had
others clear his land and cultivate it for him while he devoted himself to the description of life in the New World:
the beautiful landscapes, the democratic institutions, the

opportunities waiting to be seized.  The glowing account of the West contained in his *Bericht über eine Reise nach den westlichen Staaten Nordamerikas*, published in Germany in 1829, met with immediate response.  It was reprinted a number of times and is credited with having convinced many individuals to seek an ideal existence in the American wilderness.

Farmers from Westphalia and Hannover now came in unprecedented numbers; these were areas north of the German states that had contributed a large portion of the colonial German population.  Later groups represented a wide range of classes and occupational groups, including merchants, officers, doctors, lawyers, professors, and teachers.  Members of aristocratic families settled in the neighborhood of Duden's farm in Warren County, Missouri.  Gustav Koerner, a German diplomat who arrived in America in 1833, attempted to counterbalance the influence Dr. Duden was currently exercising in Germany by publishing a critique of the *Bericht*.  Koerner tried to present both positive and negative aspects of American life more fully and fairly so that those who were contemplating emigration would have a more realistic basis for their decision.

Ordinary farmers from Germany who settled in the West worked hard, and most of them prospered.  The well-educated professional men, scholars, and members of the nobility who came with romantic notions about farming generally fared poorly. Many who settled in the Missouri colony had been educated in German *gymnasia* and universities and were much more adept at Latin and Greek than at the practical aspects of farming.  The epithet, "Latin farmers," won currency in the 1830s and 40s for members of the Latin settlements and others equally unprepared by education and training for farming.  Some Latin farmers were able eventually to escape to cities and make their way into occupations for which they were better prepared.  There were others, however, who died in frustration and poverty.  The journal of Frederick Gustorf includes the following entry written in St. Louis on October 16, 1835:

> During the day I met many cultured Germans, former farmers, now earning their bread and butter in a very humble way.  One German gentleman from the vicinity of Hannover told me several sad stories about the sufferings and hardship of several middleclass German families in Missouri and Illinois.  Their experiences are beyond imagination.  With their wives, sons, and daughters they live wretched lives.  Imagine people from the finest German classes living in miserable huts!  Previously they had lived in comfortable houses, and now they have to eat the plainest of food and do the hardest work in the fields, surrounded by black forests and cut off from society and all the

conveniences of life.  They live in memory of the
sweet past, in contrast with the miserable present,
and in contemplation of a sad future, one illusion
after another.  It is not always easy to give the
appearance of contentment when one's heart and mind
are suffering from regret.[5]

Most immigrants and American-born Germans moved westward
as individuals or small family groups.  There were larger religious groups, however, who came with the hope of founding a
New Jerusalem in the West.  They established isolated settlements that placed emphasis on Christian teachings and a com-
munistic way of life.  Johann Georg Rapp led a group of his
followers from Württemberg to Pennsylvania in 1805, where he
founded the colony of Harmony in Butler County.  In 1815 the
Harmonists, one of the most widely known religious groups,
moved to a settlement on the Wabash River in Indiana but later
they returned to Pennsylvania to found a third colony at Economy.  The Rappist sect was successful in its industrial and
agricultural enterprises as long as the community held together.  Celibacy was an important principle of the sect, and
was strictly enforced so that the perpetuation of the colony
proved impossible in the long run.  This particular aspect of
the Rappist colony received a disproportionate amount of popular attention.

When Rapp the Harmonist embargoes marriage
    In his harmonious settlement which flourishes
Strangely enough as yet without miscarriage,
    Why call'd he "Harmony" a state sans wedlock?
Now here I've got the preacher at a deadlock.
            —Lord Byron, *Don Juan*, Canto xv

Apart from the relatively small number of religious
utopians, most of the immigrants who settled the western portion of the country scattered broadly and were integrated into
pioneer communities within a generation or two.  European languages and other more obvious cultural characteristics gradually disappeared, but not without having made some impression
on the cultural characteristics of the regions of immigrant
settlement.  The United States government refused to grant any
immigrant element special rights of settlement on any considerable portion of land.  Yet with the acceleration of immigration in the 1830s and the decades following, certain areas of
concentrated settlement did develop without deliberate design.
Norwegians, Swedes, Germans, and other groups were in some
areas so compact in their own communities that the daily contacts of individuals were largely confined to members of the
same group.  Many immigrants welcomed the economic advantages

that life in the United States had afforded them but at the
same time regretted the gradual decay of their old language and
culture with the passage of time.  Others ignored or were rec-
onciled to the signs of acculturation.  There were individuals
in most ethnic groups who not only lamented the loss of traditional culture and national identity but aspired to establish
compact and exclusive ethnic settlements.  By midcentury, as
Alan Conway notes, many Welshmen were becoming concerned that
Welsh language and culture would completely disappear in America as the immigrant generation died out unless Welsh families
could be concentrated somewhere on the frontier in compact national communities.[6]  There were groups of Germans, Norwegians,
and others who had similar aspirations for their people.

About 1830 Paul Follen (or Follenius) and Friedrich Münch
began to formulate plans for an emigration scheme designed to
establish large numbers of Germans in unsettled areas of the
Mississippi Valley.  The plans were given shape and impetus by
the despair Follen and Münch felt at the failure of the movements for constitutional government in Germany.  The American
frontier seemed to provide another chance for the Germany they
represented.  They attracted a number of university students
and teachers who were similarly opposed to the paternalism and
autocracy of contemporary German governments and who had the
same vision of a new and freer Germany in the New World.

> We must not go from here (Germany) without realizing
> a national idea or at least making the beginnings of
> its realization; the foundation of a new and free
> Germany in the great North American Republic shall be
> laid by us; we must therefore gather as many as pos-
> sible of the best of our people about us when we emi-
> grate, and we must at the same time make the neces-
> sary arrangements providing for a large body of
> immigrants to follow us annually, and thus we may be
> able at least in one of the American territories to
> establish an essentially German state, in which a
> refuge may be found for all those to whom, as to our-
> selves conditions at home have become unbearable,—
> a territory which we shall be able to make a model
> state in the great republic.[7]

In 1834 Follen and Münch sailed from Bremen to New Orleans
with two shiploads of settlers.  After explorations in Arkansas
and elsewhere, they led the newcomers, mostly from the Grand-
duchy of Hesse, to the north bank of the Missouri River in what
is now Warren County, Missouri.  This area, on both sides of
the Missouri from its confluence with the Mississippi to a
point up-river 125 miles to the north, became an area of heavy
German settlement.  In this early period, nine-tenths of the
inhabitants in Warren County were Germans.[8]

The dreams of Follen and Münch for a German state in the
United States were never realized.  Nevertheless Follen and
Münch provided the opportunity for a large number of immigrants
to establish themselves on fertile land under favorable circumstances.  These Missouri Germans prospered and left a deep im-
print on the physical and cultural character of the whole
region.  Münch gave up the promise of a brilliant career in
Germany in order to further his republican principles in
America.  In Missouri he became a leader of Missouri Germans
and a member of the Missouri legislature.

Plans for systematic, large-scale colonization were characteristically conceived in gross naivete; financing was dis-
astrously inadequate and the administration of the affairs of
such enterprises were generally seriously deficient.  In 1839
a group of Germans formed a colonization society called the
*Germania Geselleschaft* for the purpose of bringing settlers to
the Lone Star Republic.  In November of that year, the society
sent 130 colonists by ship to Galveston.  By the time they
reached Houston the enterprise was already falling apart.
Those who still had money left immediately returned to New
York.  A number of similar colonization enterprises suffered an
early demise.  German residents in the United States and native-
born Americans attempted to establish colonies on various frontier areas.  Among such enterprises were the Pittsburg Home-
stead Association, the Cincinnati German Association, and the
Chicago Land *Verein*.  Some of the ambitious schemes failed as
stable enterprises but nevertheless were responsible for stimulating the settlement of the areas.

On Whitsuntide in 1841, Friedrich Ernst along with other
German settlers in Texas founded a society called the *Teutonia
Order*.  Its purpose was to preserve the ties that bound Germans
together, which, as Ernst noted, "only too easily disappear in
a foreign land."  They hoped to preserve the settlers' feeling
for "German individuality" and to sustain and cultivate German
language and culture.[9]

Ernst had been a bookkeeper in the Duchy of Oldenburg before he left for New York in 1829.  There he bought a hotel but
was soon persuaded to abandon his new endeavor and move west
after reading a copy of Dr. Duden's book.  Arriving by ship in
New Orleans, Ernst was distracted from his intention of settling in Missouri by news of the possibility of securing a land
grant in Texas from the Mexican government.  He did indeed receive a grant of new land: what is now Austin.

Not long after he settled in Texas, Ernst wrote to friends
in Oldenburg, who had his letter published in a local newspaper.
The letter received wide circulation in northern Germany.  The
enthusiasm he showed for Texas and the opportunities existing
there created an interest in emigration among many families in
Oldenburg.  Among the immigrants who left for Texas in 1834

were Dr. Justus Kleberg and members of the von Roeder family
who, like Ernst, were to play important roles in their new
Texas homeland.

The interest that Ernst and others were creating in the
settlement of Texas soon led to larger colonizing efforts.  A
group of wealthy German noblemen, some of whom were reigning
princes, formed a corporate enterprise under the name of the
*Verein zum Schutze deutscher Einwanderer in Texas*.  The organization was known more generally as the *Adelsverein* (noblemen's
union or society) because it was formed exclusively by noblemen.  The founders hoped to realize a substantial profit from
their investment in Texas land as property values increased
with its settlement and development.  They had philanthropic
interests as well: they believed they were contributing to the
welfare of the colonists whom they recruited because they provided them land for safe settlement and prosperous development.
Prince Carl von Solms-Braunfels was sent to Texas as chief com-
missioner for the *Adelsverein*.  In 1844 the first group of settlers recruited by the *Verein* arrived at Galveston and then
sailed to Matagorda Bay where they disembarked.  The community
of New Braunfels was founded in 1845 in Comal County and,
shortly afterward, Fredericksburg in Gillespie County as well
as other widely scattered settlements.  Prince von Solms-
Braunfels and some of the other noblemen who directed the affairs of the *Verein* were determined to concentrate German settlements in Texas and to isolate them from external influence
in order to build a German state or perhaps even a sovereign
territory in the still unsettled wilderness.  The Prince, however, remained only a short time.  He was replaced by Baron
Otfried Hans von Meusebach who dropped the use of his title and
became plain John O. Meusebach as a symbol of his commitment to
democratic values.  Meusebach believed his predecessor's dream
of a separate German state to be ridiculous and the policy of
isolation that derived from it to be wrong.  He encouraged the
integration of German and Anglo-American families.[10]

The *Verein* brought 7,380 German colonists to Texas in the
period from 1844 to 1946.[11]  But in 1847 the *Verein* was allowed
to fall into bankruptcy.  The noblemen who directed its affairs
were too far removed from the realities of settling the frontier.  The administration in Texas lacked money to meet the
costs of land purchases and transportation .to the new settlements, as well as colonists' support in the initial period of
their settlement.  There were too many immigrants for the impoverished *Verein* officials in Texas to handle.  Other, smaller
colonies established in the same region of Texas endured only
briefly like the communalist colony of Bettina and the colony
of the Alsatian promoter, Henri Castro.

Many thousands of settlers had been brought to Texas
from Hannover, Braunschweig, Hesse-Darmstadt, Thuringia, and

Württemberg.  A strong migratory momentum had begun that was to
continue for decades beyond the life of the *Verein* itself.  By
the late 1840s thousands of German immigrants were arriving
each year at Galveston from European ports; large numbers came
to other ports, especially New Orleans, and made their way to
Texas.  New settlements were established as increasing numbers
of German families spread from centers like New Braunfels into
the fertile Black Waxy Prairie.  At the same time newly arrived
farmers progressively occupied lands to the north and west of
established communities.  In addition to the settlers attracted
to rural areas, many German immigrants remained in the coastal
towns and cities.  It is estimated that in 1854, one-third of
the population of Galveston was German.[12]  By 1850 the main
geographic outline of German settlement in Texas was already
apparent.  Immigration during the rest of the century served to
fill in the broad belt of high German density extending from
the coast, at some points, across the south-central portion of
the state to areas deep in the interior.

The German newcomers made quick accommodation to the physical and cultural environment.  Despite their extensive adaptation to southern agricultural practices prevailing in Texas and
to the cultural traditions Anglo-Americans brought with them
from the border and southern states from which they migrated,
the German settlers retained some cultural distinctiveness.
The Germans became Texans but retained for generations the
sense that they were a particular kind of Texan.  An important
element in this sentiment was their conviction that they were
better farmers than southern Anglo-American farmers.

The German emphasis on family and hired labor as opposed
to slave labor distinguished them from many of their neighbors
and led to experiences that contributed to the perpetuation of
a sense of special identity.  As was true throughout the country, few Germans in Texas held slaves.  The total absence of
slaveholding in some areas of their settlement there led to
widespread Anglo-American criticism of those "damned Dutch abo-
litionists."[13]  The Texas Germans did not make a public issue
of the moral and ideological aspects of slavery.  They did believe—as it was plain to observe in their daily lives—that
slavery was not only wrong, but uneconomical for them in contrast to family and wage labor.  Many immigrants worked for
wages in the cities and on farms until they had enough money
saved to buy their own land.  Ultimately a higher proportion
of German immigrants owned their farms than was true of other
segments of the population.  They had no qualms about doing the
kinds of menial farm work that according to southern tradition
were appropriate only for slaves to perform.[14]  The surprise
attack of Confederate troops against a group of young Germans
bivouacked at the Nueces River in the summer of 1862 and the
Confederate occupation of certain areas of German settlement

became parts of Texas German lore and added to a sense of special identity. Germans of Comal County supported the Confederacy not as a result of sympathy with the institution of slavery but as an indication of allegiance to their adopted state.[15]

Anglo-American newspaper editors in Texas and writers in the 1850s praised the Texas Germans for their intelligence, industry, and thrift. Frederick Law Olmsted, writing in the mid-1850s contrasted the Germans' intensive and diversified farming methods with the careless, casual practices of southern Anglo-Americans. The German settlers, as Jordan points out in his detailed account of the period, were more attached to the land and far less likely to heed the call of greener pastures in Oregon or gold fields in California than their Anglo-American neighbors.[16]

One observer in the postbellum period described the German settlements near San Antonio, noting the more settled and refined appearance of the country as one approached the German settlement of New Braunfels:

> This whole region . . . is settled very largely
> by old country Germans, and they have left their im-
> press of industry, order and economy on this section,
> as they have always done wherever they have found a
> home in the new world.[17]

Among the most valuable lessons the German-American farmer learned from his Anglo-American neighbors was the importance of innovation, improvisation, and experimentation to survive in Texas, especially in the Western counties.

An enormous increase in the Lutheran population occurred after 1840 as Norwegian, Swedish, and Danish Lutherans joined the rising tide of German Lutherans pouring into the midcontinent from Texas to Canada. German Lutherans had been an important element in the colonial and charter population of the Republic. The new, intensely orthodox immigrants, however, represented a tradition within German Lutheranism that contrasted with those of their colonial co-religionists. Moreover, Lutheranism in the late colonial and early national periods had moved away from many of its continental traditions with the passage of generations, and it began to resemble other major Protestant denominations more and more—especially Presbyterianism, Methodism, and Episcopalianism. In part this resulted from common religious interests and problems and from the deliberate desire on the part of some Lutherans to give their church more of what they considered to be the vigor of Presbyterianism and the warmth of Methodism. Because of these tendencies, Lutherans in the United States gradually lost much of their distinctiveness. Rationalist influences strongly affected them and weakened the strength of their devotion to

historical Lutheran doctrine and adherence to traditional
liturgical practices.  The doctrinal differences that set them
apart were less well defined than previously; consequently the
Lutherans' sense of their own distinctiveness diminished.  A
movement to blend and unite with other denominations became
increasingly widespread.  In New York the feeling of intimacy
between Lutherans and Episcopalians led to negotiations for the
mergence of the two churches, but this was never accomplished.
The cooperation of Lutheran and Reformed synods in Pennsylvania
led to the sharing of common hymnals and catechism.  In the
face of this so-called unionism or ecumenism, a counter movement began that sought to stimulate denominational loyalty and
doctrinal purity.  Gradually it gained strength and by the
1820s and 30s showed signs of vigor.  The revival of Lutheran
consciousness, however, resulted chiefly from the arrival of
large numbers of rigid confessionalists from Europe.[18]
     In 1817 the King of Prussia initiated efforts to bring
about the union of the two main Protestant denominations, Lutheranism and the Reformed church.  He sought to further the
union by encouraging the clergy to formulate common articles of
faith and a common liturgy.  In 1830 he issued a royal decree
that abolished the use of the old denominational books and
forced the acceptance of the new common books and liturgy,
which, of course, were neither Reformed nor Lutheran but rather
constituted a compromise.  The effort to force a union of the
two Protestant Churches led to a revival of denominational
loyalty among some groups.  Congregations calling themselves
"Old Lutherans" separated from the official State Church.  Some
elements of orthodox Lutheranism decided in favor of emigrating
to America in order to free themselves from the constraints imposed upon their religious life by the Prussian ruler and the
leaders of the State Church.[19]
     A group of orthodox Lutherans left Prussia in 1839 and
settled in Buffalo and Milwaukee.  The Buffalo Lutherans formed
their own synod in 1845 in order to maintain in vigor and
purity their rigidly defined doctrines and religious discipline.  Similar congregations of orthodox Lutheran immigrants
came with their leader, Martin Stephan, from Saxony in 1839 and
settled in St. Louis and in Perry County, about one hundred
miles to the south.  St. Louis drew a large orthodox immigration first from Saxony and later from other areas in Germany.
Some immigrants came first to the eastern seaboard; others entered the country by way of the Gulf of Mexico and sailed up
the Mississippi to St. Louis.
     Soon after the arrival of the first group of Missouri Lu-
therans, leadership fell to one of the young pastors, C. F. W.
Walther, who had accompanied them from Saxony.  From 1839 until
his death in 1887, the devout and orthodox Walther remained the
leading figure in Missouri Lutheranism and, indeed, one of the

great forces in the history of Lutheranism in America.  As the
number of German Lutherans in the region increased, efforts to
form a new synod came to fruition.  The German Evangelical Lutheran Synod of Missouri, Ohio, and other states (which became
known as the Missouri Synod) was organized with Walther as its
first president.  At the time of Walther's death almost five
decades later, the synod had expanded to fifteen hundred congregations, a fact which attests to the vigor of Missouri Lutheranism.[20]  Walther founded the journal, *Der Lutheraner*, in
1844; and its vigorous polemical discussions of doctrine attracted wide attention to Walther and the Missouri Lutherans.

The divisions among Lutherans in America gave rise to bitter controversies.  A long and sharp exchange occurred between
the Buffalo and Missouri Lutheran groups, both of whom were
conservative.  Walther also founded a monthly theological
journal, *Lehre und Wehre*, in 1855 that, under his editorship,
became the principal medium of the Missouri Lutherans for pre-
senting their position in disputes with other Lutheran bodies.
The disputants rarely encountered one another personally, but
argued out their principles in written theses and countertheses
in vituperative German.  The Missouri Synod, wishing to avoid
dependence upon European seminaries for its pastors, established its own.  A system of German Lutheran parochial education was also developed in order to defend their children
against the paganism that Lutherans believed characterized the
public schools.  The English schools and even the English language seemed to be insidious vehicles of the liberalism and
rationalism they were so strenuously seeking to exclude from
their religious thought and practice.

Unlike those who came to Missouri, Iowa, and Buffalo, the
German Lutherans who settled in Wisconsin, Michigan, and Minnesota had emigrated more because of political dissatisfac-
tions than for religious reasons.[21]  Synods were formed in
Wisconsin in 1850 and in Michigan and Minnesota in 1860.  After
lengthy discussions, they finally reached common positions on
doctrine and practice and eventually formed a joint Synod.

The Lutherans of the Iowa Synod differed from the Missourians in their assertion that certain scriptural doctrines
were not clearly defined in the Augsburg Confessions and that
therefore there could be legitimate fellowship among Lutherans
differing in these matters.  That being true, they argued, it
was acceptable to share the pulpit and altar with Lutherans
whose differences from their beliefs were of this nature.  The
Missourians opposed this as "unionistic poison that drives congregations into the arms of skepticism and infidelity."[22]
There was, they argued, only one correct interpretation of each
doctrine taken from the Scriptures.  Walther, like other leaders, hoped that ultimately a single Evangelical Lutheran Church
would emerge to embrace all Lutherans in North America, but

there could be no compromise.  In spite of a large measure of
doctrinal agreement as well as their common origin and traditions in Europe, the differences among German Lutherans seemed
too important to warrant any concessions even though they saw
the hand of Satan in the issues that divided them.

The rising tide of confessional Lutheranism aroused the
opposition of older Lutheran bodies in the United States.
Leaders of the older "American Lutheranism," like Dr. S. S.
Smucker, Dr. Benjamin Kurz, and Dr. Samuel Sprecher, President
of Wittenberg College, emphasized "religion of the spirit"
rather than "religion of forms."  The highly liturgical worship of conservative Lutherans seemed too reminiscent of the
Roman Church.  The American Lutheran movement stressed personal
piety above doctrine and all else.  Moreover, the aggressiveness and argumentativeness of orthodox Lutherans repelled the
American Lutherans.

By 1859 the American Lutheran movement had succumbed to
the new and more vigorous orthodox Lutheranism.  Controversy
among German Lutherans, however, continued to flourish, now
focusing on the divine obligation of Sunday observance, the
right to demand interest, the question of whether or not the
Pope was anti-Christ, and predestination (most bitterly argued
of all).  The Norwegian, Swedish, and German Lutheran Churches
continued to grow rapidly in midcentury and after, not only
through the migratory floodtide and the high birth rate of the
immigrant families, but also by virtue of the aggressive missionary spirit of the Churches.  Many of the Germans and Scandinavians who came to the Middle West were not identified with
any church.  They were a fertile field for the missionary activities of Lutheran synods to till.

The spirit of factionalism characterized what has been
called the Middle Age of American Christianity.  It was not
only the Lutherans who suffered internal divisions.  Controversies abounded, and religious factions frequently split from
established Churches to form new denominations.  Sectarian in-
tolerance gave rise to numerous heresy trials in various Protestant denominations during this period.  Among Roman Catholics, as well, persistent controversies focused upon the matter
of lay and clerical trusteeship of Church properties.

By the close of the 1840s the movement of Germans into
Illinois, Iowa, and Wisconsin was swelling into a great wave.
Chicago was emerging as a center of settlement.  Dubuque, She-
boygan, Davenport, Des Moines, and the fertile corn fields of
Iowa, were attracting large German populations.  Milwaukee was
already claiming to be a "German Athens" in America.  Several
immigrants from Württemberg established the first of the breweries "that made Milwaukee famous" (including Schlitz, Pabst,
Blatz, and others).  Robert W. Wells has pointed out the logical progression of events that started with the secession

and ended with the great industrial growth of Milwaukee breweries:

> If the Southern states had not seceded, there
> would have been no Civil War.  If there had been no
> Civil War, it would not have been necessary to impose
> a one-dollar tax on whisky, doubling the price
> charged in Milwaukee saloons.  If Milwaukee's thrifty
> saloon patrons had not sought to counteract this in-
> flationary trend, they would not have switched to
> beer, the breweries would have continued to be small,
> family operations, making only enough to supply the
> neighborhood trade.  And if Milwaukee had not become
> famous for its breweries—but that is too humiliating
> to contemplate.[23]

In 1850 approximately 64 percent of the population of the city was foreign born and almost two-thirds of these were natives of Germany.  The size and cohesiveness of the German-town community in northwestern Milwaukee made German influence in many ways the most distinctive feature of the city in mid-century.  The Germans were largely skilled artisans, carpenters, masons, painters, smiths, tailors, shoemakers, and saddlers; because of their skills, most of them quickly secured a comfortable living for themselves and their ample families.  Immigration to Wisconsin from various parts of Germany was stimulated by letters sent home by early settlers like Franz Neukirch and Hermann Kemper and by the books of Carl E. Hasse, Carl de Haas, and Ferdinand Goldmann, which described the soil and climate of Wisconsin as well as its favorable political circumstances.[24]  To provide additional impetus to migration, the Milwaukee city and the state governments made special efforts to attract German settlers.  In 1851 the city council appointed an alderman to go to New York and represent the advantages of Wisconsin in proselytizing efforts among immigrants entering the port of New York.  Later, pamphlets advertising the advantages of Wisconsin were distributed in Germany.  Chicago and Milwaukee competed strenuously among the hordes of immigrants for the favors of the skilled artisans and technicians.

The Roman Catholic population of Wisconsin was sufficiently large by the 1840s to justify the creation of a Catholic diocese.  The German-Swiss prelate, John Martin Henni, was appointed as the first bishop.  The creation of the bishopric with a German-speaking bishop is said to have encouraged many German Catholics to emigrate to Wisconsin.  With the acceleration in the growth of the Catholic population, an archbishopric was established in Milwaukee and Henni became the first archbishop.

At the same time that hundreds of thousands of Germans were pouring into the new western lands, large numbers were settling in the older, established cities.  By the end of 1850, there were perhaps one hundred thousand Germans in New York City.  Fifty German schools had been established.  Many German bookstores and printing establishments met the special needs of the immigrants.  Two German language daily newspapers were being published in the city.  A theater was founded for German audiences.  As in other cities throughout the country, a large number of cultural societies were formed wherever a substantial German population had congregated.  Their activities not only influenced the life of the German population but that of the general population as well.  The musical interests and activities of Germans in Buffalo, Charleston, St. Louis, and Philadelphia had an effect upon general musical tastes and activities.  The Germans introduced a type of continental leisure that contrasted quite distinctly with that of the Yankees.

There were many men of great talent and learning, known as the *Dreissiger*, among the German immigrants of the 1830s and 40s.  Distinguished scholars like Francis Lieber (author of *Political Ethics*), Franz Gräber, Karl Beck, Franz Grund, and Carl Follen became teachers at Harvard.  Among the men of singular achievement and leadership were Gustav Körner, Konstantin Hering, and Friedrich Münch.

Carl Follen was a great friend of William Ellery Channing and together with him took part in many controversial activities on behalf of freedom of speech and religion and the fight for abolition.  One of Channing's earliest biographers believed that Channing had been influenced more by Follen's thoughts than by any other personal relationship.  Follen, through his teaching at Harvard and his friendship with Channing, had great influence on the New England intellectuals of his day.  His translations of German literary works were circulated in manuscript form.  These translations and his lectures contributed to the increase of interest in Schiller and Goethe.  The influence of German theological thought on New England transcendentalism was greatly advanced by the works of Beck and Follen.[25]  Follen perished at sea on a stormy January night in 1840.

Along with the farmers, craftsmen, and mechanics, men of unusual musical and artistic talent or of scholarship were able to make special contributions to their adopted homeland.

A number of intellectuals who arrived in the 1830s and 40s had had experience in printing in Germany and were able to establish themselves as publishers of books and newspapers.  The German language press experienced a resurgence in this period.  The newspapers that began to appear in increasing numbers contributed to the binding of German-American populations into more cohesive communities.  Paradoxically at the same time they

did much to quicken the pace of acculturation into American society.  The foreign language newspapers in the United States
helped newly arrived immigrants to orient themselves to the un-
familiar physical and cultural environment they had entered.
They informed their readers about public affairs and encouraged
them (often in a very partisan manner) to take an interest in
American politics.  The foreign press made subscribers aware of
opportunities available to them.  Even advertisements conveyed
useful information.  Many editors addressed themselves vigorously to the task of countering the evils they saw in nativism,
discrimination against foreigners, slavery, and political corruption.  The foreign press had another, quite different function.  The newspapers provided the immigrant with some continuing contact with the home country.  They followed the principal
events occurring in Germany and in Europe generally.  Loyalty
to the native language and culture was stressed; readers were
encouraged to retain important aspects of their cultural heritage.  The newspapers interpreted both the old world and the
new to their readers.  Along with the church and school, newspapers were an important creative force in giving shape to the
hybrid culture that characteristically arose among immigrants
and their children.

In 1848 it was estimated that there were seventy newspapers published in the United States, and half of them were
published in Pennsylvania.  Philadelphia Germans had two German language dailies.  One of them, the *Alte und Neue Welt* was
among the most distinguished German newspapers in the United
States.  Its founder, Johann George Wesselhöft, brought a hand
press with him from Europe in 1833 and began to print books
and other materials.  On January 1, 1834, he printed the first
issue of the *Alte und Neue Welt*, which quickly won the respect
and esteem of the Philadelphia Germans.  The newspaper helped
to strengthen the journalistic standards of German language
newspapers in America.  Wesselhöft's editorials reflected the
views of liberal refugees in America.  The editor was critical
of certain aspects of American life, but took pains to show
how German-Americans could make contributions to their adopted
country.[26]

The *New Yorker Staatszeitung*, which first appeared on December 24, 1834, has maintained a position of eminence among
German-American newspapers from its beginning to the present.
Its early editors, among them Oswald Ottendorfer, won an excellent reputation for their journal, and it quickly became a
financial success.  This was an extraordinary accomplishment
considering the high mortality rate characteristic of foreign
language newspapers.  At the beginning of its publication, the
editor established its identity as an American newspaper, but
simultaneously stressed the importance of cherishing and cultivating the German language and culture.  In 1850, four German

daily newspapers were appearing in New York—more than German
cities like Berlin and Leipzig were supporting.[27]

In parts of Maryland heavily settled by Germans in the
colonial period, German-American families were being rapidly
assimilated; aspiring editors found little support for their
projected enterprises.  In Baltimore, however, the German population was increasing, and its support was vigorous.  The outstanding German language newspaper of the period was the
*Deutsche Correspondent*, published by Friedrich Raine.  The
newspaper, which appeared first in 1841, reflected the disin-
clination of its editor to make it a means of propagating his
personal political views.  Raine devoted most space to the pre-
sentation of succinct news reports, and editorial opinions were
restricted to modest proportions.

The rapidly growing German population in Cincinnati and
its environs encouraged the birth of numerous journalistic enterprises.  The most eminent German newspaper of the period was
the *Cincinnati Volksblatt*, which was founded in 1836 and continued publication until it succumbed to the anti-German feeling of the First World War.

St. Louis was becoming the center of a great surge of
German immigration in Missouri.  In 1835 Heinrich Bimpage established the *Anzeiger des Westens*, which, under the editorship
of Wilhelm Weber, soon won recognition as the leading German
newspaper in the region.  The paper gained much from Weber's
ability to persuade eminent German Americans like Körner and
Münch to contribute articles.

In 1844, when Milwaukee had a population of sixty-four
hundred, Moritz Schoeffler founded the *Wisconsin Banner*.  He
began publication at an opportune time, for the German population in Wisconsin was growing rapidly.  Many of the German
residents had become incensed at the rise of American nativism
and looked forward to having a newspaper that could fight back.
The editor of the Irish *Courier* welcomed the *Wisconsin Banner*
as an ally in the struggle against nativism.

Newspapers for German readers appeared in a large number
of communities all over the nation: in Canton, Galveston, New
Orleans, Charleston, Reading, and elsewhere.  The German-
American press contributed much to a sense of social unity
among members of the German community.  Old files of such well-
edited newspapers as the St. Louis *Anzeiger* contain an interesting portrait of the lives of German residents in that period.  The newspapers not only helped to bind immigrant families
into a German-American community and to remind them of the
value of their cultural heritage, but also encouraged and
guided their accommodation to American society.

## GERMAN SETTLERS LOOK AT AMERICA:
## A MIRROR FOR AMERICANS

German-Americans, like other immigrants, came to America
with their own individual anticipations of what it would be
like to live and work in America.  These expectations provided
motivation for emigration from their homeland.  They had been
shaped by the accumulating folklore about America, by letters
and tales from friends and relatives there, and by the advertisements posted by immigrant recruiters.  The anticipation of
life in the United States was generally highly positive in the
balance, but there were often grave concerns and skepticism
about some aspects of life in the New World.

Just as the native Americans observed the immigrant groups
and made judgments about what they were like and how they be-
haved, new settlers made observations of the land and people
among whom they settled.  The newcomers quickly set about the
task of putting some order to their observations about America,
about the physical and social attributes of the country.  The
notions that they formulated provided them some cue as to how
to treat Americans and how to accommodate themselves to the requirements of the new environment in such a way as to secure
advantage for themselves.  The culture that new settlers
brought with them constituted a perceptual screen through which
they viewed Americans and American society: it provided them
with a framework with which they could make some systematic
comparisons of life in the old and new lands.  But it served
also to distort the image of America.

What most immigrants saw was that part of American life
that touched them most directly in their own daily life.  Few
Europeans in America had the chance to move around the country
in all sections and regions and see people in various circumstances or different classes and groups as did the rich and influential visitors like de Tocqueville or Harriet Martineau.
Nevertheless their observations gave insight not only into the
processes of their own accommodation to America but also into
the social character of ordinary America.

They observed the native Americans with whom they came
into contact, and other ethnic groups as well, although these
were rarely as important in their lives as the more numerous
old Americans.  They learned how the others were different from
people they had known before or from members of their own group
in America among whom they may have settled.  Their observations and their interpretations were pragmatic, but often revealed shrewd and perceptive comparisons of peoples.  Their notions, were, however, no more than unrefined generalizations
that, however valuable in guiding them in their practical,
daily interaction with others, were likely to show distortions,
misconceptions, and exaggerations.  This is also true of the

notions or stereotyped conceptions the old stock Americans had
of various ethnic groups in their midst.  Apart from sentiments
of malice or intentions to take advantage of members of another
group, there was inevitably much confusion, uncertainty and
doubt as the culturally different groups came into contact.
When the newcomers found themselves in particular difficulties
in such contact, they tended to pull back into their own group
where their personal relationships could be comfortable and
spontaneous rather than tension-laden and calculated.  When
tensions were relieved they felt freer to form new associations,
to govern their behavior according to other (American) models
rather than the traditional models of their group.

There was, of course, great diversity among Germans in
America in their views of American society.  While they shared
a general cultural tradition that tended to determine the way
they saw America, this cultural tradition was itself characterized by subcultural variation.

What later generations know about the experience of German
and other immigrant groups in accommodating themselves to American society comes largely from diaries, journals (published
and unpublished), letters, and books written to guide those in
the homeland considering emigration.

### Family Life in America

American family patterns were of great interest to the
German settlers: the details of domestic life, the raising of
children, the relationship of husband and wife, and the economic functions of the family.  The child-oriented family life
and the characteristic independence of undisciplined children
were frequently (and critically) observed and recorded by
German-Americans.  Some American parents seemed incredibly in-
dulgent of their children according to standards of behavior
that seemed sensible to German-Americans.

> Many parents, who like to think of themselves as
> emancipated individuals, want their children to expe-
> rience the same freedom and permit them not to attend
> school.  When these children grow up, they become use-
> less loafers and rowdies, roving in bands on the
> streets and swayed by political demagogues.[28]

Over and over, German-Americans made a point of empha-
sizing how much women were honored in the United States.  It
seemed that women expected and received deference.  While they
worked hard at cleaning and ordering the household (sometimes
even helping in the garden), the farm females never worked with

their men in the fields.  Some observers were sure that American women had little to do and were dull and indolent.

> The husband must buy the groceries, start the
> fire, and milk the cows.  Outside of doing the wash,
> the American wife is more or less free.  The general
> respect for womanhood causes parents to spoil their
> daughters and neglect teaching them the necessary
> skills for managing a household.  It is little wonder
> that they often attend such ridiculous women's rights
> conventions where they praise woman's noble position
> in society, even though one can find nowhere else so
> few good housewives as in America.[29]

It was natural for German-Americans to look at the families of their neighbors largely in terms of their own traditional beliefs about the way family life should be, how the
tasks should be divided among family members, and what the relationships should be.  The judgments they made about American
families were often a mixture of perceptive observations, sur-
face impressions, and silly interpretations, which is precisely
what occurred when native Americans observed the newly settled
German-Americans in their midst.

> The American women stay at home and are quite
> modest.  They have a good practical sense, but one
> misses the heartiness in their activities and their
> relationship with their husbands.  The lively ex-
> change of ideas among members of the family which is
> characteristic of German homes is lacking.  American
> women like to sit in their rocking chairs.  They en-
> joy being at home . . . The husbands let the wives
> become rulers of the house and they tend to control
> all household affairs.  The conduct of American women
> is somewhat more free than in Europe.  Marriage seems
> to be more of a business than anything else to them.[30]

The German-Americans generally placed great stress on the
family as a humanizing and socializing agency.  Putting strong
emphasis upon the internal workings of their own domestic life,
they were likely to be very observant of the differences they
witnessed in the native-born families surrounding them.  Their
own children, often perplexed by the differences they witnessed
in the family patterns of their American friends, brought questions and points of confusion to their parents for explanation.
Despite all the acculturation and assimilation that occurred
among German families in the United States, some characteristic
differences in family life continued to exist, sometimes into
the third and fourth generation beyond the immigrant generation.

*Money and Social Classes in America*

One of the most frequent characterizations of the American people of all classes was that they were inordinately interested in money and preoccupied with amassing wealth.  The tendency to judge people and things in terms of their estimated pecuniary worth was a corollary of this fault.  Americans, Frau Bylandh wrote, hate no one; they just love money.  Cleverness is admired even when it is demonstrated in ways that are obviously not altogether ethical.  So, Frau Bylandh observed, America is a land where one never saw a smooth brow, a cheerful look, or a pleasant smile; where joyful song never quickened one's heart; where everyone worshiped money and men were always contending with each other for it, climbing, falling, and climbing again, never being contented to be at rest.  Nevertheless, immigrants largely attracted to America by the better chances for economic advantages, as well as the older German-American settlers, valued highly the opportunity of improving their economic circumstances, or at least of trying to do so.  No one could really claim that this was exclusively an American fault.  Moreover, there were a number of virtues that Germans found in the American people that acted as a counterweight.  One of these positive characteristics (and this at least in part argues against some of the allegations above) was that in America people were generally treated in more human terms than they were in Europe.  No one was expected to show his subservience to another human being.  No man, however rich, was regarded as a different kind of human being from those less affluent around him.  The frequency with which this is mentioned by German-Americans speaks eloquently about the memories of their social experience in Germany.

> The American farmer is free and he knows it.  He
> and the President of the nation and all of the public
> officials are simply fellow citizens; none is better
> or worse than the others.  Here you find neither the
> pride of the rich German farmers nor the cringing
> servility of the poor German peasants.  American
> farmers, regardless of how much wealth they possess,
> still treat each other as equals.  These farmers will
> be the salvation of the Union in its time of peril.
> They will rise and show all American citizens where
> their interests really lie, and destroy the corrupt
> party machines.[31]

A German living in Texas found that workers were much more sincerely attached to their employers in this region than in Europe since they were treated as equals rather than as creatures on a lower rung of the social ladder.  Any one coming to

the United States with plans to farm on a grand scale might
very well find unresolvable problems.

> No land is less suitable for European gentleman-
> farmers than America, where the feudal system and
> peasant servitude do not exist.  All farmers in Amer-
> ica have equal rights and no one is suppressed or
> wronged by his neighbor.  Former gentlemen-farmers
> must not only change their view of the nature of the
> social order, but must also learn completely new
> methods of farming . . . The whole system of levies
> and special privileges for gentleman-farmers is
> repugnant to Americans. . . . [32]

Neighborliness, the willingness of the people to help
those in need, seemed a most admirable trait.  If the social
welfare agencies in Germany provided some kind of help for
victims of disaster or bereavement, in America such aid came
mostly from neighbors.

> One very praiseworthy characteristic of Ameri-
> cans is their willingness to help each other in time
> of need.  When a farmer is sick, others harvest his
> crops for him; when a house burns down, charitable
> neighbors often more than cover the destitute family's
> losses.  This is true in the cities as well as in the
> country.  However, general charities, as one finds
> them in Europe, are not well known here.  Perhaps
> that is because beggars are still not common here,
> because of the almost universal prosperity.  Also as
> a consequence of this prosperity, Americans seldom
> lock their doors and farmers let their stock wander
> in the open.  Thievery is not nearly as common here
> as in Europe. [33]

Americans appeared well aware of their principal national
virtues and were extravagantly appreciative of them.  This led
some European visitors to conclude that Americans were certainly the most conceited people anywhere on earth.  Others
found this pride or even self-assertiveness to be of no great
defect.

> As Americans lounge easily in their taverns,
> they have an air about them which says: "I am a
> citizen of the Land of the Free and the Home of the
> Brave and recognize no higher power on earth over me.
> No one can limit me except the laws, which I myself
> make." [34]

Despite apparently easy confidence, Americans often showed
uncertainty about themselves and their country in terms of European comparisons, which at times revealed an almost pathetic
desire for the approval of strangers of the new nation and its
institutions.

The American disposition to keep busy and to invent new
ways of doing things was noted and, generally speaking, appreciated as an appropriate adaptation to life under the social
circumstances existing in the country.  As Victor Bracht
pointed out to his German compatriots in Texas, one cannot ap-
ply European patterns of behavior and systems of value to circumstances existing in newly settled areas of America.  Americans seemed inclined to spend their time with the most obvious
and immediate tasks involved in making a living and devoted
less time to reflection or appreciation of nature than many
German Americans thought they should.

> Americans do not appreciate the beauties of
> nature and view the most beautiful and most odious
> landscapes with the same indifference.  Indifference,
> even-temperedness, and shrewdness are unmistakeable
> characteristics of the American mentality.  The high-
> est interest in their life is to satisfy their desire
> to accomplish something, to undertake something.
> They are more interested in expressing themselves in
> the external world than in receiving impressions.[35]

Perhaps the love of activity characteristic of American
life was responsible for the proliferation of laws.  If new
settlers were sometimes dismayed by the widespread disregard
for law in America, they were equally dismayed by the abundance
of laws and the manner of their application in the courts of
the land.  Making laws and engaging in litigation seemed at
times to be two favorite American pasttimes.  The apparent enjoyment of litigation, as a form of legitimatized hostility,
seemed strange.  The amount of disputation in the courts, especially over issues involving land, appeared staggering in its
proportions.  In Europe land titles were most stable.  Perhaps
that was because ordinary people felt they lacked the same access to the courts of the richer and more powerful elements in
the population.  German-Americans tended to be very conservative in this matter; they were frequently warned by their compatriots to be careful to secure legal titles when they purchased land.  The contentiousness of lawyers and the strangely
informal and haphazard forms of securing justice through the
courts in America seemed to provide little encouragement for
the German-Americans to emulate the native-born in their love
of litigation.

> A lawyer's main goal is to cloud the issue, not
> to establish the truth.  The state legislatures meet
> every year for several months to pass new laws in un-
> believable quantity; many states' law books are big-
> ger than those of European countries hundreds of
> years older . . . Because of the corruption existing
> in the party system, the saying: "the small thief is
> hanged, the big thieves are let go" is often true.
> In New York the courts, the jails and the police de-
> partment are corrupt—mainly because the party system
> permits offices to be given as political rewards
> rather than on the basis of ability.[36]

The convulsive political activity that regularly occurred
a month or so before each election was uniformly followed by a
long period of complete political indifference and lethargy on
the part of the public.  This behavior seemed to many German-
Americans to represent a clear invitation to elected officials
to behave without a proper sense of accountability.  During
the prime period of electioneering, the heat of battle brought
forth an incredible avalanche of personal invective against opposition candidates, all of which seemed to many new settlers
to be beneath the dignity of a mature and democratic people.
The press, which appeared to play such an important part in the
formation of political attitudes, was often charged with irresponsibility and malice.  As one German writer said caustically:

> All education in America tends toward training
> men to be merchants.  If one fails as a merchant, one
> practices with a doctor or lawyer and then sets up
> one's own practice.  Failing in this, one becomes a
> newspaper man and publishes a newspaper with seven-
> teen columns of advertising and three columns of
> slander against the government.[37]

### The Military

German settlers frequently expressed wonder at the marked
contrast existing between the kinds of military provisions being made in the United States and those generally found among
the German principalities.  It seemed strange that the United
States with its vast territories maintained only a small standing army—no more than a few thousand men.  Happily, military
expenditures did not place a grave burden upon the populace,
nor did military personnel bring a curse upon the people near
whom they were stationed.  There was actually little contact
with the troops, which, in the absence of a threat from Indians
or foreign dangers, was an unquestioned advantage.

The same kind of observations were made with regard to naval forces:

> The American navy is unimpressive when one con-
> siders America's position as the second greatest mer-
> chant nation in the world.  Still in one year America
> could transform her merchant marine into naval war
> vessels.  In as much as almost every man along Ameri-
> ca's coasts is a natural born sailor, there would be
> no lack of willing sailors for an American naval
> fleet.  America need fear no European naval power.[38]

A further contrast that was often noted lay in the forms of military dress and deportment.  German-Americans could write home that there was none of the ridiculous pomp or exaggerated military pride that so generally characterized the officers and men in the armies of the German states.

There was some humor in these circumstances, as well as gratitude.  The raggle-taggle dress of state militias could not help but bring amused smiles to many German faces; the awkward-ness of military exercises and maneuvers also provoked amuse-ment, as Beyer noted in 1838.  At least, he concluded, America was not a military state, and the American people were to be envied for that.  Johann Jakob Rütlinger noted that the uni-formity of military dress, the shining metal of muskets, the even array of buttons of the same size and shape in truth made little difference when the homeland was in danger.  What im-pressed him most, he wrote, was that the people were proud of their freedom and appeared willing to defend it, and that was what was crucial to the preservation of the nation.[39]

There were, however, other observers among the German-Americans who had misgivings about the small standing army and the poorly trained state militias: they feared that one day the nation might have to pay dearly for its lack of military and naval forces.  The present standing army was made up of only a few thousand men, mostly Irish, Frau Bylandh noted with con-cern; and these were scattered across the North and the West. This was not enough for the defense of the country.  The state militias were often laughable in that they had almost as many officers as troops.  At least, she concluded, their quaint pa-rades served, on occasion, to break the monotony of everyday life.[40]

> The Americans do not hold their promises to the
> Indians as binding.  Why else does America pay its
> small army, made up mostly of Irishmen, to protect it
> from the Indians with whom it supposedly has diplo-
> matic relations?  Only because the army cannot really
> control the Indians, do Americans find it necessary

at times to make concessions to the Indians.  An Indian army travels faster than an American courier.
Because of these circumstances, European settlers in
the West serving in the militias are well-practiced
in quick retreats and Christian patience.[41]

One German-American writer in the 1850s expressed the conviction that America was well able to defend itself with its
state militias, its sharpshooting farmers inspired by love of
freedom.  Yet he gave a warning.

America should always remain neutral and never
wage an aggressive war because graft makes America's
army one of the most expensive in the world and the
nation could not afford a long war.  Moreover, America needs its youth too desperately to man its industries, and the economy would be seriously damaged
if too many workers went away to war.[42]

*The Relationships between the Races*

Most German immigrants saw people of African origin for
the first time when they entered the American port cities of
Baltimore, Boston, New York, and New Orleans.  What generally
impressed them most was the squalor and degradation characterizing the life of this segment of the population even outside
the deep South.  What they observed was hard to understand in
the light of the nation's ideals, although sometimes the inferiority of the Negro social position in the north was attributed to their lack of initiative and ability.  Apart from
German communities in Texas, Germans settled largely in areas
where there were relatively few Negro families.  The reasons
for avoidance of the Southern states is reflected in a German
settler's comment on the comparative advantages and disad-
vantages of various sections of the country:

Which American states are most suitable for German immigrants?  All Southern states should be
avoided.  The climate is unfavorable, the ground has
been exhausted by the plantations, and slavery is
practiced there.  Moreover manual labor is looked
down upon as something which puts one in the same
class as the slaves.  The eastern states are already
densely populated and the ground is too expensive.
The New England states should be avoided; not only is
a hypocritical puritanical spirit very much in evidence there but it is the stronghold of anti-foreign
feeling.  For common workers and farmers, the best

opportunities lie in Ohio, Wisconsin, Illinois and
Michigan. Iowa and Minnesota are also promising, but
they are prairie lands with unfavorable weather conditions. Kansas and Nebraska will soon offer good possibilities, but one should wait until the political
(and racial) situation there is more settled.[43]

Addressing himself to the question of what people who were
contemplating coming to the United States should be concerned
with in making a decision in this important matter, Franz
Brauns in 1829 answered by speaking frankly of the racial situation. To ignore the inequities that the African-Americans
faced would, he believed, invite the disillusionment of those
who would come to America expecting a kind of utopia.

> Two million of America's twelve million inhabit-
> ants are Negro slaves; how then can one call America
> the land of equality? Not only are the sufferings of
> the slaves great, that is, they are whipped, they re-
> ceive little or no religious instruction and they are
> sold like cattle. Degrading as this is to the Ne-
> groes, it damages the whites as well.
> According to a Virginian, whenever the fire-bell
> rings, everyone is filled with terror at the thought
> of a Negro uprising. In the North, the free Negroes
> seem almost incapable of obeying moral laws and com-
> mit many crimes. In America the whites may not as-
> sociate with Negroes and if they do they become out-
> casts.[44]

While German settlers, particularly members of sectarian
groups, were characteristically sharp in their condemnation of
the institution of slavery, there were some who expressed the
judgment that the actual conditions of life among some classes
in western European countries were as bad as those of the Negroes in America. This was by no means a justification of
slavery itself or, for that matter, the conditions of life endured by slaves or free Negroes in America.

> So far, the Negroes (in Texas) comprise only a
> small fraction of the total population. Almost with-
> out exception they are treated well and aside from
> the terrible thought of a lifetime of servitude,
> their lot is undoubtedly far better than that of many
> servants and most factory workers in Europe.[45]

When Germans observed the conditions of other ethnic
groups with whom they came into contact and made comparisons

with members of their own group, they frequently made bitterly
critical remarks about some of the recent German immigrants.

> Naturally the various races in Texas stand on
> different cultural levels.  At the lowest level stand
> the copper-colored peons who seem incapable of being
> politically educated.  The newly arrived, coarse Ger-
> man peasants and workers are not much better, but
> there is at least some hope for making good citizens
> out of some of them.[46]

Germans should not have been too offended at the crudity
of their fellow German immigrants in America, two of their compatriots warned in 1839, since after a few years in the atmosphere of democratic social equality, which America provided,
their fellow German-Americans would acquire a reasonable amount
of decorum.[47]

German travellers in America often published accounts of
their travels for the benefit of European readers with a
strange combination of outrageous fantasies and common sensical
observations of Indians and Indian life.  In any event, the accounts provided a very sketchy and inadequate representation of
Indian life.

> The aged receive great respect.  Only through
> merit can one attain a high position in the tribe.
> They are quite hospitable and invite you readily into
> their house to sup with them.  The old customs in
> dress and paint are changed only after much delibera-
> tion . . . The female Indians, and not the males,
> make the declarations of love.  The females are quite
> forward and could make a youth from Berlin blush.
> The women seldom have more than two or three children.
> They know of a plant which serves to inhibit concep-
> tion.  They do not tend to their children every time
> they begin to cry, so that the children soon learn to
> become self-sufficient.[48]

People who had more than casual relationships with Indians
had to know a great deal more about them and their particular
tribal values and customs if they were to have any kind of success in their social intercourse.

Apart from the Moravians and other sectarians who often
worked long and successfully among the Indians, relatively few
Germans had the interest and special understanding that would
have permitted them to see the Indians in terms different and
more favorable than those of the old-American families among
whom they settled.  One is not surprised to find Victor Bracht

speaking of his experience with Indians in Texas (which he con-
fesses to be very limited) in ways that reflect the stereotypes
of the region, i.e., their coarseness, wildness, treachery, cunning, cowardliness, and cruelty.  But, he adds, it is likely
that they had not been exactly improved in their social and
personal characteristics by their contact with the white man.
Yet one still cannot, he says, find a beautiful and poetic side
to them.[49]   Nevertheless, there were some settlers, like Johann
Jakob Rütlinger, who, although he had no special relationship
with the Indians, wrote in the 1820s of their capacity to living according to decent conceptions of duty and responsibility.
It one treated them fairly, he observed, there was no need for
fear of them.  If, however, the Indians were cheated and un-
fairly dealt with, one can well expect their animosity and
desire for revenge.[50]

One of the most extraordinary accounts of the Indians and
whites on the frontier in the later 1840s and early 1850s comes
from the journal of the German-Swiss artist, Rudolph Friedrich
Kurz.  The notes that he took during his years of painting
Indians in the upper Missouri Valley reveal an amazingly sophisticated understanding of Indian culture and the nature of the
impact that the spreading influence of American culture was
having upon the Indians.  The artist-anthropologist understood
the consequences that ensued from the increasing dependence of
Indians upon various kinds of metal ware: knives, guns, axes,
and other objects and commodities such as blankets, coffee, and
sugar that had become indispensable.  Kurz described the Indians in realistic but sympathetic terms.  He felt there could
be no solution of the problems arising between Indians and
whites until the latter were prepared to accept the Indians as
human beings of equal intelligence and capacity.[51]

### A Final Thought

The contrasts and incongruities in the American social
character sometimes confounded many of the German settlers.  As
the German-Swiss school teacher, Johannes Schweizer, wrote in
the 1820s, one minute you might rejoice at your good fortune to
be a citizen in the happy land whose political institutions were
so wisely devised and whose spirit was so free and independent.
The next moment you might want to flee from a people whose
lives seemed formless, governed by materialistic interests, and
the people themselves to have been thrown together by a strange
whimsy of fate, which left them capable only of drifting, un-
guided by traditions or even fixed principles.[52]

At the end of his journal Rütlinger tells his friends in
Europe that if they were now to ask him if he were happy in
America, he would say yes, but it would be a qualified affirma-

tive. The precious freedom one could enjoy, the chance for making a more secure life, the freshness of the country stood in favorable balance against the futility and tired resignation characteristic of so many lives in Europe. But the gravest question remaining in Rütlinger's mind concerned the wisdom and discipline that Americans would be able to demonstrate in the exercise of their freedom and opportunities. America had, he concludes, a great potentiality, but it was a potentiality for good *or* evil. Whichever of the two it should prove to be would be on such a scale as to affect the future of other peoples.[53]

## THE ERA OF EUROPEAN REVOLUTIONS AND THE AMERICAN CIVIL WAR

The year 1848 was marked by revolutionary upheavals throughout Europe. The uprising in France in February of that year came suddenly, with few signs to foretell the approach of national crisis despite the ferment of unresolved political problems and a crescendo of popular dissatisfaction. A single fusilade on the streets of Paris in the evening of February 23 unexpectedly transformed a riot into a revolution. Within a short time the news of events in Paris had set a spark to powder magazines of popular unrest in almost all areas of continental Europe. Austria, the Germanys, and the Italian states were to be profoundly affected by the Revolution in France. But it is likely that some kind of social upheaval would have occurred in the Germanys within a relatively short time without the stimulation of the uprising in Paris.

The Congress of Vienna had organized the thirty-eight states in Germany as the Germanic Confederation. A Diet was established at Frankfurt that functioned as a forum for representatives of the rulers of the sovereign German states. The representative of Austria was named permanent president of the body. The two most powerful states within the German Confederation, Austria and Prussia, contended for predominance of influence and power. The Habsburg emperor ruled over a multinational empire of Austrian-Germans, Czechs, Slovaks, Hungarians, Poles, South Slavs, Italians, and Romanians. Although the Austrian-Germans were the predominant element in the heterogeneous population of the Habsburg empire, other nationalities were numerically superior. This complex situation presented tragically difficult issues to those who sought the unification of the Germanys. Increasingly, those who worked for a liberal, unified Germany looked to the ruler of Prussia for leadership.

The quickening of industrial activity and the expansion of commerce by midcentury had served to alter significantly the social and political balances in Germany. The proletariat, although increasing, still remained without any clear voice. The

middle class was becoming larger and more powerful, but it
lacked an appropriate political representation. The dissatisfaction of the bourgeoisie was becoming broader and more intensive. The fragmentation of German states permitted a system of
tariffs that was highly inimical to the development of trade
and industry. The persistence of feudal privileges retarded
necessary changes in agricultural production and in other sectors of the economy. The social arrogance and the bureaucratic
indifference of the nobility, the military establishment, and
public office holders increasingly antagonized other classes.
Liberal elements desired an end to arbitrary power and police
espionage; they wanted an end to absolutism and sought to secure in Germany the kinds of political rights and forms of
popular representation that existed in Great Britain.

The ferment in the Germanys in early 1848 led to the election of eight hundred representatives of the people chosen by
manhood suffrage. The Frankfurt Parliament met in May to consider the form of government most desirable for the proposed
German national state. It had to address itself to difficult
territorial questions, the most crucial of which was the issue
of whether non-Germanic territories of Austria should be included or excluded in the new Germany.

There were divisions among the delegates as to the specific kinds of political institutions most appropriate for a
united German state. Some favored a constitutional monarchy;
radicals wanted an end to monarchical institutions and pressed
for a republic. The political struggle within the Frankfurt
Parliament and beyond was characterized by impressive debates
on political theory and practice. Equally impressive were the
popular demonstrations of the spirit, idealism, and vigor of
those elements seeking reform, particularly the *Turner* movement
and student organizations.

The lack of actual political experience among liberal elements in Germany had tragic consequences. The inability to
reconcile differences and to deal with the extremely difficult
problems facing the Parliament weakened the forces of revolution, as did the high-minded flights from practical reality
into philosophical fantasy. When the test of strength with the
established order finally came, the advocates of liberal reform
lacked the military arms and equipment as well as the food and
the trained military leadership they needed. When Frederick
William IV refused to accept the position of leadership of the
German federation, the hopes of the revolution were destroyed.
The revolutionary conflagrations in Germany and in Europe as a
whole had risen swiftly in early 1848, and now quickly receded.
The poorly led revolts quickly lost their momentum and failed,
leaving frustration and bitter disillusionment. "The revolution," Pierre Joseph Proudhon said, "had come before its time."

The failure of the revolution in Germany gave further
impetus to German immigration to the United States.  The Germans who came to the United States because of the collapse of
the revolution were to have a profound effect upon American
social and intellectual history.  There was no immigrant group
with which it can be compared except, in some measure, the
movement of refugees from Germany in the era of Hitler.  The
German "Forty-eighters" brought a vigor, talent, and spirit
that transformed the German-American population in the two
decades that followed.  They also exerted an important influence upon American cultural history.

The Forty-eighters included men and women who had actually
taken part in the liberal or radical movements that produced
the uprisings in 1848 and 1849 and who fled the consequences of
defeat.  There were liberals, republicans, and radical reformers of widely divergent kinds among them.  A large number were
university professors and students, pastors and theologians,
lawyers and judges, physicians and scientists, writers and musicians, educators and journalists.  Along with the university-
trained men and women of social standing there were, of course,
many very ordinary people among the Forty-eighters.

There is no way of determining the numbers of Forty-
eighters even in rough approximation.  In any case, they were
a small proportion of the immense migratory stream that left
Germany for the United States in the 1850s.  German immigration
reached flood tide proportions in that decade.  The foreign-
born element in the American population increased 84 percent
and the German-born increased 119 percent.  The peak of German
immigration in the period came in 1854 when 230,000 German immigrants were admitted to the country.  The size of total immigration in this period in its proportion to the current population of the country was higher than at any other decade in
the nineteenth or twentieth centuries.

The political conditions of Germany in the decades of the
midcentury period cannot alone explain the emigration of many
hundreds of thousands of people.  Economic motives were paramount even among most political refugees.  The existence of
relatively extensive economic opportunities on the land and in
the rapidly growing cities of the United States was becoming
increasingly known in Germany.  In addition to those who came
of their own free will, there were some who came because judges
often sentenced guilty political offenders to either emigration
or a prison sentence.  Local governments sometimes gave indi-
gent families who were considering emigration a small stipend
to encourage them to leave, hoping thus to relieve the community of the need to provide for them.  All but a small proportion of the immigrants from Germany came with the training and
vigor necessary to take advantage of the opportunities in

America to make a decent living.  Some did fail and either returned to their homeland or joined the swelling numbers of
urban indigents.

De Tocqueville's *De la Democratie en Amerique* had appeared
in 1835 and was soon widely circulated and read throughout
Western Europe.  It was quickly recognized as a significant
work on a subject that fascinated many Europeans, namely, the
growing young republic in North America.  Its style was clear
and its analysis seemed objective and penetrating.  De Tocqueville's description of the United States added to the impulse
to emigrate.[54]  America seemed to be the land of freedom.  Because of the large numbers of fellow countrymen who had already
settled in America, the German-born could hope to find themselves in an environment where the German language and culture
retained much strength and vitality.  For many immigrants, the
part American and part old country life that they encountered
among their compatriots who were long-term residents of the
new world served to ease the travail of their accommodation to
American society.  To them America was a land not wholly
strange or alien, but one in which a piece of the homeland was
deeply imbedded.  Yet many were to experience the longing expressed by the German-American poet, Carl Heinrich Schnauffer:

> Reichtum suchen, Hütten gründen
> Könnt ihr wohl an jeden Strand.
> Aber eine Heimat finden
> Kann ich nur im Vaterland.[55]

The refugees of the Revolution of 1848 had an immediate,
galvanizing effect upon German communities throughout the
United States.  An immense broadening and intensification occurred in the social, intellectual, and cultural activities of
America's German population.  Indeed, in every community where
large numbers of Forty-eighters settled, but particularly in
major cities, they stimulated new activities in drama, music,
science, education, and, most visibly, journalism.  Zucker
maintains that more Forty-eighters went into journalism than
into any other occupation or profession.[56]  Often, however, the
journalists were at the same time practicing artists, doctors,
translators, tutors, lawyers, educators, merchants, and book
salesmen who willingly devoted whatever leisure they had to
editing journals or writing for them.  The impact of the refugees was quickly obvious.  This was in part due to the nature
and scope of their activities, and in part due to the fact that
their penchant for journalism allowed them to give their activities and views wide circulation.  Almost all segments of the
German population in every part of the country were soon affected by the quickening of political currents and cultural
activities.  But there was a new divisiveness and strife

introduced as well.  For a time, indeed, friction was so
serious between the Grays (those who had arrived before the
Revolution) and the Greens (newly-arrived immigrants) that the
cohesiveness and coherence of German-American communities were
jeopardized.  The Greens were characteristically impatient to
achieve the kinds of reform for which they had worked in vain
in the revolutionary period in Germany.  There were many irre-
sponsible radicals as well as high-minded reformers among them
who could not, in their zeal for change, bother with tact or
concern for other people's sensitivities.

Despite their revolutionary past and their present democratic pretensions, they often showed little compassion for
the limitations of those who were less educated than they.
Some Forty-eighters spoke with undisguised disparagement of
farmers and artisans.  They denounced clerics and clerical influence in terms more appropriate to European than American
social contexts.  They criticized contemporary German leadership in the United States for its failure to become an effective force on behalf of the kinds of political reform they
thought appropriate.  They charged that it had failed to take
issue with clerical influence in political and social affairs
of the country (although there was no established church in
the United States, as there was in Germany).  Added to these
were the further charges that the established leaders had not
provided the kind of direction in efforts to raise the standards of public schools that should have been expected of them.

An inter-generational conflict emerged quickly.  Some of
the established leaders of German-American communities who had
won recognition for their accomplishments were embittered by
such criticisms.  Older settlers in general felt that they had
worked hard and successfully to achieve economic and social
well-being in America and that their accomplishments deserved
respect rather than disparagement from the newcomers.  Moreover,
the sharp criticisms often directed against American institutions and values seemed to them to have been made in lamentable
ignorance of the American social system.  The criticisms on the
part of newcomers seemed presumptuous and discourteous, and the
Grays found it easy to imagine that the American public generally would quickly become disenchanted not only with the newly
arrived refugees from Germany but with all Germans in the
country.  The eagerness with which the Forty-eighters raised
controversial religious issues gave offense to many of the
older German-Americans.  Their support of new biblical criticism in Germany as well as their uncompromising anticlericalism
offended both the Lutherans and the German Catholics.  The St.
Louis *Lutheraner* and German Catholic newspapers like the *Katho-
lische Kirchenzeitung* of Baltimore and the *Wahrheitsfreund* of
Cincinnati found common cause in fighting the attacks upon re-
ligions and religious institutions.[57]

The Forty-eighters were openly scornful and contemptuous
of the editors of existing German-American newspapers.  They
made it clear that they found the style dull and the grammar
atrocious.  The newspapers' editorials were condemned as characteristically shallow, devoid of any fixed principles, and
spineless in posture.  The newspapers founded by the Forty-
eighters, or taken over by them, were generally better written;
in a few years their quality began to raise noticeably the
journalistic standards of the German-American press.  A number
of the Forty-eighters who edited newspapers in the 1850s, or
who wrote for them, won positions of national significance in
journalism or in other fields.  Karl Douai, for example, who
was for a time editor of the New York *Demokrat*, became a distinguished educator.  Carl Schurz was another editor who
achieved prominence and national renown in other fields as well
as journalism.  Joseph Pulitzer, a young German-speaking, Hungarian Jew began his long career in American journalism as a
reporter for a German-American newspaper.

In addition to the larger German language daily newspapers
appearing in major American cities, there were large numbers of
small radical papers published in all parts of the country.
Many of them were created by refugees who had little money but
an abundance of hope and dedication to their principles.  Many
such sheets appeared in the 1850s, only to succumb to debt and
editors' frustrations in a relatively short time.  Some hoped
to save humanity through the conversion of an ever-widening
circle of readers, and in this pursuit endured great hardship.
Some of the more radical and zealous lost themselves in feuds
with those who had rival panaceas.  Personal invective and
abuse reached lamentable dimensions.  Johann Most, editor of
*Freiheit*, gained wide notoriety as one of the few advocates of
anarchism among American editors.  After the assassination of
McKinley, *Freiheit* was suppressed after Most republished an old
article that gave sanction to tyrannicide.  A few of the editors of the small radical newspapers, like Karl Heinzen, won
widespread respect for their unselfishness of purpose, the high
intellectual level of their writing, the fire and spirit with
which most of their journals discussed public issues.  Rarely,
however, were the writings of radical journalists graced with
humor, which would have made palatable their stern convictions
and biting invective.[58]

The German-Americans were not unmindful of the frailties
of their press just as Americans in general were concerned with
the way journalists performed their functions.  Readers sometimes viewed with suspicion reporters' inclinations to pursue
petty personal controversies and to distort descriptions of
persons and events or to dignify triviality with the vestments
of significance when they were unable or unwilling to find
something more noteworthy to occupy their attention.  A poem

in the Buffalo County (Wisconsin) *Republikaner* of July 2, 1870, expressed the criticism humorously:

> Gefährlich ist's den Leu zu wecken
> Verderblich ist der wüste Soff
> Jedoch das Schrecklichste der Schrecken
> Das ist ein "Reporter" ohne Stoff.
>
> Dangerous it is to arouse a lion
> Ugly drunkenness is ruinous
> But the most terrifying thing of all
> Is a reporter out of news.

In the first decade of their residence in America, an agonizing ambivalence toward the United States was often manifested by many of the Forty-eighters. The country of their adoption was the land of Jefferson, the Constitution, and religious tolerance. But they were distressed about the serious imperfections they saw and refused to accept them quietly: the dirtiness, ugliness, and congestion of Eastern cities; crime and prostitution in urban slums; astrology for sale and gross popular superstitions; preoccupation with the accumulation of wealth; fits of free-for-all political activity around election time followed by longer periods of political apathy; and irresponsibility and tolerance of corruption. The Constitution contained a great Bill of Rights about which the world had heard much, and yet slavery was legal. Many German Republicans found it worthy of concern that the president of a democracy held greater executive power in his hands than most of the reigning monarchs of the old world. The Forty-eighters lamented the fact that while Americans were creatively innovative in business affairs and in industry and invention, they seemed loathe to accept innovations in education and in many areas of cultural and intellectual life.

There was an almost universal opposition among German language newspapers to the temperance movement and to such specific manifestations as temperance legislation and Sunday closing laws that appeared to them as infringements upon citizens' personal liberties. Wilhelm Weitling's labor newspaper, *Die Republik der Arbeiter*, might have scolded the workers sharply for having nothing more elevating on their minds during their days off work than drinking beer, but it vociferously defended their right to spend their free time as they chose.[59] Opposition to what they considered to be temperance fanaticism and Sabbatarian narrowness became all the more vehement because they were seen basically as manifestations of an increasing American xenophobia. German-American communities became highly sensitive to various expressions of nativism among the Anglo-Americans. They were especially concerned when their interests

appeared directly and immediately involved.  At times a certain
ambivalence to expressions of nativism appeared when the special target was the Irish population; because many Germans were
convinced that the Irish were dominated by clerical influence
they were haunted by the thought that nativism directed toward
controlling that influence might not be altogether bad.  The
German-language press reflected the popular sensitivity among
its readers by frequent editorials opposing nativism and by
extensive news coverage of popular demonstrations or riots directed against foreign elements.  When in 1859 the Massachu-
setts legislature passed the so-called two-year amendment that
kept naturalized citizens from voting or holding office for two
years after acquiring citizenship, there was a flood of protest
from German communities in all parts of the nation.  Their
press condemned the "Know-Nothing" influences that prompted the
legislature and denounced the obvious intent to reduce the foreign-born citizens to second-class citizenship.

The Forty-eighters intended to convert the cultural wilderness of America into a garden in full bloom—and quickly.  Even
if they were wrong in some of their judgments about American
society and made their share of tactical mistakes, their zeal
and talents resulted in amazing accomplishments.

The Forty-eighters generally acknowledged that the American educational system provided for a larger proportion of
youths than was true in Germany and that this was potentially a
great advantage.  Their criticisms, however, focused upon the
evidence of low educational standards that they felt had accompanied the wide extension of educational opportunities; super-
ficial instruction, thin and poorly balanced curricular fare,
poor texts, the primacy of utilitarian over intellectual values,
and in some instances inadequate school buildings and equipment.
Many were shocked that so few Americans were aware of the contemporary progress of pedagogical theory in western Europe.
Some worked to make the new theories better known and more
widely applied.  Many educated German immigrants directed their
efforts at improving the quality of public education.  German
private schools of high quality were established in many communities, both to serve the needs of the German-American families and to provide models of curriculum design and instruction
for study and emulation (*Anschauungsunterricht*) by the general
public.  Many hoped that German private schools would not only
provide excellent instruction, but that they would also have a
significant effect in preserving German culture undiluted by
the process of cultural hybridization that comes with prolonged
contact of immigrant and host country cultures.  German schools,
secular and religious, appeared in communities all over the
country.  Later institutions like the German-American Teachers
Seminary in Milwaukee were founded to help the German schools
maintain high standards and to provide them with well-trained

teachers.  One of the most able teachers of his generation was
Peter Engelmann, who directed the German-English Academy in
Milwaukee, which for a quarter of a century was widely recognized as the finest school in the city.  The success of his
methods was reflected in changes in the public school system;
in exerting this influence and in other ways, the former editor
of a revolutionary journal in Germany contributed significantly
to the intellectual life of the growing urban center.  In other
areas, other refugee intellectuals played similar roles.  The
German and English Institute established by Friedrich Knapp in
Baltimore applied the educational theories of the Swiss educator, Heinrich Pestalozzi, and won widespread recognition.  A
number of educational institutions of their nature were established in cities in various parts of the country.  The number
of Forty-eighters who taught in public and private schools was
large, and the quality of their teaching remained generally
high.  The kindergarten was introduced from Germany in the
early 1850s by people well acquainted with the principles established by Friedrich Fröbel.  The first kindergarten was
started in Wisconsin by Margaretha Schurz, wife of Carl Schurz.
Others were established in the 1850s in Columbus, Ohio, and
Boston, and later in Hoboken, Newark, New York, and, as the momentum of interest grew, in many other cities.  A number of the
leaders of the movement were German-Americans, like Dr. K. D. A.
Douai and Frau Marie Kraus-Boelte.

The Forty-eighters were able to spread their influence
among German language elements throughout the country by means
of exhibits of arts and crafts, newspapers, books, specialized
periodicals (such as educational journals), and the lecture
platform.  Even relatively small communities held lecture series, debates, and forums.  Among the speakers most favored by
German audiences were celebrities like Carl Schurz, Friedrich
Hecker, and Reinhold Solger, along with a host of less notable
itinerants.  The festive observance of such events as the hun-
dredth anniversary of Schiller's birth in 1859, and a decade
later the birth of Alexander von Humboldt, did much to sustain
national pride and to encourage cultural activities.  There was
an almost incredible response of cultural leaders in German
communities across the country.

German bookstores flourished and the establishment of German libraries contributed much to the availability of reading
material published both in the United States and Germany.  Labor leaders like Wilhelm Weitling, editor of the labor newspaper *Die Republik der Arbeiter*, supported libraries in the
workers' halls in New York and promoted their utilization by
workers.  Similar efforts were made in other cities with large
German populations.

Many Forty-eighters, like Theodor Griesinger and K. D. A.
Douai, wrote of their experiences in the United States princi-

pally for readers in Germany.  Gustav Struve wrote a three-volume work on ancient and medieval history.  The wandering musician and writer, Otto Ruppius, wrote a number of novels in German using American settings, especially the prairies.  His novels were comparable to those of the more widely known Charles Sealsfield (Karl Anton Postl).  Oswald Seidensticker, one of the *Dreissiger* leaders, published a large number of historical works dealing with early German settlements in America. Heinrich Rattermann was also a prolific and respected writer on German history and literature in the United States.  The lawyer and editor, Konrad Krez, who became a general in the Civil War, was possibly the ablest German-American poet in his period.  He published a volume of verse, *Aus Wiskonsin*, in 1875, and a second edition appeared in 1895, which attested to its appeal to German-American readers.  There were many other poets and writers; some were men of considerable literary talent; others had more literary ambition than talent but were nonetheless widely read and appreciated.  Literary journals and reviews appeared, and a national association of German-American writers was founded to promote their interests and the quality of their literary production.  Circles of free thinkers and other groups with special interests and perspectives had their own publishers.

The range of contributions of the Forty-eighters defies easy description.  There were men who made contributions to the cultural life of their adopted country in art, sculpture, music, and lithography.  Many German lawyers successfully adjusted to the American legal system, which was radically different from that of Germany, and established notable careers in law.  A number of German doctors, scientists, and engineers achieved distinction in teaching, research, and public service.  The professional and technical skills of the German immigrants, the Forty-eighters in particular, proved to be of advantage to the United States not only in peacetime but during the Civil War as well.

The German-American population contained a heterogeneous body of educated men and women who supplied leadership for a wide variety of intellectual and social purposes.  Its leadership elements were diverse in their functions and in the basic social and intellectual values that they espoused.  Unlike most nineteenth century national groups that entered the United States, German intellectuals and technological trained elite were well represented among the larger body of farmers, workers, artisans, and traders.  A new elite or a new leadership class did not have to be created in the new world out of the lower class and lower middle class elements predominantly represented in most immigrant groups.  Various religious and secular groups were served by their own corps of leaders, prophets, and writers.  There was, however, no clearly defined national leader-

ship that could claim the loyalties of the German-Americans
collectively.  The German-American population was too large and
too heterogeneous in social characteristics and interests to
permit the emergence of a body of national German-American
leaders.  Yet no immigrant group had more active, constructive
and diverse leadership.

The Germans of all classes in the United States were opposed to slavery, except, perhaps, some segments of those who
settled in the south.  Knowing little of American history and
the complexity of sectional differences, the German immigrants
responded to the public issues arising out of slavery in an
unequivocal way; however, they were concerned about competition
from cheap labor if 3,500,000 slaves were suddenly freed and
moved northward.  Beyond their general condemnation of slavery,
they were divided in their views of political measures and
party platforms.  In the election of 1860, Wisconsin Germans
were divided in their party support.  The spirited support of
Lincoln's candidacy by some of the Forty-eighters did not win
over some of the more conservative elements; especially the
German Catholics who nurtured strong suspicions of the free-
thinking Forty-eighters and were likely to hold themselves
aloof from any cause with which they were identified.  After
the election, some *Achtundvierziger* emigres bitterly denounced
Lincoln for his delay in issuing the emancipation proclamation.

When the Civil War broke out, German volunteers enlisted
in the Union forces in numbers considerably beyond their proportion in the national population.  Of the two million men who
served in the Union Army, it has been estimated that 176,817
were of German birth.  Benjamin Gould, the actuarian of the
United States Sanitary Commission, in his *Investigation in the
Military and Anthropological Statistics of American Soldiers*,
(1869) notes that the Germans in the Union Army were proportionately a larger group than were the Irish or native Americans (who were more often able to pay for substitutes who enlisted for them).  Among the foreign-born soldiers, the Irish
were next most numerous, with 144,221, followed by the British
with 45,508.  (Far more numerous than the foreign-born Germans
were the native Americans of German origin.)

The Germans, Irish, Norwegians, and Swedes all preferred
to serve in regiments and companies that were composed wholly
or mainly of their fellow countrymen.  The urban German and
Irish youths who were frequently engaged in street fighting
found it amusing to be fighting on the same side if not in the
same military units.  The Army in its recruitment acknowledged
their preferences and promoted the enlistment of foreign-born
groups in their own military units.   Thus, in the area of Wisconsin, the Ninth Regiment was composed largely of Germans, the
Fifteenth of Scandinavians, and the Seventeenth of Irish.
There were also German regiments and companies in New York,

Pennsylvania, Ohio, Indiana, and Missouri.  Native American troops in general disliked serving under foreign-born officers, and this fact lent further strength to the tendencies of ethnic segregation.  As the Civil War progressed, the former preferences became less important as they were weakened or overcome. A large number of foreign-born troops fought in mixed contingents, and the proximity of Germans, Irish, Swedes, and Anglo-Americans in combat did much to weld ethnic components together.

Some German immigrants in southern areas like Texas and South Carolina enlisted in the Confederate Army, but their numbers were much smaller than those who fought for the North. Sometimes families were divided in their loyalties; one of the sons of the scholar, Francis Lieber, fought for the Confederacy and two other sons fought in the Union Army.  F. W. Wagener, a civic leader in Charleston, served as a general in the Confederate forces; there were other officers, like the cavalry officer, Heros von Borcke, who commanded southern troops.

At the beginning of the Civil War, the German element in St. Louis proved to be a crucial factor in preventing the pro-Confederate governor and his supporters from swinging the state to the Southern cause.

The rank and file of German soldiers fought well.  Many German immigrants had had extensive military and engineering training and practical experience in the armies of the German states.  This was particularly true among the Forty-eighters. The Union Armies suffered from a lack of trained and experienced military men, and so were eager to utilize the services of the foreign-born officers.  Approximately five hundred German officers of senior rank served in the Union Army, and a far larger number as junior officers.  One of the most notable was General Carl Schurz, a friend of Lincoln and a distinguished leader of German-Americans, who had had little previous military experience.  Some, like General Adolph von Steinwehr, proved to be able military leaders.  Major General Franz Sigel, a popular and well-qualified officer, seemed plagued throughout his military service by misfortunes.  The question of his military capability was raised and generated a long and bitter controversy that lasted through the war years.  Some German-American newspapers, like the Illinois *Staatszeitung*, defended him against what they considered to be unjust attacks.  There were editors who blamed criticism upon newspaper correspondents and West Pointers.  The question of Sigel's military abilities was never really resolved, but for a time the German language press glorified him as the symbol of German-American group loyalty and he was indeed a popular hero to many of them.

Major General Joseph Asterhaus enlisted as a private despite his military training in Europe and won quick promotions by virtue of his service.  He fought in thirty-four battles, and in no battle where he fought independently of another's command did he lose.  The Prussian army officer, August von Willich, supported the Revolution of 1848 and, as an extreme radical or communist, was forced to flee Germany.  The Prussian nobleman was a brilliant military leader.  He served the Union cause well in such battles as those at Chickamauga and Liberty Gap.  After taking Missionary Ridge, General Willich and his brigade, largely German regiments from Indiana, Kansas, Ohio, and Wisconsin, were sent to Texas.  Another distinguished general was Alexander von Schimmelpfennig, who whipped his Pennsylvania troops into what was generally regarded as an elite military unit.  Not all German officers proved to be distinguished in their talents or fortunes (which was similarly true of native officers), but the general standards maintained by both senior and junior officers were high.

Some of the most notable Union officers were of German origin although born in the United States; among the many such officers were General William Rosencrans, General Herman Haupt, and a dashing and glory-conscious cavalry officer named George Armstrong Custer.

Almost two hundred thousand soldiers of German birth fought in the Civil War.  The manner in which they responded to the national crisis gave testimony of their commitment to their adopted country.  In the army the sharpness of their criticisms diminished; they became far more aware of the heterogeneity of the American population and the diversity of its cultural patterns; they came to a greater understanding of the strengths and weaknesses of the American character.  Their service in the Civil War bound them, by common wartime travail, to their fellow citizens.

An especially important contribution to the military forces was made by scientists and engineers who brought unusual and needed talents to the war effort.  Among the physicians and surgeons who contributed to the Union forces were Dr. Gustav Weber and the Vienese physician, Julius von Hausesn.  Count Zeppelin, a cavalry officer and engineer, joined the Union Army in 1863.  He experimented with lighter-than-air crafts and made the first ascent in a military balloon in the United States.

Of all the Germans who came to America in the midcentury period, the most widely respected and personally esteemed was Carl Schurz (1829-1906).  Sixteen years after the twenty-three-year-old Bonn University student had arrived in the United States, he had served his adopted country as Minister to Spain, as an officer of general rank during the Civil War, and had become a United States Senator from Missouri.  During the years from 1877 to 1881 he served as Secretary of the Interior under President Hayes.  Schurz later served in an editorial capacity for the *Nation* and *Harper's Weekly*.  Among the many things that distinguished his public career were his presidency of the Civil Service Reform League and his practical civil service

reforms during the period he was Secretary of the Interior.  He
worked for systematic and practical conservation and for the
establishment of a national park service.  Schurz was one of
the first leaders in efforts to gain reform in the management
of forest resources, a movement much more advanced in Europe.
As Secretary of the Interior he addressed himself to the
desperate plight of the Indians.  An advocate of the assimilation of German immigrants into the mainstream of American life,
he judged the wisest course for the nation to be the rapid absorption of the Indians "by legal means" into the general citizenry, and when this assimilation had occurred, to "treat them
in all respects" like any other citizens of the country.

Soon after Schurz's death, Mark Twain wrote a stirring
tribute in the *Harper's Weekly* of May 26, 1906.  The following
is a small excerpt:

> I had the highest opinion of his inborn qualifica-
> tions for the office: his blemishless honor, his
> unassailable patriotism, his high intelligence, his
> penetration. . . .
> I have held him in the sincerest affection,
> esteem, and admiration for more than a generation.
> I have not always sailed with him politically, but
> whenever I have doubted my own competency to choose
> the right course, I have followed him through without
> doubt or hesitancy.  By and by I shall wish to talk
> of Carl Schurz the man and friend, but not now; at
> this time I desire only to offer this brief word of
> homage and reverence to him, as from grateful pupil
> in citizenship to the master who is no more.

During his lifetime, Schurz was more widely acclaimed and
respected than any other German-American, although there were
others whose accomplishments were equal to his.  To many German-
Americans, he symbolized their participation in national life;
the recognition he won among the populace at large was viewed
symbolically as a recognition of the important place German-
Americans had won in public affairs.  Long after his death and
as long as the German-Americans preserved a sense of their collective identity, he remained a legendary character who person-
ified more fully than anyone else their collective contributions to American society.

## YEARS OF EXPANSION:
## GEOGRAPHIC AND SOCIAL MOBILITY

The period of the Civil War and the succeeding two decades
were characterized by agricultural, industrial, and geographic

expansion.  The common belief in the advancing prosperity of
the nation and in the abundance of opportunities for individual
betterment kept at minor proportions any misgivings concerning
the increasing foreign-born population.  The heavy transatlan-
tic migration of the 1850s was resumed after the end of the
Civil War and grew to even more impressive dimensions.  Improved communication facilities and the spread of railroad
transportation lines into central and eastern Europe contributed to the expanding number of emigrants and to the emergency
of more diverse patterns of European emigration.  The time and
travail of the Atlantic crossing were reduced with the appearance of steamship lines catering to the swelling contingents of
immigrants.  Ships left European ports on regular schedules for
passenger convenience.  The new, fast ships of the Hamburg-
American Line sailed from Hamburg to New York in the average
time of eleven days by the 1870s.[60]
    The immigrants from Germany continued to represent the
largest ethnic contingent as they had in the 1850s; those from
Britain were the next most numerous, replacing the Irish at
that rank.  Settlers from Scandinavian countries began to come
in large numbers.  They followed the patterns of settlement
that earlier Norwegian and Swedish groups had established, most
of them going to the upper Mississippi Valley.  An annual influx of approximately 130,000 German immigrants arrived in the
United States each year in the period from 1866 to 1873.  The
possibility of securing economic advantage in an expanding
economy acted as a stimulation to emigration.  The social and
economic consequences of three wars waged in less than a decade
added to the motivations for leaving the homeland.  When economic conditions in the United States became less favorable,
the rate of immigration was soon affected.  Hard times in America from 1873 to 1882 led to a decline in German immigration.
As economic conditions improved in the 1880s, it quickened
again.  In the single year of 1882, a quarter of a million Germans entered the United States.  The economic crisis that began
with the panic of 1893, as in past crises, reduced immigration.
At the same time, Germany's industrial system was reaching a
high state of development and prosperity.  Requirements governing German military service became less severe, a fact that reduced some of the migratory pressures.  Moreover, the social
legislation instituted by Bismarck eased some of the hardships
and suffering that in the past had encouraged people to emigrate.  At the same time the disappearance of free land in
America diminished its attraction.  Increasingly larger immigrant populations from Asia and eastern Europe heightened competition on the American labor market.  The disparity in the
rates of upward social mobility between the United States and
Germany was rapidly diminishing during this period; this also
diminished migratory pressures.  The peasant aspiring to

improve his class position could expect similar opportunities
whether he chose to move to Essen or Chicago.

After the early 1880s, immigrants came in larger numbers
from regions of Europe that had hitherto yielded little population to the United States. From that period to the outbreak of
the war in Europe in 1914, millions of immigrants came from
southern Italy, Austria-Hungary, and the Russian Empire. What
became known as the "New Immigration" added immensely to the
religious and cultural heterogeneity of the American republic.
Italians, Poles, Hungarians, Lithuanians, Russians, Slovaks,
Jews, and Romanians came in impressive numbers. They swelled
the Catholic, Orthodox Christian, and Jewish populations in
the predominantly Protestant nation. But the first large-scale
movement from eastern Europe curiously was a movement from German settlements in Russia.

In 1873 the first large group of Germans from colonies in
Russia arrived in the United States. They represented the
vanguard of a population that was ultimately to number perhaps
four hundred thousand. Prior to their first migratory influx,
scattered Russian-German families had settled in various parts
of the United States. Johann Bette and several other emigrants
from Johannestal, Worms, and Rohrbach in southern Russia near
Odessa had settled in Sandusky, Ohio, in 1847-48. Bette's
visit in 1872 to his native community did much to stimulate
interest in emigration. The enthusiasm engendered spread
throughout the vast Russian territories where German colonies
existed.[61]

Empress Catherine II, herself of the German royal line of
Suhalt-Zerbst, began the systematic settlement of German farmers and artisans along the Volga River in 1763. Her purpose
was to promote the settlement of the borderlands lying beyond
the frontiers of Russian settlement. As Russia expanded its
territory in the late eighteenth century at the expense of Turkey, the Russian government continued to settle Germans on the
land in an effort to repel Tartar nomads and make Russian sovereignty secure. At the same time it was anticipated that the
Germans would introduce modern agricultural methods to the advantage of all segments of that frontier population. They were
allowed to form almost completely autonomous communities. The
German colonists were guaranteed freedom of religion, exemption
to taxation for a stipulated number of years, loans for tool
acquisition, thirty to sixty hectares of land, and exemption
from military service.

In 1804 Alexander I expanded the program of German settlement by opening the Black Sea region to carefully selected farmers and artisans who by dint of training, personal qualities,
and financial position were considered by Russian officials to
be ideal settlers. Most of the colonists were members of the
Lutheran and Reformed churches, but there were also many

Mennonites, Hutterites, and Roman Catholics.  The German settlers were primarily drawn from the Palatinate, Württemberg,
Baden, Alsace, and Switzerland: territories from which most of
the German-speaking immigration to the United States had thus
far proceeded.  Ultimately the German population in Russian
colonies was to reach several million.  From 1763 to the 1820s,
Russia competed with America in the recruitment of German settlers.

In the Russian-German colonies, despite many serious problems,
were relatively prosperous and expanded into Bessarabia, the
Crimea, and the Caucasus.  The large German families sent children forth to found daughter colonies, but all of the colonies
retained their rights of autonomous life.  In large part they
successfully maintained separateness from surrounding Russian
communities.

On June 4, 1871, Tsar Alexander II issued a decree that
served to abrogate the guarantees the earlier rulers had extended in order to encourage German settlement in what had been
a vast wilderness.  By the decree of 1871 and subsequent de-
crees, the autonomy of German colonies was increasingly under-
mined.  Their young men became subject to military service in
the Russian army.  The threat of Russification profoundly dis-
quieted the Russian-Germans.  Beginning with a small group in
1873, emigration from the Russian steppes brought hundreds of
thousands of German colonists to America despite the general
prosperity of the colonies then and in the succeeding decades.
Economic factors were of basic importance in the emigration.
But the size and continuity of the movement suggest that ac-
celerating Russification also played an important part in the
decisions people made in favor of emigration.

In 1872 three small advance parties set forth from the
neighboring Black Sea colonies of Worms, Rohrbach, and Johannestal to survey possibilities of settlement.  They spent the
winter in Sandusky, Ohio, while exploring land in several
states before eventually pushing westward.  They focused upon
two prospective areas: Sutton in Clay County, Nebraska, and
Yankton and Bon Homme Counties in Dakota Territory.  It was to
these regions that the first group of Germans from the Black
Sea came to settle in the summer and autumn of 1873.  They long
continued to be the focus of settlement and dispersion for the
expanding Russian-German settlement of the Canadian prairie
states and provinces.

In the autumn of 1873 a newspaper in Yankton, the capital
of Dakota Territory, expressed the general favor with which the
people met the early influx of Russian-Germans:

>     Over 200,000 of these people will come to Amer-
>   ica within the next two years.  They are very desira-
>   ble settlers, and no effort within the power of Dakota

to put forth, should be spared . . . With one half of
these people settled in Dakota, we shall be ready to
take on the habiliments of Statehood.

German Mennonite communities also sent delegations to the
United States in the same year.  They were charged with the
task of finding good land at low prices.  They also had the
more difficult task of exploring the possibility that the government of the United States would be willing to affirm officially that the pacifist Mennonites would forever be free from
liability to military service.  In 1874 the Congress came near
to abandoning its traditional policy of denying special concessions or privileges to any immigrant group.  The Mennonite
delegations returned to their home colonies to report that the
issue had not been successfully resolved.  This fact dissuaded
many Mennonites and Hutterites from coming to the United States.
However, within a decade eighteen thousand Mennonites had arrived and spread their closed communities into Nebraska, Kansas,
Minnesota, Dakota Territory, and the Canadian provinces.  Later
settlements were formed in the West, and among them a colony
has survived in the southern San Joaquin Valley near Fresno.
Hutterites established three colonies between 1874 and
1877 in Bon Homme County near Yankton.  Later, the three groups
known as *Dariusleut, Lehrerleut,* and *Schmiedeleut* spread out
into surrounding states and Canada.
Germans from the Volga colonies had a somewhat different
pattern of settlement from the larger Black Sea groups.  First
settling in Kansas, Nebraska, and Colorado, they moved into
Idaho and Montana following the expansion of the sugar beet industry.  The Volga German immigrants more frequently than other
Russian-German groups turned to urban employment in Midwestern
cities.
The first years on the American prairies brought severe
hardships to many of the Russian-German settlers as well as to
the Norwegian and Czech Hussite farmers among whom they settled
on the prairies.  New arrivals on the sparsely treed plains
often had to improvise homes quickly from blocks of sod in
order to protect themselves from the weather.  These shelters
were half carved out of the earth and half built above ground
level.[62]  Hastily built log cabins that often replaced them in
the first several years of settlement were little improvement.
Equally hazardous to the health and well-being of the settlers
was the devastation of many of the grain fields in the first
three years that resulted from successive grasshopper plagues.
One of the most widely held conceptions about German immigrants is that they were not the hardy souls who first staked
out farmlands and put them to the plow, but that they preferred
to buy the land after the Scotch-Irish and Anglo-Americans had
made the initial improvements.  According to this traditional

view, the German immigrants transformed the farms into prosperous enterprises through their knowledge of farming, hard work,
and stubborn determination to succeed.  There is much validity
to the general proposition, but it was not invariably true.
In Dakota Territory and Nebraska, for example, the German immigrants were just as numerous on the frontier as the Anglo-
Americans and just as much involved in the travail of being the
first to settle the land.

The migratory movement continued to grow after 1878, and
the Russian-German farmers spread out almost explosively.  They
sought lands suitable for growing wheat and other small grains
and were far less attracted to cattle ranching areas.  Row
after row of townships were settled by Russian-Germans and Norwegians who were the predominant ethnic groups in North Dakota
and in many areas of South Dakota.  Some counties were predominantly settled by Russian-Germans; McIntosh County in North Dakota, for example, was perhaps 90 percent Russian-German in the
beginning decades of its settlement.  They established farms.
Others took part in founding the small towns and villages that
began to appear on the face of the prairies in the 1880s and
during the succeeding two decades.  By the early decades of the
twentieth century, sons of immigrants were becoming merchants,
mechanics, preachers, and professional people in the communities.  In some areas German or the Swabian-German dialect was
not only the language of the home, but of the streets and mar-
kets well into the 1930s.  The Church remained the chief bulwark of language and culture.  Newspapers like the *Dakota Freie
Presse*, founded in Yankton in 1874, kept its readers informed
not only about the colonies in Russia from which they had come,
but also helped them to sustain their language and culture in
America.  At the same time the German-language press introduced
them to many important aspects of Midwestern life unknown to
them.  The compactness of their communities in Nebraska, the
Dakotas, and the San Joaquin Valley in California made it possible for them to preserve their identity and much of their
cultural distinctiveness for several generations.

The frontier was rapidly contracting and was soon to disappear.  An increasing proportion of German immigrants went to
the cities.  Yet in 1900, as the census records, farmers of
German parentage owned more than half a million farm homes, or
almost three times more than those of British parentage, the
next largest national group.

The Germans, in general, have contributed as much as any
group to the development of American agriculture.[63]  The range
of their agricultural interests has been particularly broad.
They were responsible for introducing many new crops, plants,
vegetables, and trees.  From early colonial times, German farmers were generally recognized among their fellow American citizens for the particular care they gave their fields and their

THE GERMAN ELEMENT

Proprietorship of Homes, Distributed According to Parentage[64]

| States, Territories, and Counties | Total Private Families | Total Farm Homes | Free | Owned | |
|---|---|---|---|---|---|
| | | | | En- cumbered | Un- known |
| Total of all in United States | 14,083,882 | 4,906,911 | 2,270,194 | 1,042,859 | 11,926 |
| Parentage in U.S. (or unknown) | 8,091,658 | 3,579,240 | 1,683,461 | 628,262 | 84,405 |
| Austria-Hungary | 192,068 | 34,870 | 16,261 | 10,629 | 655 |
| Canada (English) | 207,580 | 49,971 | 19,837 | 16,952 | 1,029 |
| Canada (French) | 159,590 | 24,401 | 10,095 | 8,529 | 417 |
| Germany | 1,982,917 | 522,252 | 227,266 | 156,253 | 10,054 |
| Great Britain | 835,513 | 183,157 | 87,786 | 49,278 | 3,987 |
| Ireland | 1,234,108 | 176,968 | 85,320 | 52,651 | 3,734 |
| Italy | 141,635 | 5,321 | 2,091 | 1,005 | 139 |
| Poland | 121,971 | 12,478 | 4,795 | 5,725 | 227 |
| Russia | 128,206 | 13,416 | 7,216 | 3,212 | 374 |
| Scandinavia | 437,516 | 174,694 | 70,788 | 64,873 | 4,170 |
| Other countries | 322,495 | 81,292 | 34,967 | 20,802 | 1,691 |
| Mixed foreign population | 228,625 | 48,851 | 21,311 | 14,688 | 1,044 |

farm animals.  No group of immigrants was more important than the Germans in introducing new methods of agricultural production.

In the midnineteenth century and succeeding decades, German nurserymen were instrumental in the introduction of new plants and their adaptation to American conditions.  John Rock of Oberhessen brought new fruits, plants, and trees to California.  Earlier, Johann Sutter, the German-Swiss pioneer of New Helvetia, had encouraged the cultivation of fruits and plants little known outside of the mission gardens.  Eugene W. Hilgard, trained at the Universities at Freiburg, Zurich, and Heidelberg, was one of the most distinguished contributors to the effort to make agriculture more scientific.  This purpose was reflected in his work with governmental agencies and in his teaching and research at the Universities of Mississippi, Michigan, and California.  Although few agricultural scientists achieved his international recognition, there were many others, like Charles Goessman of Göttingen University, who made notable contributions.

From colonial times, settlers from the Rhineland had made attempts to grow grapes and produce good wines in the New World.

In the late nineteenth century, the soil and climate of California encouraged many Rhinelanders to plant vineyards. Julius Dresel, once a law student at Heidelberg and a Forty-eighter, laid out his vineyards in Sonoma County in 1858. Soon he was able to produce a wine resembling that of his native Rhine Valley. Dresel and others engaged in experimentation to discover varieties most suitable to California conditions. Charles Krug, who had returned to the country of his birth to lend support to the Revolution of 1848, fled Germany after nine months of imprisonment. He arrived in San Francisco and became editor of the *Staatszeitung*. In 1860 he moved to the Napa Valley to establish vineyards and a winery that for over a century has enjoyed a reputation for the excellence of its wines. William Palmtag in Hollister and J. Beringer in the Napa Valley and many other German viticulturalists were important in the development of the wine industry. There were also immigrants from France, Italy, Hungary, and Italian Switzerland who made contributions to it. Professor George Husmann, born in Bremen, accomplished as much as any man in advancing the cultivation of California vineyards. It was the discovery made by a firm of German nurserymen in Bushberg near St. Louis that prevented the wholesale destruction of European vineyards attacked by the dreaded plant disease, phylloxera. They found that a certain American riverbank vine was immune to the insect-carried disease currently raging in Europe. By proving that European vines could be grafted onto the sturdy, phylloxera resistant stock, the experimenters provided the means and methods with which the threatened destruction could be prevented.

It would have been amazing, indeed, if German entrepreneurs and their brewmasters from Germany and Bohemia had not played a leading role in producing beer in the United States. Names of leading brands like Anheuser-Busch, Pabst, Schlitz, Blatz, and Burgermeister have been household names all over America for generations, attesting to the influence of German tastes and talents in the brewing of beer.

A large number of German craftsmen came to the United States in the late nineteenth century. Apprenticeship training, which craftsmen had to endure in order to learn their trade in Germany, even in the nineteenth century had a certain archaic atmosphere and rigorousness of the medieval guild system. German carpenters, masons, cabinet makers, painters, shoemakers, and printers had long held a reputation in America for the quality of their work in the cities, towns, and villages where they settled. It was sustained generation after generation, although there were many individual craftsmen who failed to live up to the general standards of quality and honesty. Craftsmen were generally quite keenly aware that their occupational reputation as a group among their American fellow citizens affected the income they received from their services.

They often gave warning to prospective emigrants in Germany
that if newcomers were not prepared to work hard and well they
should stay at home.  America, they warned, was no haven for
the shiftless.  Their general reputation appeared to have mar-
ketable value to the individual craftsmen.  When someone did
something to impair that reputation, other craftsmen in the
community were likely to suffer.

The German craftsmen were characteristically slower but
more thorough than native American craftsmen were likely to
be.  The European-trained artisan's insistence on quality work
sometimes placed him at a disadvantage in competition with
American labor when price rather than quality was the principal concern of the consumer.  But while finishing work was
required in the construction industry, German-trained craftsmen
were in demand where quality work was required.  Many a German
artisan looked with sadness and despair upon his son who
adapted himself too readily to American standards of workman-
ship in his trade.

German technical and professional education in this period
enjoyed the reputation of being as high in general quality as
any in the world.  Technical schools of various levels, the
*Hochschulen*, and the universities trained men in technical
fields, in engineering, in scientific research, as well as in
other professions.  Many such well-trained young men chose to
seek careers in the United States, despite opportunities for
men of their skills in European industry.

The gigantic industrial revolution in the United States
required a vast reservoir of cheap, unskilled laborers for its
expanding mills, smelters, foundries, and factories.  Hundreds
of thousands of poor peasant youths were recruited from all
parts of Europe, but particularly from the rural slums of
southern Italy, Hungary, and the Russian Empire.  Nonetheless,
there was a smaller but crucial need for skilled toolmakers,
machinists, engineers, and many technical categories.  Along
with native-born Americans, many European immigrants with technical training and experience were recruited, especially from
industrially developed countries like Great Britain, Belgium,
Switzerland, and Germany.  Successful performance by men of
such groups tended to stabilize the demand for them in industry.
Moreover, skilled immigrant craftsmen who became supervisors
often gave preference in their hiring to young men of their own
national origin whose training and experience were like their
own.  When foreign-born supervisors were able to establish
their own businesses, these new entrepreneurs were in a position to hire those whose technical skills and attitudes were
acquired in the same or similar schools as those they themselves had attended.  European countries like Germany and Switzerland provided certain kinds of technical and professional
instruction that could not be found anywhere in the United

States.  German skilled technicians, engineers, and scientists
were drawn into American industrial enterprises, large and
small, in every major field of manufacturing, in every region
of the country.  Their contribution to the industrial development of the United States was extraordinary.

All but a few of those German immigrants who made such
contributions in industry, construction, or transportation are
no longer remembered for their own personal accomplishments.
By mentioning a few one may illustrate important dimensions of
immigrant accommodation to the United States.  One finds in
this period, as in all others, German immigrants in the most
humble circumstances performing the most menial kinds of tasks
and others acquiring national recognition and public acclaim
for their accomplishments.  What was most significant about
the German immigrants was the high quality of their general
performance.

Great advances in American bridge building were achieved
by several Germans: John A. Röbling invented the suspension
bridge and Charles C. Schneider developed the cantilever bridge.
The former became best known for his construction of the Brook-
lyn Bridge, the latter for his cantilever bridge at Niagara
Falls.  Joseph Baermann Strauss aided in the construction of
the Arlington Memorial bridge over the Potomac River in Washington, D.C., and the George Washington suspension bridge over
the Hudson River in New York.  His greatest achievement as a
bridge builder came near the end of his life in his work as
chief engineer in the construction of the Golden Gate Bridge
between San Francisco and Marin County.

In the field of electrical engineering, Charles Steinmetz,
born in Breslau in 1865, stands out particularly among German-
born men in his field.  Steinmetz won a reputation as something
of a wizard.  Henry Ford once asked him to check out a new generator that was not operating effectively in his Ford's River
Rouge plant.  Steinmetz surveyed the generator, asked for a
piece of chalk, made a mark on its side and told the workers to
cut off precisely sixteen windings from the cable coil.  He
later sent Ford a bill for $10,000.  Ford demanded an itemized
account.  Steinmetz sent him a statement with two notations:
"Making chalk mark on generator 1 dollar.  Knowing where to
make chalk mark $9,999."[65]

In mining engineering, the work of Adolph Sutro in California seemed particularly outstanding to his generation.  In
chemical, mechanical, electrical, and civil engineering eminent
men of German birth and German origin could be listed exhaus-
tively to illustrate the essential point that in a time when
the need for people trained in applied and theoretical fields
of science was great, German immigrants were among those who
most abundantly responded to that need.

Germans were strongly represented in most major areas of
business and manufacturing.  In certain fields of enterprise
they were much more numerous than in others.  Germans were
particularly noted as manufacturers of musical instruments;
the names of Steinway and of Knabe in piano manufacture illustrate the eminence that some of their enterprises attained.
Germans also played an important role in developing agricultural industries.  As colonial Pennsylvania Germans were known for
their fruits and vegetables and for the preserving of foods,
Germans in the nineteenth century became leaders in food proc-
essing industries.  The business enterprise established by H.
J. Heinz began as a pickling firm.  In 1856, Ferdinand Schu-
macher of Hannover introduced the manufacture of oatmeal.  His
firm, the American Cereal Company, developed "Rolled Oats and
other cereal foods."  William Ziegler founded The Royal Baking
Powder Company, which provides products used in most American
households.  Claus Spreckels became the leading sugar producer
in this country.  Germans were able to establish themselves in
a variety of fields of business and manufacturing, and many of
their enterprises endured remarkably.

In music and the arts, western European nations had vastly
richer traditions than America.  But American tastes were
changing with an impetus determined in part by large numbers of
European musicians and music lovers who wished to play and hear
music in their new homeland.  German immigrants played an important part in the development of musical traditions in the
United States.  German immigrant musicians and Americans
trained in German conservatories of music were important in developing musical training in the United States and in establishing conservatories in Boston, New York, Chicago, and St. Louis.
The Philharmonic Society of New York gave its first concert in
December 1842.  Among the notable men who directed the work of
the Philharmonic in the early decades were Theodore Eisfeld,
Carl Bergmann, Dr. Leopold Damrosch, Adolph Neuendorff, Anton
Seidl, Walter Damrosch, and others, mostly Germans.  In 1865,
seventy of the eight-one musicians in the orchestra were Germans; twenty-five years later, eighty-nine out of ninety-four
were Germans.  Similarly, the early orchestras in Boston and
Chicago were composed largely of German musicians.  They taught;
they performed; they set standards of musical accomplishment.
Even in relatively small cities and towns, the German cultural
emphasis upon instrumental music and choral singing often had
some influence upon public tastes and musical activities.

German-Americans supported a wide range of periodicals designed to improve the practice of various occupations and professions.  From the time of the early German settlements in
Pennsylvania, advisory farming almanacs and journals had been
published.  By the late nineteenth century, there were numerous
farm publications published in German for the advantage of

people in a variety of agricultural specialties, such as the
*Geflügel Züchter* for those engaged in raising chickens and
other fowl. The *Bierbrauer Zeitung* was published for brewers;
vineyardists had the *Deutsch-Amerikanische Weinzeitung*; bakers,
tailors, and others had their special journals. In the late
nineteenth century doctors and pharmacists were engaged in a
war against patent medicine frauds that had become something
of a national nuisance. Reputable pharmacists tried to raise
standards of the profession, and in an effort to accomplish
that purpose, several pharmaceutical journals were founded.
The *American Journal of Pharmacy* was edited from 1871 to 1893
by the German immigrant, Johann Maisch. The *Deutsch-Amerikanische Pharmaceutische Zeitung* was its German language counterpart. There was no effective legislation regulating the training and licensing of pharmacists. German pharmacists were the
only ones professionally trained at that time. In many an
American city, the "Deutsche Apotheke" was the only reliable
apothecary. ·

The Christian and democratic affirmation of the common
humanity of all men and their equal rights prevailed in the
1870s and 1880s. These beliefs supported the conviction that
all the exceedingly diverse streams that had poured and were
continuing to pour into the American sea of population would be
absorbed into one nation.[66] In America, Herman Melville af-
firmed, "all tribes and peoples are forming into one federated
whole . . . This seed is sown, and the harvest must come."
More cosmopolitan conceptions than those that had earlier prevailed were being fashioned in the American consciousness, a
sense of nationality that recognized the common humanity lying
beyond obvious cultural and racial differences but which fore-
saw the evolution of the diverse elements into a unique national amalgam.

In all human societies there are manifestations of nativism or zenophobia. The existence of a substantial population
of African descent, the influx of unprecedented numbers of
European immigrants, and the new immigration from Asian countries inevitably raised doubts in some segments of the population as to the ability of the nation to absorb all those who
had already come and would come in the future. Nativism in
this period tended to diminish or increase with fluctuations in
the health of the national economy and the confidence of the
citizenry in the basic strength of the nation. Urban poverty
and dependence, congestion and crime, corruption in municipal
governments, labor dissatisfaction and social unrest, the advocacy of radical theories, and the political use of violence all
seemed to grow more acute. To several quite differently oriented segments of the American population, this fact was linked
to the appearance of large ethnic enclaves in the cities. To
some it suggested the need for practical sociologists and

social reformers to address themselves to the problems of the immigrant. To others it suggested the need to restrict immigration by quantitative and qualitative measures. That the large-scale influx of diverse contingents, largely poor and little trained for urban occupations, presented problems to the stable governance of urban communities could only be denied out of excessive sentimentality. The belief that the problems mentioned existed only because of the presence of the foreign-born is patently false. Nevertheless this conviction was widespread, particularly in the depression years of the mid-1890s, during which time it occasionally rose to dimensions of hysteria. In general, however, the American public retained its confidence in its ability to assimilate the new elements into a stronger and larger national population.

Native-born Americans tended to look most favorably upon those nationalities that seemed most like themselves. British and Anglo-Canadians seemed most acceptable despite traditional American hostility toward the British government and aristocracy. The Germans, among major immigrant groups, fared almost as well. Their obviously successful assimilation and their tangible contributions to American life were widely recognized. Their reputation for thrift, honesty, industriousness, and serious, orderly living was well earned and reflected the general response of most of the Germans in their midst. The eminence of Germany in European science, medicine, and other fields of learning was recognized and reflected in America in popular attitudes not only toward Germans but German-Americans as well. But by no means did Germans escape personal or group encounters with antiforeign distrust and hatred in this period. Children of immigrants, including the Germans, often suffered ridicule from their peers for their dress or accent or strange ways (or for those of their parents).

German Jews came to the United States in substantial number in the 1840s. Their early experience in the country was satisfactory enough to encourage them to write favorably about emigration to relatives still in Germany, and the German Jewish immigration into the United States increased rapidly. Characteristically the young men who came with meager resources became itinerant peddlers in the towns and villages of the East, the Midwest, and the South.[67] In areas where farms and small villages were relatively isolated, peddlers made a decent living and often saved enough, by grave austerity, to establish themselves as proprietors of small mercantile enterprises in towns and regional trading centers. Many of these merchants prospered, settled into the community, and became part of it in time. Others, also prosperous, were able to expand their interest into other enterprises. There were some young men who had had some experience with moneychanging in Germany or who had acquired some rudimentary knowledge of banking and were able to put that knowledge to use in the rapidly expanding economy of the United States. The fact that family members were often scattered in various regions of the country facilitated their operations in banking. The Seligman family, which was once regarded as the leading Jewish family in the United States, came from a line of weavers in Baiersdorf, Bavaria. Several Seligman brothers became peddlers in Pennsylvania, but in three years had saved enough to establish a store in Lancaster where they could sell their goods. Other Seligmans became peddlers in the South; they put up tents under shadetrees to display their wares. They saved enough to move to New York and establish themselves in the import business. Eventually the Seligman family spread into banking, clothing manufacture, and other branches of business and manufacture.

German Jews in cities like New York and Philadelphia also employed themselves in street peddling, but were increasingly drawn into the sale of secondhand clothing, which became a substantial business before the Civil War. This involvement in the clothing business brought some enterprising German Jews into clothing manufacture. Levi, Strauss and Company by 1850 had begun to manufacture the blue jeans (Levis) that were to become a standard part of American apparel on the western plains and farmlands, Pacific mining fields, and, later, alas college campuses. The demand for ready-made clothing increased rapidly in the Civil War period. The Seligman family contracted with the government to supply the Union Army with uniforms, and undertook the difficult task of paying themselves by selling United States bonds on the European market. The Horatio Alger-like fortunes of Nelson Morris were also advanced by wartime military needs. He arrived in the United States in 1856 at the age of fifteen and got a job at $5 a month in the Chicago stockyards. When the Civil War broke out the young man was able to contract with the government for the purchase of livestock. After the war he was a leader in developing the shipment of frozen meat to distant markets. His financial interests became immensely successful.

A number of Jewish banking firms grew to national significance: Kuhn, Loeb & Co., Lehmann Brothers, August Belmont & Company, and others. Simon Guggenheim came from his native Switzerland in 1847 to join his son who was working as a peddler in the anthracite region of Pennsylvania. Beginning in textiles, they ultimately branched into mining and other enterprises in Colorado.

Many German Jews achieved amazing success in the American eocnomy; some were considered among the wealthiest men in the country. German Jews who had amassed great fortunes began to make outstanding contributions to philanthropic causes: to the support of the Metropolitan Opera, to Negro education, to educational institutions, as well as to Jewish benevolent societies and cultural institutions.

Some of the Jews maintained contact with German life.  It
was not unusual for children to be sent to Germany for part of
their education or training.  German governesses or instructors
were sometimes employed by rich families for their children.
For many German Jews, German remained the language of all family discourse.  In the Jacob Schiff family this was still true
in 1915 when his daughter had to remind him that speaking German in public might no longer be wise.

There were Jewish intellectuals of the 1848 generation and
businessmen of education and cultivated tastes.  Some of the
German Jews who achieved great success from humble beginnings
were men of little education and culture.  Like their Christian
counterparts they showed the limitations of the nouveaux riches
in their pretentiousness.

While the German Jews as a group prospered to a degree one
could hardly have anticipated, the majority nevertheless remained in modest circumstances.  Sometimes men who began as
itinerant peddlers ended their lives as itinerant peddlers.
While some became men of influence in business and government,
most lived out their lives modestly.  When the German Jews began to arrive in the United States in the 1840s, the American
Jewish community was composed mainly of Sephardic Jews.  The
small Sephardic community looked askance at the poor, unculti-
vated, and aggressive young Jewish men and women from Germany.
In the 1880s when Eastern European Jews began to arrive in
large numbers, they found the German Jews equally uneasy and
critical.  The bonds of mutual interest and sentiment were not
easily established among them.

Ethnic rivalries and hostilities were by no means exclusively characteristic of native-born Americans.  Immigrant
groups brought with them nationalistic sentiments of pride and
exclusiveness as well as traditional antipathies toward other
national groups.  Some of the most virulent manifestations of
antiforeign feeling have appeared among segments of the foreign-
born.

In the 1880s a bitter controversy raged within the Catholic Church in the United States that had its origins in the
diversity of traditions among various national Catholic populations.[68]  The Polish-, German-, Irish-, French-, and Italian-
Catholic traditions that the immigrants brought with them were
distinctly different.  At the level of popular worship these
differences were important.  Catholic bishops had to deal with
the complications that arose when Irish priests served parishes
that were predominantly Italian, Polish, or German.  The major
conflict among national Catholic populations flared between the
two largest groups, the Irish and the Germans; but it spread so
that it ultimately involved Hungarian, Polish, Czech, Slovak,
Italian, Polish, and other Catholic populations.  The Irish-
Catholic leadership favored a policy that was directed to what

they considered to be the Americanization of the Church.[69]   To
Archbishop John Ireland this meant "harmonizing ourselves with
our surroundings," which would lead to the recognition that
Catholicism was not an alien faith incompatible with American
life and identity.   Some Irish clerics opposed what they considered "the Germanizing process" in the province of Milwaukee;
Irish priests protested against what seemed to be the intentions of German priests "to perpetuate a young Germany here."
German Catholics accepted the fact that ultimately German
Catholics would become assimilated and lose their national
identity.   But for the present they believed that their religious traditions were inextricably bound up with their cultural traditions; if one were lost the other would soon be
threatened.   The German-American Catholics resented being lectured on Americanism by Irish Catholics who were as much alien-
born as they themselves were.   "Do the Irish think" they would
ask, "that because they happen to speak English they are closer
to being truly American than we?"   There was a variety of reasons for antagonism.   Half of the Catholic bishops in the
United States were Irish.   The German, Austrian, Swiss, French,
English, Dutch, Spanish, and others had the other half.   German
bitterness over underrepresentation evoked fears among Irish
priests that Germans aspired to dominate the American episcopa-
cy.   This fear persisted until the First World War.   The fiery
advocacy of temperance by Irish Catholic prelates aroused resentment among German Catholics.   It encouraged ridicule among
Germans who felt they knew how to use liquor moderately.   Father Peter Abbelen pointed out that German-American Catholics
were surrounded by German Protestants who were trying to lure
them from Catholicism.   So, he argued, if German Catholics were
made to feel that they were second-rate Catholics, they might
well abandon the church altogether.   The difficult issues of
national parishes and ethnic representation in the church hierarchy that arose with the Cahensly movement reached a climax
in 1891-2 and then slowly became diminished in the early twentieth century.   There was, however, no clear resolution of the
problems that occupied the arena of conflict.   But the competition of the Irish and German priests in the American-Catholic
hierarchy ended clearly with an Irish advantage.   American
Catholicism became strongly marked by Irish-Catholic tradition
rather than that of continental Catholicism.


### NOTES

[1] John W. Wayland, *The German Element of the Shenandoah Valley
of Virginia* (Bridgewater, Virginia: Carrier, 1964).
[2] Charles A. Johnson, *The Frontier Camp Meeting: Religion's Harvest Time* (Dallas: Southern Methodist University Press,
1955) 29, 85, 147, 181.

[3]Wentz, *op. cit.*, 66.

[4]Marcus Lee Hansen, *The Atlantic Migration*, 1607–1860 (Cambridge: Harvard University Press, 1940) 280 ff.

[5]Fred Gustorf and Gisela Gustof, eds., *The Uncorrupted Heart: Journal and Letters of Frederick Julius Gustorf* 1800–1845 (Columbia, Missouri: University of Missouri Press, 1969) 76–77.

[6]Alan Conway, ed., *The Welsh in America: Letters from the Immigrants* (Minneapolis: University of Minnesota Press, 1961) 10.

[7]Faust, *op. cit.*, vol. I, 443.

[8]*Ibid.*, vol. I, 444–445.

[9]Gilbert Giddings Benjamin, *The Germans in Texas, A Study in Immigration* (Philadelphia, 1909).  Reprint from *German-American Annals*, vol. VII, 7.

[10]See Irene Marshall King, *John O. Meusenbach: German Colonization in Texas* (Austin: University of Texas Press, 1967).

[11]Terry G. Jordan, *German Seed in Texas Soil: Immigrant Farmers in Nineteenth-Century Texas* (Austin and Landau: University of Texas Press, 1966) 45.

[12]*Ibid.*, 50.

[13]*Ibid.*, 109.

[14]*Ibid.*, 111.

[15]*Ibid.*, 185.

[16]*Ibid.*, 196.

[17]H. H. McConnell, *Five Years a Cavalryman: or, Sketches of Regular Army Life on the Texas Frontier* (Jackboro, Texas: J. N. Rogers, 1889) 144.

[18]Wentz, *op. cit.*, 106.

[19]*Ibid.*, 119.

[20]*Ibid.*

[21]*Ibid.*, 272.

[22]*Ibid.*, 211.

[23]Bayrd Still, Milwaukee, *The History of a City* (Madison: The State Historical Society of Wisconsin, 1966) chapter 6. See Carl E. Hasse, *Schilderung des Wisconsinsgebietes in Nordamerika* (Crima, 1841); Carl de Haas, *Nord-Amerika. Winke für Auswanderer* (Iserlohn, 1848); and F. Goldmann, *Briefe aus Wisconsin in Nord-Amerika* (Leipzig, 1849).

[24]Wittke, *The German-Language Press, op. cit.*, 43.

[25]See Siegfried B. Puknat, "Channing and German Thought," *Proceedings of the American Philosophical Society* CI, no. 2 (April 1957); and his article, "De Wette in New England," *ibid.*, CII (August 1958).

[26]Wittke, *The German-Language Press, op. cit.*, 43.

[27]*Ibid.*, 75.

[28]Translated and paraphrased from L. v. Baumbach, *Neue Briefe aus den Vereinigten Staaten von Nordamerika* (Cassel, 1856), seventh letter.

[29]Translated and paraphrased from *ibid.*, ninth letter.
[30]Translated and paraphrased from Viktor Bracht, *Texas im Jahre 1848* (Elberfeld und Iserlohn, 1849) 108-110.
[31]Translated and paraphrased from Baumbach, *op. cit.*, ninth letter.
[32]Translated and paraphrased from Franz Brauns, *Belehrungen und Ratschläge für Reisende und Auswanderer nach Amerika* (Braunschweig, 1829) chapter 12.
[33]Translated and paraphrased from *ibid.*, tenth letter.
[34]Translated and paraphrased from M. Beyer and L. Koch, *Amerikanische Reisen*, vol. II (Leipzig, 1839) 32-33.
[35]Translated and paraphrased from *ibid.*, vol. I, 286.
[36]Translated and paraphrased from Baumbach, *op. cit.*, seventh letter.
[37]Translated and paraphrased from Frau Bylandh, *Bilder aus dem gesell-schaftlichen Leben der Nord-Amerikaner* (Reutlingen, 1835) chapter 13.
[38]Translated and paraphrased from Baumbach, *op. cit.*, seventh letter.
[39]See Johann Jakob Rütlinger, *Tagebuch auf einer Reise nach Nord-Amerika im Jahre 1823* (St. Gallen, 1826); this is translated in full in Robert Billigmeier and Fred Picard, eds., *The Old Land and the New* (Minneapolis: University of Minnesota Press, 1965); see reference on page 244.
[40]See Bylandh, *op. cit.*, 55-59.
[41]Translated and paraphrased from *ibid.*, chapter 17.
[42]Translated and paraphrased from Baumbach, *op. cit.*, seventh letter.
[43]Translated and paraphrased from *ibid.*
[44]Translated and paraphrased from Brauns, *op. cit.*, chapter 1.
[45]Translated and paraphrased from Bracht, *op. cit.*, 116.
[46]Translated and paraphrased from *ibid.*, 116-117.
[47]Translated and paraphrased from Beyer and Koch, *op. cit.*, vol. II, 5.
[48]Translated and paraphrased from *ibid.*, 142-145.
[49]Translated and paraphrased from Bracht, *op. cit.*, 115-116.
[50]See Rütlinger's journal in Billigmeier and Picard, *op. cit.*, 248.
[51]Rudolph Friedrich Kurz, *The Journal of Rudolph Friedrich Kurz* (Fairfield, Washington: Ye Galleon Press, n.d.). The journals were published along with some of the artist's representations of Indian life well over a century after Kurz's death.
[52]See Rütlinger's journal in Billigmeier and Picard, *op. cit.*, 265.
[53]*Ibid.*
[54]Eitel W. Dobert, *Deutsche Demokraten in Amerika, Die Achtund-vierziger und ihre Schriften* (Göttingen: Vandenhoeck & Ruprecht, 1958) 17-18.

[55]Carl Heinrich Schnauffer, *Neue Lieder für das Teutsche Volk* (Rheinfelden, 1848). Roughly translated it means: To seek one's fortune/to establish one's dwelling/can be tried on any shore/but finding a homeland/I can only do in the land of my birth.

[56]See A. E. Zucker, ed., *The Forty-Eighters, Political Refugees of the German Revolution of 1848* (New York: Columbia University Press, 1950); Carl Wittke, *Refugees of Revolution, The German Forty-Eighters in America* (Philadelphia: University of Pennsylvania Press, 1952); and Carl Wittke, *We Who Built America, The Saga of the Immigrant* (The Press of Western Reserve University, rev. ed., 1964). See also Frank Friedel, *Francis Lieber, Nineteenth Century Liberal* (Baton Rouge, 1947); Gustav Körner, *Das Deutsche Element in den Vereinigten Staaten von Nordamerika, 1818-1848* (Cincinnati, 1880); and Chester V. Easum, *The Americanization of Carl Schurz* (Chicago, 1929).

[57]Wittke, *The German-Language Press*, op. cit., 79. The most authoritative work on the subject is Karl John Arndt's *German-American Newspapers and Periodicals, 1732-1959; History and Bibliography*, rev. ed. (New York: Johnson Reprints, 1965).

[58]*Ibid.*, 121-126.

[59]*Ibid.*, 135.

[60]Henry Fry, *The History of North Atlantic Steam Navigation* (London: Sampson Low, Marston and Company, 1896) 211, 220.

[61]Georg Rath, "Die Russlanddeutschen in den Vereinigten Staaten von Nord-Amerika," *Heimatbuch der Deutschen aus Russland* (Landsmannschaft der Deutschen aus Russland) 1963. For Catholic settlements, see George P. Aberle, *From the Steppes to the Prairies* (Bismarck, N.D., 1963).
See also Joseph S. Height, *Paradise on the Steppe, a Cultural History of the Kutschurgan, Beresan, and Liebental Colonists, 1804-1944* (North Dakota Historical Society of Germans from Russia: Bismarck, 1972); Georg Leibbrandt, *Die deutschen Kolonien in Cherson und Bessarabien* (Stuttgart, 1926); and Karl Stumpp, *Die Russlanddeutschen* (Freilassing, 1964).

[62]See John J. Gering, *After Fifty Years* (South Dakota: Pine Hill Printery, 1924).

[63]Faust, in his second volume, gives a detailed account of the men who contributed to various occupations and professions.

[64]*Twelfth Census of the United States*, 1900, vol. II, Population, part 742, table CXIV.

[65]Richard O'Connor, *The German Americans* (Boston: Little, Brown, 1968) 373.

[66]See John Higham, *Strangers in the Land, Patterns of American Nativism, 1860-1925* (New York: Atheneum, 1963).

[67]See Eric E. Hirschler, ed., *Jews from Germany in the United States* (New York: Farrar, Straus and Cudahy, 1955).  A highly interesting portrayal of German-Jewish families in the United States may be found in Stephen Birmingham's *Our Crowd, The Great Jewish Families of New York* (New York: Harper & Row, 1967).

[68]See Philip Gleason, *The Conservative Reformers, German-American Catholics and the Social Order* (Notre Dame: University of Notre Dame Press, 1968).

[69]One of the most valuable sources in this area is John Tracy Ellis, *The Life of James Cardinal Gibbons* (Milwaukee: Bruce, 1952) vol. 1.

# 3

## THE PENNSYLVANIA GERMANS
## FROM THE AMERICAN REVOLUTION
## TO THE FIRST WORLD WAR

Like the English in New England, the Pennsylvania Germans have created one of the most distinctive and stable regional cultures in the United States. The first German and Swiss settlements in Pennsylvania were a century old by the time of the American Revolution. They were firmly attached to the soil of Pennsylvania and their culture and social system were well defined. By the beginning of the nineteenth century it was becoming more generally recognized that these "dumb Dutch" were not simply an ephemeral ethnic component of the American population. It was amply clear that there were important cultural and religious differences among the Lutherans, Reformed, Amish, Schwenkfelders, and other groups among them; but their common origins and the extensive similarities of culture and social characteristics justified the use of the appellation "Pennsylvania German" (or "Pennsylvania Dutch" or "Dutchmen") to embrace them all. By this time the Pennsylvania Germans had developed a clear sense of their collective identity as Americans rather than as Germans—but *as a particular kind of Americans*, to be distinguished from their Anglo-American and Scotch-Irish neighbors. The narrow and arbitrary definition of Americanism in exclusively Anglo-American terms yielded slowly to their claims. However, even some of their distinguished compatriots like Benjamin Franklin and Horace Greeley, along with legions of others less well known, found it difficult to accept the proposition that the Pennsylvania Germans had either the right or the capacity to remain a more or less permanent, differentiated subcultural entity in the nation's population. Their stubborn persistence in using a foreign language was widely viewed as a mark of queer and boorish indifference to decent education and general advancement. Immigration continued to swell the German population of the Dutch counties in the nineteenth century, but by this time the regional identity within the general American identity was well established, and the ties binding the Pennsylvania Germans to Germany were

undoubtedly weaker than those binding Anglo-Americans to Great
Britain.

The Pennsylvania German territory embraced the counties of
Berks, Bucks, Carbon, Dauphin, Lebanon, Lehigh, Lancaster, Monroe, Montgomery, Northampton, Northumberland, Schuykill, Snyder,
and York. These counties include more than eight thousand
square miles and had a population of more than one and a quarter million.[1]  A number of other counties in Pennsylvania were
less distinctively Pennsylvania German in character, but nevertheless had areas of Pennsylvania German settlement.  Outside
of Pennsylvania, particularly in Maryland and Ohio, there were
important communities of Germans established by migrants from
Pennsylvania.

The culture and social character of the Pennsylvania German population in the nineteenth century remained much as Benjamin Rush had described them in the eighteenth century.  A
majority of the population continued to be strongly bound to
the land and to farming as a way of life.  Towns like Lancaster,
York, and Reading were county seats and expanding shopping centers for the rich farming hinterland surrounding them.  They
prospered and attracted new commercial and industrial enterprises.  With economic development came new and varied elements,
yet the towns retained their basic Pennsylvania Dutch character.
Bethlehem, which was founded in the eighteenth century by the
pacifist Moravians, paradoxically became an important center of
steel manufacture and munitions production.  The growing operations of Bethlehem Steel transformed the face of the city, but
enough of the traditional culture remained to permit the city
still to preserve a special character of its own.  As Allentown
attracted manufacturing enterprises, many foreign-born workers
settled in the community; but it retained a strong Pennsylvania
German character and even among the Pennsylvania Germans themselves it was known for its "Dutchness."[2]  Frederick and Hagers-
town, Maryland, remained almost as Pennsylvania German as Lancaster and York.  Even the smaller towns of the Pennsylvania
German territory experienced the encroachments of electric
power plants, steel mills, and factories.  The towns and cities
remained, as they had in the past, educational and trading centers and the market places for the urban and rural populations.
But the great reservoir of strength for the Pennsylvania German
culture was the farm family.

Most of the Dutch farms have been handed down from generation to generation, from fathers to sons.  Many of the children
of farm families, however, have acquired educations in other
parts of the country and some have settled away from home.  The
Pennsylvania Germans have contributed many distinguished men
and women to the nation.  There are a number who made notable
contributions to medicine in the nineteenth and early twentieth
centuries, among them Caspar Wistar, Samuel Gross, William

Pepper, and William C. Gorgas.  An impressive number became
eminent in business, and some of their family names are familiar to most Americans: Widener, Wanamaker, Frick, Schwab, Stude-
baker, Seiberling, Cunard, and Henry Ford, whose mother was a
Pennsylvania German.[3]  If there were rich men like Charles T.
Yerkes whose financial success was marred by graft and corruption, there were others like Jane Addams who devoted themselves
to succoring the victims of social injustice.

Pennsylvania Germans produced a substantial number of
judges, supreme court justices, and cabinet members.  At least
two presidents, Herbert Hoover and Dwight Eisenhower, were of
Pennsylvania German origin.  For a people characteristically as
peaceful as the Pennsylvania Germans, especially the sectarians,
it is surprising how many military leaders have come from the
Dutch country.  A number of major American writers descended
from Pennsylvania German families, including Pearl Buck née
Sydenstricker, Willa Sibert Cather, Thomas Wolfe, Elsie Sing-
master, Stephen Vincent Benet, and others.[4]

The Pennsylvania German dialect or language is one of the
most conspicuous aspects of Dutch culture and became symbolic
of the culture as a whole.  The early immigrants from southwestern Germany and German-speaking Switzerland brought with
them the closely related popular dialects of their areas.  In
Pennsylvania the eighteenth century German settlers maintained
the linguistic patterns that characterized their homelands:
standard literary German was reserved for formal discourse and
for written communication; the dialect was used for informal,
daily communication.  The dialect was the language of the family and community life and was loved for its warmth and earthi-
ness and for its intimate connection with the most personal and
important aspects of human existence—outside the realm of religious experience.  German dialects are not, of course, a corruption of the standardized literary language, but indeed ante-
dated it.  The Pennsylvania Germans of the colonial period and
the early nineteenth century read standard German and used it
as they had in Europe for formal occasions; their Bible, hymn
books, and prayer books were printed in literary High German.
*Deitsch*, as the Pennsylvania Germans called their language,
closely resembled Pfälzisch, the dialect of the Rhenish Palatinate, although it absorbed certain influences from the closely
related dialects of surrounding areas.  In Pennsylvania counties like York and Lancaster, however, the popular dialect reflected the fact that Swiss settlers had predominated there in
the beginning days of settlement.  In time *Deitsch* (from
*Deutsch*) assimilated influences from English, but did not become a mish-mash of English and German elements.  It remained
essentially a German dialect very similar to that spoken even
now in the areas of emigration.  American English also reflected the regional patterning of English emigration.  It also
continued to evolve in the New World.

In the eighteenth century many of the Pennsylvania Germans were trilingual as they acquired fluency in English.  In the nineteenth century the use of standard German receded as English increasingly absorbed the functions of formal communication.  The establishment of a system of universal, compulsory education accelerated the language changes.  *Deitsch*, however, remained as the language of daily life in most communities in the Dutch country.  English gradually replaced standard German first among the Lutherans and Reformed Pennsylvania Germans; the transition was initially noticeable in the towns and cities before it became evident in the villages and farmlands.  The Amish retained the use of literary German and continued to teach it to their children throughout the nineteenth century and beyond.  They are the most Bible-centered, the most attached to the German Bible translated by Martin Luther.  They are bound more tightly into a separate community life than were the Lutherans or Reformed; to fail to cultivate written German would, they realized, weaken the attachment of the people to the German Bible, which would, in turn, cause an erosion of the sentiments that bound the people to their religious principles and communal life.

The Pennsylvania Germans in the eighteenth century provided schools for their children that compared well with those existing among other portions of the population.  The Mennonites established schools soon after Germantown was founded.  The Baptists of Ephrata founded a school and printed numerous textbooks in various subject areas.  Moravians were perhaps the most active in providing schools for their children.  The Schwenkfelders had the reputation of being the best educated among the Pennsylvania German groups.  The Lutheran and Reformed congregations maintained in aggregate more than three hundred schools by the end of the third decade of the nineteenth century.  In addition there were many neighborhood schools not connected directly with any denomination.[5]  Nevertheless there were provisionary defects in Pennsylvania Dutch community schools, as in others: a chronic lack of sufficient financial support, paucity of qualified teachers, inadequate provision of texts, as well as absenteeism among students.  A major weakness was their tendency to neglect secondary and higher education.  In many communities, children of Pennsylvania German families who wanted to study beyond the elementary school level had no alternative to but attend English language high schools and colleges.  The proportionately small numbers of those who became scholars, intellectuals, and professional people received their training through the medium of the English language and therefore were often drawn into a largely English-speaking milieu.  This tended to interpose a wedge between the intellectual groups and the largely monolingual, German-speaking majority.  The educated groups often became

lukewarm or indifferent about the preservation of Pennsylvania
German culture and the cultivation of German.[6]
   To meet the deficiencies in the state's educational system, the Pennsylvania legislature enacted a series of bills in
1834-6 that established a public system of basic education.
Opposition to the legislation was widespread among the Lutherans, Reformed, Mennonites, and others because they saw the
secularization of the school system potentially destructive to
church schools and the German language.[7]  The state superin-
tendents and the Pennsylvania legislators, however, did not
move very hastily to enforce the compliance of Pennsylvania
German communities with regulations governing the use of German
in the schools.  Many communities did indeed take a long time
to comply with the provisions.  Among the Pennsylvania Germans
themselves there were some influential people and public officials who stressed the advantages for all the "Dutch" to know
English fluently, even though they were devoted to the use of
*Deitsch* or *Pennsylvanish* in their homes and in community life.
The conviction was widespread among Pennsylvania Germans that
the important aspects of their lives were so largely confined
to home and community relationships that no other language besides their dialect was needed.  Or as Harbaugh expressed pa-
rental concern for what a son might discover in the world
beyond the community:

> Es is all Humbuk owwe draus
> Un er werd's selwert seh'!
>
> All is humbug in the world outside
> And he'll see it for himself.

   Farmers saw no value in exposing sons who wished only to
remain farmers to public school anglicization.  At the same
time there were many others who expected that their children,
or some of them at least, would leave their communities for
higher education elsewhere and would eventually find jobs and
careers in other parts of the country.  Hence a mastery of
English was far more important for them than *Deitsch*.  Community resistance to the spreading use of English and to other
aspects of anglicization, on the other hand, was often led by
ministers, who were most conscious of the mutual dependence of
language, church, schools, and rural farm life.  The use of
English did spread, but *Deitsch* remained largely unthreatened
in its function as medium for the common transactions of daily
family and community life until the turn of the century.  As
the Pennsylvania Germans would describe the situation: "Mir
hen Englisch in der Schul awwer Deitsch daheem" (We learn English in school but German at home).  Zealous advocates of wider
use of English (among both Anglo-Americans and Pennsylvania

Dutch themselves) attempted to force the replacement of *Deitsch* quickly and completely and resorted to ridicule in an effort to loosen the bonds of sentiment that tied the Pennsylvania Germans to their language.  Others cultivated the language in poetry and prose, both because it pleased their readers and because it lent strength and vitality to the language and culture.  The language remained an important part of the cultural life of the Pennsylvania Germans and a symbol of their special identity.  Pennsylvania Germans who abandoned the use of *Deitsch*, however, did not automatically discard all other aspects of their heritage or cease to identify themselves as Pennsylvania Germans.

In 1862 an alliance was formed between the German language press in Pennsylvania and widely different German-American groups and clubs (including radical elements).  This organization, the *Verein der Deutschen Presse von Pennsylvanien*, was effective in a variety of enterprises on behalf of preserving German language and culture: it secured the passage of a bill in the Pennsylvania legislature making it mandatory that official notices be published in German in designated counties; it worked effectively to preserve the German Sunday School and in some instances succeeded in restoring anglicized Sunday Schools to German Schools; it was instrumental in the establishment of bilingual schools in some towns and the introduction of German instruction in others.  Much of the momentum of the movement was lost when the *Verein's* founder and director, S. K. Brobst, died in 1876.

Charles Calvin Ziegler insisted that there were things that, if they are to be done well, have to be done in Pennsylvania German:

> Will ich recht ve'stannig schwetze
> Eppes auseinnanner setze
> A, B, C, un eens, zwee, drei
> So dasz jeder commoner Mann
> Klar un deitlich sehne kann
> Wel' as Gold is un wel Blei,
> Nem ich gute deitsche Worte,
> Weis un schwarze, weech un harte
> Noh vollbringt die Sach sich glei.[8]

> (If I want to speak with sense
> separate one thing from another
> A, B, C, and one, two, three
> So that every common man
> Can see clearly and distinctly
> Which is gold and which is lead
> I take good German words
> White and black, soft and hard
> then the matter is accomplished quickly.)

In the 1840s, German language newspapers in Pennsylvania
began to publish popular verses composed for special occasions,
humorous notes, love letters, and advertisements in the dialect.  More serious literary attempts began with the publication of "Abendlied," written by the Moravian pastor, Emanuel
Rondthaler, in the *Deutscher Kirchenfreund* in 1849.  The Dutch
loved to sing, and an important part of their poetic literature
is devoted to song.  A contemporary of Rondthaler, Louis Miller,
wrote songs in dialect that were widely sung in the area of
York County.  Many singers and music teachers composed songs
and wrote lyrics about the ordinary experiences of life: the
joy experienced at the birth of a child; nursery rhymes; forag-
ing in Mother's pantry; the seasons; and the important holidays
like Easter, Christmas, the Fourth of July, Thanksgiving,
school days, and weddings.  Some poems dealt with themes of the
village miser, braggart, clown, or beggar.
    The most widely known and best loved of the Pennsylvania
German dialect poets was Henry Harbaugh, born in 1817.  He was
a widely experienced man and was able to write authentically on
many aspects of the life of his people.  He spent his youth on
a farm, worked at carpentry and various other skilled trades;
he attended college and theological seminary and served as a
preacher in several communities before becoming a professor in
the Theological Seminary at Mercersburg.  He was invited to
submit a poem for publication and offered "Heemweh" (Homesick-
ness), which was published anonymously in 1861.  It immediately
won a warm and enthusiastic response, and his readers and his
example encouraged many others to write in the dialect.  Professor Richard Hess Reichert recalls that a generation ago the
volume of Harbaugh's poems, the *Harfe*, still frequently lay by
the side of the family Bible in the homes of Pennsylvania German farmers.[9]  Some of the poets who followed him were better
poets than he but none of them ever evoked such a warm response.
Edward Hermany wrote dialect poems, some of which were satiri-
cal.  Henry Lee Fisher, who became a lawyer and lived in York,
wrote poems that provided interesting insights into the manners
and customs of the Pennsylvania Germans of his time.  Eli Kel-
ler won favor among dialect readers in Pennsylvania and in
Ohio, where he lived, for his portrayal of the seasonal tasks
of farm life, particularly in "Es Mehe Mit der Deitsche Sense"
and in the long poem, "Vum Flachsbauer," which describes the
cultivation of flax.  Col. Edward H. Rauch wrote prose pieces
in dialect and made translations of selections from Shake-
speare's work.  In 1883 he published, in the dialect, a bois-
terous two-act version of Rip Van Winkle.  A Moravian pastor
and teacher in Bethlemen, J. Max Hark, set himself the task of
proving the versatility of the dialect for respectable literary
purposes; he wrote poems in a variety of meters and on serious
and humorous subjects.  He was not able to complete the task in

the measure he had originally contemplated, and his work was
taken up by others.

Col. Thomas Zimmerman made some notable translations from
High German.  He is best known, however, for his translation in
1876 of "The Night Before Christmas."  John Birmelin translated
Mother Goose rhymes into the dialect, as well as selections
from the poems of Robert Louis Stevenson.  His own works were
written principally for children.  One of the best of the dialect writers was Charles Calvin Ziegler who, although born in
Pennsylvania German country, spent much of his adult life in
St. Louis.  His poetry dealt with a wider variety of subjects
and the forms of poetic expression more varied than that of
most other dialect writers.  His works did not evoke the warm
response that Harbaugh achieved.  Nevertheless Ziegler was a
skillful poet, and his works remained highly prized by those
who knew them.

Dialect writers in Pennsylvanish did not keep in touch
with writing styles and orthographical norms established in
this period among the people of Rheinpfalz and Baden-Württem-
berg whose alemanic dialects most closely resemble the dialect
of the Pennsylvania German descendants of emigrants from that
region.  Today there is a resurgence of dialect writing in
Southwestern Germany and the orthographical sophistication of
contemporary dialect authors makes one realize and regret the
crude borrowings and improvisations from English orthographical
models made by Pennsylvanish writers.  These made Pennsylvanish
look more like a humorous German-English mish-mash than what it
was or could have been with more respectful cultivation, namely
an alemanic dialect capable of versatile and sophisticated communication.  What this fact most clearly demonstrates is how
little contact there was by the turn of the century between
writers and intellectuals in general in Southwest Germany and
the Pennsylvania German region.

The *Pennsylvania German Magazine* was founded in 1900 in
an effort to make the Pennsylvania Germans better informed
about their history, literature, and culture, as well as to
record the achievements of their people.  The editors wished to
combat the sense of inferiority that developed among a people
who for generations had suffered remarks about the "dumb
Dutch."[10]  The *Pennsylvania German Magazine* published many dialect poems and short prose, to give encouragement to aspiring
writers and to preserve specimens of the dialect should it one
day die out.  The Pennsylvania German Society was established
in 1891 with many of the same objectives.

For those who knew the Pennsylvania Dutch country and
loved it, it was difficult then and remains difficult still to
imagine the region anglicized and stripped of all the important
cultural and physical characteristics that set it apart from
the rest of the nation.

As German language newspapers and periodicals in Pennsylvania began to die out, there were fewer opportunities for dialect writers to publish their works.  English language newspapers in the area, however, continued to publish occasional poems and articles in dialect, and a new genre of the "Zeitingsbrief" developed in Pennsylvania and spread to German and English language newspapers in the Middle West and Canada.[11]

Pennsylvania Germans' regional cultural heritage, Frederic Klees notes, was discovered by the rest of the United States in the 1930s.[12]  The resurgence of interest among other Americans in the folk arts and crafts of the Pennsylvania Dutch happily matured before the products of their skills had been lost or replaced by machine-made articles.  The Americans, enamored of their techniques of mass production, came to appreciate the fact that common, hand-wrought articles of daily life, often crudely made and naively decorated, can be both beautiful and pleasing to live with.  Their simplicity, freshness, and unjaded quality are appealing.  The Pennsylvania Germans love color and beauty and have taken the time to embellish the common objects that surround them in their daily lives with tulips and hearts, distelfinks and peacocks, doves and pelicans, unicorns and horses, and other decorative subjects favored by the Pennsylvania Germans.  Their folk traditions reflect their sense of design and their willingness to allow their imaginations to be playful.  The inscriptions on their houses and the hex signs on their well-designed barns reflect the Pennsylvania German willingness to do things just "for fancy" and their insistence that their daily lives be relieved from strictly utilitarian concerns.

Birth certificates (*Geburtsscheine*), baptismal certificates (*Taufscheine*), and marriage certificates (*Trauscheine*) were customarily written in illuminated writing and embellished with designs that they called *fraktur*.  The finest examples of illuminated writing appear in the works of the monks and nuns of Ephrata.  The Pennsylvania Germans made their own glass; the most prized pieces are those produced by Heinrich Stiegel.  Ironmasters produced stove plates with Biblical representations or designs of tulips.  They produced trivets, latches and hinges, weathervanes, andirons, and crosses to mark graves.  The Pennsylvania German smiths vied with one another in their creation of elaborate designs.  Human figures, men on horseback, and unicorns are among the designs frequently appearing in their sgrafitto plates and pie plates.  Painted designs and carving add beauty to dower chests and bridal boxes, trays and platters, chairs and settees.  Their artistry is apparent even in the most common objects of kitchen use: pitchers and sugar bowls, coffee pots, and cooky cutters.  The wealth of Pennsylvania German folk art lies in the expression of artistic impulses on innumerable objects that are part of their daily life.

The importance of the folk art traditions to social historians lies not in the beauty of the objects themselves but what the traditions reveal about the values and way of life of the Pennsylvania German people.

When the Pennsylvania German Society was established in 1891, it took as one of its major goals the task of putting Pennsylvania German history in a proper perspective. Pennsylvania Germans have been largely ignored by most professional historians. The attention they have received in state and national historical writing has often focused simply upon a few of the more picturesque events of their history and has ignored the more basic and enduring aspects of their collective experience. A number of Pennsylvania German historians and linguists, among them eminent men like Seidenstricker, Learned, Kuhns, Faust and others, made scholarly studies that make possible a more adequate view of the role the Pennsylvania Germans have played in the history of Pennsylvania and the United States.[13]

### NOTES

[1] A. F. Buffington, "The Pennsylvania German Dialect," in Wood, *op. cit.*, 262.

[2] Klees, *op.* cit., 257.

[3] *Ibid.*, 265–266.

[4] *Ibid.*, 268–269.

[5] Clyde S. Stine, "The Pennsylvania Germans and the School," in Wood, *op. cit.*, 111.

[6] Heinz Kloss, "German-American Language Maintenance Efforts," in Joshua A. Fishman, et al., *Language Loyalty in the United States* (The Hague: Mouton, 1966) 217–223.

[7] *Ibid.*, 116.

[8] Harry Hess Reichard, "Pennsylvania German Literature," in Wood, *op. cit.*, 169.

[9] *Ibid.*, 175.

[10] Ralph Wood, "Journalism among the Pennsylvania Germans," in Wood, *op. cit.*, 157–158.

[11] *Ibid.*, 159.

[12] Klees, *op. cit.*, 381. See Cornelius Weygandt, *The Red Hills: A Record of Good Days Outdoors and In, With Things Pennsylvania Dutch* (Philadelphia: University of Pennsylvania Press, 1929).

[13] Richard H. Shryock, "The Pennsylvania Germans as seen by the Historian," in Wood, *op. cit.*, 239–258.

# 4

## THE EFFECTS OF HYPHENIZATION AND TWO WORLD WARS

GERMAN-AMERICAN LITERATURE AND POLITICS
AT THE TURN OF THE CENTURY

The Germans in America created a literature of their own that in some measure mirrored the manifold complexities of their daily lives as immigrants and children of immigrants in a rapidly changing society. The very diversity of the German population in the United States meant that there were many conflicting interests to be satisfied through literary activity and many different German reading publics. The writers who sought to stimulate interest in reading and satisfy it were themselves diverse in their literary interests and in the quality of their talent. No German-American writer of the late nineteenth and early twentieth century acquired a substantial reputation in continental German literature of the period, although some of their works still may be read with interest and enjoyment.

There were some themes in both popular and serious poetry that were common to every generation of German-American writers. One such common theme expressed love for the homeland and a lament that circumstances had forced emigration from it. Love for the new country and feelings of excitement in the face of its challenges were expressed in widely different forms, but so frequently that only the best writers could escape banality. Immigrants in Pennsylvania, Missouri, and Texas, or wherever else they settled gave frequent poetic expression to their attachment to the soil of their new homeland.

The German-Americans were so dispersed geographically and so extraordinarily diverse in their interests that it is remarkable that a sufficient reading public could emerge to consume the numerous publications of German-American writers. The scores of writers were sustained by people in New Braunfels and Milwaukee, Yankton and Philadelphia, by farmers, craftsmen, engineers, physicians, clergymen, professors, villagers and

city dwellers, by Mennonites, Lutherans, Catholics and German
Jews, by Württembergers and Pomeranians, and by "assimilators"
and cultural traditionalists.

Aside from the matter of pride in the cultural activities
of writers from their own communities, the German-Americans
gained from their journalists, poets, and writers a fuller
sense of their personal membership in a large and productive
segment of the American population. With others of German
origin they shared common experiences that bound them together
and contributed to the emergence of a special body of traditions that, for a time, distinguished them as a distinct kind
of American. One cannot overlook the deep and often bitter
divisions that remained among them, as those between Lutherans
and Catholics, Christians and Freethinkers, conservatives and
socialists, Prussians and Bavarians. Nevertheless, the German
language press and literature provided one means by which recognition of shared experiences could develop and a sense of
common identity could be sustained. In reading the poetry and
short stories of their writers, German-Americans learned much
about what they shared with others of similar origins who were
now both German and American. Paradoxically, the German language press and literature, because they reflected much of
what was occurring in general American society, served ultimately to advance the accommodation of the German-born to that
society.

Books of poetry, travel, reminiscences, descriptive accounts of pioneer life, autobiographies, and stories of the
travail of immigrant life on the farms and in cities bulging
with newcomers were published in substantial volume by German-
American writers. In addition to *Novellen*, tales and poetry,
popular history was recounted, serious historical accounts
were written by scholars, and an extensive literature of social
commentary and polemics came from their pens. Many writers
wrote in praise of democracy but denounced the social evils and
inequities they believed they discovered in their new homeland.
Many of the writers, however, wrote simply to entertain; they
expressed their feelings and ideas without pretensions of extraordinary literary merit; those who were successful as writers of popular poetry and prose were content with the knowledge
that their works were met with favor.

Some writers like Konrad Krez and Konrad Nies were widely
read and much respected among German-American communities
throughout the country. Konrad Nies arrived in the United
States in 1883 and tried his hand at acting, teaching, writing,
and publishing. He wrote several *Novellen* and published three
collections of his verse. His last volume of poetry, *Welt und
Wildnis*, was published after his death in San Francisco in 1920.
For years Nies tried to enlist the support of German-Americans
for a magazine of high literary standards, but he found little

practical encouragement.  Finally he began the publication of
*Deutsch-Amerikanische Dichtung* in 1888, but the enterprise cost
him serious financial losses, and he was forced to abandon it
after two years.  Although many of his ambitions were frus-
trated, he was regarded by many as the most gifted of the
German-American lyric poets of his generation.

Frontier life was a frequent subject of both fiction and
nonfiction.  Among the most prolific writers was Heinrich
Möllhausen who wrote scores of romances based on life on the
western frontier.  Gert Göbel wrote a notable work on the early
days of Missouri, *Länger als ein Menschenleben in Missouri*.
Reinhold Solger is particularly remembered for his portrayals
of American life, in which he displayed unusual skill in repro-
ducing the patterns of common American speech and the dialectic
peculiarities of groups like the Irish immigrants.  There were
writers who stressed the contributions that German culture
could make to that still evolving in the United States.  Johann
Rittig was notable among them.  One of the most gifted and
original prose writers was Hugo Betsch.  Robert Reizel was a
writer of substantial merit.  But in many instances, the literary style of German writers in America suffered as the years of
their residence outside of Germany was extended.  Some writers
like F. Kenkel and Lotte Leser, however, were widely respected
as stylists.[1]

The German-American public bought and read with enjoyment
the works of their authors.  Many of the educated classes, however, preferred works of more substantial literary value that
were written in Germany and were therefore less directly related to their lives in America.  German literary classics and
new works by well-known writers in Germany were available in
urban book stores that specialized in such publications.  The
families that did not have the works of Goethe, Schiller, and
Lessing on their bookshelves could find them in public libraries in Milwaukee, St. Louis, or Philadelphia.  The place that
literature and song had in adding to the Gemütlichkeit and
fellowship of such families is illustrated in the reminiscences
of Hermann Hagedorn.

> I don't know when German poetry and German folk
> songs entered my consciousness.  I suppose the folk
> songs came first—the best of them not actually folk
> songs at all, having been written by Goethe, Uhland
> or other recognized poets, with music composed by
> trained composers, but adopted by the Volk as their
> own.  *Heidenröslein* was among the earliest I knew,
> *Ich hat einen Kameraden, Freut euch des Lebens*, and
> the haunting *Muss i denn* . . . Their simple words and
> melodies, reflecting the raptures and the brooding,
> the merriment and the exaltations of ordinary men and

women in their passage from the cradle to the grave,
entered into my innermost parts, leaving an emotional
influence that seventy-eight years of life in America
have not wholly overcome.  The heart of the German
people as I knew it, at its best, as a boy—warm, com-
passionate and true—speaks to me through them still.
    Certain quotations of Schiller's poems were such
time worn cliches of the family talk, that I can't
remember when the poems themselves first entered my
world; but a letter that Mother wrote Father . . . the
summer I became six, indicates that, one rainy day
she was keeping us children occupied by reading Schiller to us.  The old classic standbys became part of
me early and I can't remember the time when *Der Hand-
schuh* wasn't familiar . . . [2]

It was for the most part very difficult for German-
American writers to avoid the artistic stultification that came
with isolation from continual contact with the mainstream of
German intellectual life and literary activities.  This isolation was not usually compensated for by an extensive assimilation of literary influences from the mainstream of American
intellectual life.  Too often German-American literary crea-
tions reflected more the period of their gymnasial training in
Germany than the intellectual and literary movements current
in the Germany of their adult years—from which they were
largely isolated.  By the turn of the century the accommodation
of German-Americans to general American society was proceeding
at an ever more rapid pace.  The reading of German-American
poetry and short stories was clearly diminishing while the
preference for Germany's classical and popular writers on the
one hand or American writers on the other became increasingly
more general.  Children and grandchildren of German immigrants
began to appear among the ranks of major American writers;
among the most distinguished in the early part of the century
were Henry L. Mencken and Theodore Dreiser.
    The German theater was still important in larger German-
American communities in the years immediately before the First
World War.  It had begun to develop in New York, Cincinnati,
Milwaukee, St. Louis, and other American cities in the 1840s.
It flourished particularly in the 1870s and '80s, but continued after the turn of the century.  Theatrical clubs were organized in cities like Columbus in the mid-1880s as large
contingents of Forty-eighters and other German immigrants made
their homes there.  Permanent German theater or stock companies
were organized in several cities; among the most successful was
the *Deutsches Theater* of Philadelphia.  In the early years of
German theater in America the plays were often presented in un-
pretentious circumstances.  Audiences in Milwaukee had to sit

on rough board benches that sorely tested their interest and
endurance as theater lovers.  The plays were serious and the
Germans took great pride in the fact that they were adding to
the cultural tone of their adopted country.  Dancing after performances helped to make the theatrical occasions important social events for them.  In Milwaukee in the 1870s one could buy
a season's ticket for $13.50 to $30.  During the theatrical
season, serious dramas were often presented on Wednesday evenings and lighter works on Fridays and Sundays.

Most of the plays presented for German audiences were
classics of German dramatic literature; Schiller's plays perhaps had the most enduring success on the German stage in
America.  There was also keen interest in new plays by contemporary dramatists in Germany.  Some of the plays written by
German-American authors were presented.  Geza Berger's play,
*Barbara Urbyk*, met with warm response.  Some of the German-
American plays dealt with American themes, like Viktor Precht's
*Jacob Leisler*, Friedrich Ernst's *Peter Mühlenberg; oder Bibel
und Schwert*, and Friedrich Schnake's *Montezuma*.  Playwrights
like Kaspar Butz and Ernst Zündt used other historical themes.
German theatrical groups and musical societies presented or
sponsored German operas in the larger cities, but not often
without financial loss.  A large number of farces and comedies
written by contemporary popular writers in Germany were translated and adapted for general American audiences.

In addition to New York, more than a dozen other cities
had well-established theaters in German: New Orleans, Balti-
more, St. Louis, Cincinnati, Milwaukee, San Francisco, Chicago,
Ithica, Rochester, Buffalo, Philadelphia, Pittsburgh, Reading,
Newark, Columbus, Cleveland, Belleville and Peoria, Kansas City,
Missouri, Detroit, Clinton and Plain View, Michigan, Davenport,
Denver, St. Paul, Omaha, Boston, Indianapolis, Evansville,
Louisville, Austin, and Galveston.[3]  Heinrich Conried, director
of the Irving Place German Theater in New York, often lectured
on German drama at eastern universities, and on the same occasions he presented some of the best acting talent in his German
company to the university community playing the works of Schiller and other major dramatists.  In cities throughout the country German social clubs and societies helped keep the German
amateur and professional theater alive.  At best the theater
was excellent, but sometimes the repertoires included sentimental melodramas and stupid farces.  Yet, as Henry A. Pochmann points out, "The high cultural aspirations of the German-
speaking theater in America, its extraordinary vitality and
perseverance and the general respect that it won among play-
goers and critics even outside the German circles made it a
considerable factor in the history of the American drama."[4]
The contributions, however, are in no way comparable in magnitude to the great enrichment that German-American musicians,
conductors, and composers made to American music.

By the turn of the century, German immigrants constituted
a large part of the total foreign-born population in many areas
of the Middle West, including states like Missouri, Illinois,
Wisconsin, North Dakota, South Dakota, Minnesota, Iowa, and
Nebraska.   In 1890 almost three-quarters of the population of
Wisconsin was either of foreign birth or was born of foreign
or mixed parentage.   Germans represented 37 percent of the
state's inhabitants.   The next largest ethnic segment, the
Scandinavians, comprised 11 percent of the population.   Laws
governing the franchise made the participation of the foreign-
born in the political affairs of their state relatively easy.
Wisconsin law, for example, permitted immigrants to vote after
one year's residence in the state, with the further requirement
that the immigrant declare his intention of becoming an American citizen.   The German element participated extensively in
the political and economic affairs of Midwestern states, yet
there is little reliable data on the precise nature of their
influence on politics.[5]

As early as the 1850s, political observers had noted a
special affinity of German-born Americans for the Republican
Party, which had recently emerged out of the debris of the Whig
Party.[6]   President Lincoln believed that the German language
press and German-American voters had played an important part
in determining the results of the election of 1860.   Lincoln's
administration honored the obligations it felt it owed German-
Americans by the appointment of numerous men of German origin
to public office (not as many as they thought they deserved,
but nevertheless a large number).   During the remaining decades
of the nineteenth century, practical politicians of both major
political parties tended to accept the existence of this special affinity with the Republican Party.   The persistence of
this notion was aided by the fact that a number of Forty-
eighters, like Carl Schurz and Gustav Körner, were eminent Republican leaders at the national political level, and it was
widely assumed that the political elite was representative of
the political affiliations of the rank-and-file.   The belief in
the Republicanism of German-Americans as a sustained historical
characteristic still persists today among some historians and
political scientists.   Some recent scholars, however, have examined German-American political behavior with more sophisticated methods of research and have cast doubt on the existence
of a pronounced attraction to either the Republican Party or
the Democratic Party enduring over any considerable period of
time.[7]

The political behavior of the foreign-born is determined
by a number of factors, among which the cultural values brought
from the homeland and the political attitudes of the communities of settlement are crucially important.   Customarily the
naturalized citizen learns about current political issues and
about the existing machinery of political participation in

essentially the same manner that he learns about other aspects
of culture.  Political orientation is a phase of the broad
process of acculturation.  Recent studies by careful scholars
working with voting statistics on a precinct level reveal the
tendency of naturalized Germans to vote Republican in counties
with traditions of Republican predominance and, conversely, to
vote Democratic in counties that generally favor the Democratic
Party.  Frederick C. Luebke has pointed out that, in general,
voters of German background in Nebraska have shared the political interests and perspectives of the predominant population of
the communities in which they resided.  That does not mean,
however, that the patterns of their political behavior remained
indistinguishable from those of the surrounding majority.  As
is true of the Irish and other ethnic groups, the political interests and activities of German-Americans show certain divergent tendencies that reflect differences in cultural background
and experience.  But the German-Americans in these states did
not vote as an ethnic bloc.  There were, of course, significant
differences in political interests, attitudes, and voting behavior that were related to contrasts of social class, education, income, urban and rural residence, and religion among
groups of German-Americans.

Until after the First World War, the German vote tended to
fluctuate.  In Baltimore the German-American Jefferson Club competed with the German-American Republican Lincoln Club and the
German-American Roosevelt League.  Party loyalties were not
firmly fixed or imbedded in family traditions.  Strong political figures like Cleveland and Theodore Roosevelt were particularly effective in attracting support from those who normally
voted for the opposing party.

Practical politicians in many areas of the country regarded the Germans like the Irish, as a political factor with
which they reckon.  By 1900 in cities like St. Louis and Baltimore or in states like Wisconsin, party leaders found it ex-
pedient to make certain that German candidates appeared on
party tickets.  In some areas the German-Americans involved
themselves enthusiastically in local, state, and national political campaigns; in other areas their participation tended to be
less marked.  Where political interest and activity were at a
high level, the German-Americans became aware of the potenti-
alities of their political influence.  In the years immediately
before the outbreak of the First World War, efforts were made
to consolidate German-American political power more effectively.
In Baltimore the Independent Citizens' Union (*Unabhängige
Bürgerverein*) was founded by John G. Tjarks to stimulate broader participation in political life and to sharpen interest in
specific issues involving school administration, taxes, civil
liberties, constitutional rights, and so on.  German societies
from various sections of the country met in Philadelphia in

1901 and, under the leadership of Charles J. Hexamer, founded
the National German-American Alliance.  The organization hoped
to strengthen German-American political influence by coordinating the efforts of German societies throughout the country.
The task of coordination was not easy.  There was an old saying
that when two or three Germans were gathered together they
formed a society.  Later a corollary was added that when a
fourth appeared, he won over one of the original three and together they formed a rival organization.  It was at least possible for Hexamer to gain widespread support from individuals
and societies in all sections of the country.  Despite the
heterogeneity of the German-American voters and their party
divisions, they tended to define certain particular issues in
somewhat different terms than did the native-born Americans in
the same communities.  For example, from the 1850s until the
repeal of Prohibition in 1933, most German-Americans actively
opposed legislative control of alcohol as attempted by state
and federal statutes.  It was indeed the threat of Prohibition
that more than anything else drove German-American societies
to submerge their differences and found the National German-
American Alliance.

The efforts of well-meaning temperance groups (including
a small body of German Methodists) to convert the Germans met
with utter failure.  The efforts reveal the distinctive differences that existed in the patterns of sociability and
leisure time activities between the German-Americans and the
Anglo-Americans in that period.  To many Germans, Sunday was
the proper occasion for a visit to the beer garden and to enjoy
the *Gemütlichkeit* of relaxed sociability among friends and relatives.  Some Americans developed a grossly exaggerated notion
of social activities of German societies perhaps because they
were strange and conspicuous and they viewed Germans as "in-
satiable celebrators."  In any case many ordinary people could
be observed on Sunday engaged in a number of activities: picnics and dances, musical and theatrical performances, poetry
competitions, sharpshooting contests, bowling, or gymnastic
trials of the *Turnvereine*.  These activities offended certain
of their Anglo-American neighbors who were strict Sabbatarians.
Major Horace Chase, a pioneer Yankee settler in Milwaukee, succeeded for a time in banning Sunday dancing at places like
Mozart Hall in response to public feeling against "these Sunday
orgies."[8]  The Germans often showed little concern for such
sensibilities, feeling that the more Puritanical of their
neighbors needed emancipation from their narrow ways.  German
observances of popular holidays were flamboyant, often fea-
turing displays of flags and gay decorations.  No occasion was
truly festive without patriotic German and American songs by
choirs and general singing by all the guests.  Even the celebration of the Fourth of July was often done more spectacularly

than was customary among the Anglo-American population.  Many
contemporary references, however, indicate that the enjoyment
of the Sängerfeste and band concerts spread among many elements
of the population of such communities as Milwaukee, Cincinnati,
and St. Louis, even if these were presented on Sunday and even
if German families were enjoying, generally in fair moderation,
their glasses of wine or beer.

As P. J. Kenny noted in his *Illustrated Cincinnati* of 1875,
Americans enjoyed spending leisure hours with their German
neighbors at Wielerts or the Lowen Garten in the German district of Cincinnati called by Germans and Americans alike "Over
the Rhine."  To enter "Over the Rhine" (across the canal) was
like being suddenly and pleasantly transported to the Rhineland
where life seemed to move at a slower and more gracious tempo.
Here Kenny found German faces, German manners and customs,
dances and music, even German gossip, and of course German
recipes along with the inevitable beer and wine.  People being
served at the tables among the shady trees of the gardens not
only had the advantage of German music, he noted with rapture,
but often the visual treat of busts of Beethoven, von Weber,
Mendelssohn, Schumann, or other great musicians as well.  Kenny
remarked at the fact that despite the love of wine and beer
there was less crime and less drunkenness in "Over the Rhine"
than elsewhere in the city.  He quoted the words of Luther:

> Wer liebt nicht Weib, Wein and Gesang
> Er bleibt ein Narr sein Leben lang.

And as Thackeray translated it:
> Who loves not wine, woman and song,
> Remains a fool his whole life long.

But Kenny noted as well that the old Adamic curse and the
consequences of Eve's experimentation with the apple in Eden
were reflected in "Over the Rhine" as elsewhere.

Attempts to pass laws limiting the sale and use of alco-
holic beverages, restricting the issuance of liquor licenses,
or providing for local option aroused the ire of most German-
Americans.  These laws were viewed not only as an unjustified
interference with personal freedom but, worse, as a deliberate
attempt to force acceptance of the dominant Anglo-Americans'
cultural values.  This effort seemed a crude manifestation of
ethnocentrism.

German voters characteristically associated prohibition,
Sabbatarianism, women's suffrage, and nativism with reformist
Republicans and Populists.[9]  They regarded these issues as important, and the positions that the state political organization (and the state and local candidates) took on these matters
influenced their behavior at the polls.  National issues such
as the tariff question, free trade, civil service reform,

monetary policies, and federal regulation of big business, although they were regarded as important, seemed less immediate and more abstract to ordinary voters—including the ordinary naturalized Germans.  The more acculturated Germans and the better educated members of the group, however, were generally more fully informed and more interested in major national issues in contemporary politics.

In Nebraska in the 1880s, beginning with proposals to raise the cost of liquor licenses in 1881, a series of issues arose that contributed to a drift of German voters to the Democratic Party.  It reached a high point in 1890.  In 1894 the free silver question seemed to dispel the tendencies of the previous decade, and no clear ethnic pattern was apparent.  The reintroduction of the prohibition issue in 1907 and succeeding elections again result in the shift of Midwestern Germans to the Democratic Party.

The ethnic and religious patterns of response to specific political issues and programs were often complex.  In Nebraska, as in the Dakotas, German Lutherans along with German and Bohemian Catholics (Czechs) were severely divided on issues relating to religion but nonetheless cooperated in their opposition to prohibition.  Methodists, including the relatively small number of German Methodists, and Scandinavian Lutherans favored prohibition or took little interest in the political contention it evoked.  When prohibition legislation was passed by the North Dakota legislature, enforcement proved difficult in the areas of German and Russian-German predominance.  There was widespread objection to submission to a law that in their view was forced upon them by Red River Valley Scandinavians.  German-American opposition continued even after the Prohibition Amendment was passed until its final repeal.

Another issue that concerned a large segment of the German-American population was the position of private schools.  A substantial number of parochial and other private schools had been established in the 1850s and '60s.  Some were founded by liberal secularists.  The Missouri Synod Lutherans and the Roman Catholics were the most active in establishing parochial schools in areas where large German-born concentrations were forming.  The nonreligious schools were established to provide educational facilities of high quality for families who could afford the tuition; the curriculum reflected the concern of educators and parents that the education be excellent and that it train the students in the German language.  Some of the private schools like the Knapp Institute of Baltimore and Peter Engelmann's German-English Academy in Milwaukee enjoyed national reputations.  Even the best of the private schools were not uniformly successful in instilling love of German language and culture among the youth enrolled.  In his autobiographies, H. L. Mencken tells of his youthful struggles at Knapp's

Institute with German conjugations and declensions and his firm
conviction that "German was an irrational and even insane
tongue, and not worth the sufferings of a freeborn American."
He added his conviction, many years after the ordeal, that "the
German language is of a generally preposterous and malignant
character."[10]

In the 1880s interest in the private secular schools diminished and by the 1890s they largely disappeared despite the
fact that German-American life seemed to be developing vigorously.  In large part they disappeared because of the introduction of German instruction in the public schools in many communities with large German populations.  In 1867 the Milwaukee
school board made German a part of the regular curriculum in
recognition of the fact that more than half of the city's population spoke German.  Four years later, more than 46 percent of
the pupils enrolled in the public schools were studying German.[11]
Other communities with large German-speaking populations also
introduced German into the public schools.

In 1873 an experimental English-German Public School was
founded by the Baltimore schools system.  Children enrolled in
the school received instruction in both languages every day.
Most students came from German families, but Anglo-American
families interested in having their children well instructed in
German also enrolled their children because they were convinced
of its commercial utility or cultural advantage.  In two years,
five new English-German public schools were opened, enrolling
some three thousand pupils.  By the turn of the century they
enrolled seven thousand or about 10 percent of Baltimore's
school population.  After that, however, they declined rapidly
and finally disappeared in 1917.[12]  Campaigns against the
teaching of German in the public schools were having marked
success even before the nineteenth century ended.  Louisville
dropped German instruction in 1887, and St. Paul abandoned it
about the same time.

The Roman Catholic and Lutheran parochial schools continued to exist, but their German character also weakened with
time.  Other Catholic children were introduced into the Roman
Catholic parochial schools, and the Missouri Synod Lutherans
preserved their traditions longest; they were particularly
strong in St. Louis and other areas of strong Lutheran concentration.  Before the decline in the ethnic-parochial schools
became obvious, the question of their educational inferiority
or superiority as compared with public schools was warmly de-
bated in some areas of the country and occasionally grew into
a sensitive political issue.  To the *Kirchendeutsche*, as church-
oriented Germans, the religious elements in the parochial
school curriculum were crucially important and worth defending
even though the program of studies was in many respects similar
to that of the public schools.  The ethnic parochial schools

stressed instruction in the traditional language and sometimes literature and culture. Their greatest importance, however, lay in their contribution to the social unity of the immigrant communities and their continuity over a period of several generations. As William I. Thomas and Florian Znaniecki point out in *The Polish Peasant in Europe and America*, the separate ethnically oriented schools represented an institutional bond among the families it served and bound the old and young generations together. A stronger sense of community was fostered by the participation of the parents and extended family in the activities and festivities of the schools. For the immigrant generation and their children these schools were a valuable expression of the impulse of the ethnic community for self-preservation and self-development. Children who went to public schools were much more likely to become estranged from their immigrant parents. Even though the private and parochial school curricula were not radically different from the public schools, they succeeded in instructing their students with more of the traditional culture and in inculcating respect for the traditional values.[13] Peer group associations in such schools were more likely to reenforce ties to tradition and the sense of group identity. Except for a brief period, the public schools took little note of the ethnic background of the students and discovered no particular need for curriculum adaptations or specialized modes of instruction for the benefit of the second generation children.

When educators, public officials, and legislators raised questions about the quality of private and parochial schools, German-Americans interested in the future of such schools generally became zealous in their efforts to prevent the rise of any legitimate criticism concerning educational quality that might be used to justify further legislative or administrative regulation of their schools. For that reason the German-American Teachers' Seminary in Milwaukee had been founded; it contributed substantially to sustaining the quality of curricular offerings and the professional standards of the teachers. Other objections raised against the schools were focused on the alleged inhibiting effect they had upon acculturation and assimilation of immigrant groups.

In 1889 a bill sponsored by Assemblyman Michael J. Bennett passed the Wisconsin legislature without debate. The law ostensibly was directed against the employment of children under thirteen. The legislation required children to attend school for at least twelve weeks per year. Several months after its passage, German Protestant groups discovered in Section V of the Bennett Law certain wording that they interpreted to be an attack upon German religious organizations, parochial and other private schools, and, moreover, upon their language and culture. When the "Yankee" trick was discovered, a Wisconsin historian notes, "the sauerkraut really hit the fan."[14]   The provision read:

> No school shall be regarded as a school, under
> this act, unless there shall be taught, therein, as
> part of the elementary education of children, reading,
> writing, arithmetic and United States history in the
> English language.

The inclusion of the phrase ". . . in the English language" took on a foreboding aspect for those Germans struggling with the difficult task of preserving at least some part of German language and culture in their community life in Wisconsin.  The Republican newspaper, *The Milwaukee Sentinel*, sharpened the concern of the German element with its frequent and vehement denunciation of what it called "those American-born adults unable to read or write English, or even to speak it properly."  The strong position taken by this newspaper and other Republican journals evoked a sharp political response, not only among German Protestants but also among German Catholic churchmen as well.  By March of that year the latter interpreted the Bennett Law, and its defense, as manifestations of a desire to put parochial schools under state control and, moreover, ultimately to destroy the system of parochial education. Noting the zeal and swelling fervor of the united opposition among the German denominations against the Republican position during the political campaign before the local elections of April 1890, *The Milwaukee Sentinel* tried unsuccessfully to divide the opposition by playing up fears among German Protestants of Catholicism and of the formation of a Catholic political bloc.

In the election in April, German Lutheran votes made it possible for Democratic mayoralty candiates in Milwaukee, Eau Claire, Chippewa Falls, Ripon, and other cities to carry normally Republican districts and win.[15]  The Wisconsin Germans saw the vote as a testimony of their determination to preserve some measure of cultural pluralism, which they found in no way incompatible with Americanization.  Many Wisconsin Germans still hoped to preserve the German language as a second language. The Bennett Law seemed to threaten the symbol of their culture and their ethnic origin, the German language.

The state election campaign in the summer and fall of 1890 produced the most open and obvious appeals along ethnic and religious lines of Wisconsin's history.  Republicans stuck to the defense of their position and tried to rally loyalty to the principles embodied in the law by representing the opposition as a dangerous peril to the "Little School House" and public education in general.  The Democrats sought to take advantage of the situation the Republicans had created.  The result of

the campaign was a Democratic landslide.  The Republican governor was defeated.  The entire Democratic state ticket was
swept into office.  Both houses of the legislature became predominantly Democratic.  Large defections from Republican support were registered not only in the various closely knit
German enclaves in rural Wisconsin, but also among German-
Americans in urban centers, both large and small.  German-Swiss
areas like Buffalo County and Green County with its concentrations in the New Glarus colony showed similar political patterns.
    There were, of course, various national issues that were
reflected in the election, among them the unpopularity of the
McKinley tariff policy.  But in the German segment of the
state's population, the issues arising out of the Bennett Law
were paramount.[16]  The election indicated the political power
of the German voters when their interests seemed threatened and
when they could establish cooperation across the denominational
and other lines that divided them.
    In Nebraska and other states similar restrictive legisla-
tion was proposed.[17]  In 1913 a Nebraska school law permitted
the teaching of German only above grade 4 and only for one period a day.  Such legislation stood in stark contrast to the
bilingual schools that had been established thirty-five or
forty years earlier in Baltimore, Cincinnati, Indianapolis, and
Milwaukee and that had flourished for several decades before
their decline.  Texas Germans, perhaps because the divisions
between liberals and church-oriented people were less acute and
because they had a particularly strong sense of group loyalty,
were able to sustain their bilinguality more effectively than
most other German-American communities.[18]
    The visible strength of the German-Americans and the ap-
parent expansion of their influence and power in the years from
1880 to 1914 obscured incipient weaknesses.  The German language newspapers still dominated the foreign language press but
their circulation was diminishing as the immigrant generation
suffered mortality and as the pace of acculturation accelerated.
The superabundance of German clubs and societies, a legacy of
several generations of the *Vereinsdeutsche* organization building, provided a focus for social and cultural activities for a
substantial proportion of the club-oriented German-Americans.
The Roman Catholics and major Lutheran communities held themselves largely aloof from the secular clubs.  If all segments
of the German-American population were conscious of a collective German-American identity, the areas of intimate and persistent collaboration in politics or cultural activities or
even in maintaining the German language between liberals and
socialists on the one hand and the church bodies on the other
were limited.

## THE FIRST WORLD WAR AND THE
## TRANSFORMATION OF GERMAN-AMERICAN LIFE

At the turn of the century, Germany appeared to be, in the eyes of most Americans, a stabilizing element in the seething ferment of European political life.  Its military prowess, which remained formidable throughout the Bismarckian and Wilhelmian periods, impressed Americans as it did Europeans. There were, it is true, curious incongruities in the portrait of Germany that was taking shape in the American mind.  Germany's military and diplomatic power seemed to be a general stabilizing factor despite the Emperor's outbursts about German *Drang nach Osten*.  But the traditions of its military caste and the disposition of its governing elite left disquieting uncertainties in the minds of some Americans.  Germany was not an advanced democracy even by contemporary continental standards, yet its social legislation was far more progressive than that of some of the leading democracies, including the United States. The Social Democratic Party was becoming the most powerful political party, a statistic which seemed to forecast future political transformations.  The fact remained, however, that even sober and responsible Americans knew little of continental politics and of international relations.  The reputation of Germany's scientific achievement and learning was widely appreciated in the United States; large numbers of students and scholars from all over the world, including America, were attracted to Germany.  Its universities and erudite publications had for a generation exerted a deep influence upon American academic life.  There were close ties of friendship between members of the German upper classes and eminent Americans.  The Emperor was very generous but sagacious in his bestowal of official honors and decorations to distinguished citizens of the United States.  Like many others, Theodore Roosevelt sought and was flattered to receive an official invitation from William II to visit Berlin.  On his way back to the United States from his hunting expedition in Africa, Roosevelt visited the Emperor and was met with cordiality.

No one dreamed of the possibility of war between Germany and the United States.  In the German language press in the two decades preceding the outbreak of war in Europe, there was not the slightest indication of any difficulty between the two countries.  As was true of the foreign press generally, more attention was given to news from abroad than was true of the American press.  In German language newspapers more items concerning Germany were understandably published.  Yet no extraordinary attention was given to continental politics.  There seemed no obvious need either to defend or to criticize Germany's role in international affairs.  A deepening German-American suspicion of Great Britain was reflected in their newspapers.  Fears of a secret treaty between the United States and Great Britain periodically surfaced in the editorial comments of many German-American editors.  The persistence of these feelings strengthened the apparent rapprochement between Irish- and German-Americans.  German-American editors also occasionally expressed concern over what they alleged to be Russia's aspirations to dominate Western Europe.  The internal strains that threatened the stability of multinational Austria-Hungary could not fail to be noted by newspapers with any broad coverage of continental affairs.  With all this, however, it remains true that the main focus of their journalistic attention was upon the domestic affairs of the United States.

By the turn of the century, the German-language newspapers had become very much like other American newspapers both in form and in content.  Coverage was appropriately given to major national, state, and local issues and events.  The activities in Congress and in state legislatures were regularly reported.  Major attention was focused upon local affairs: municipal government; public lectures, concerts, and other cultural events in the community; crime; labor news and issues; financial news and market reports; sports; and advice to the lovelorn.  Considerable attention was given to social activities and cultural affairs in the German-American community.  German societies were indeed dependent upon these newspapers for communication with their members, and it was in the interest of editors to provide space for these societies.  Presumably the newspapers reflected the fact that German-American readers were primarily concerned with what was going on in their community in particular and in their ethnic group in general.

Henry L. Mencken, whose parents were part of the Baltimore German community, wrote about the German newspapers in the city (two dailies and four or five weeklies) and especially about their writers who were, he noted, some of Baltimore's "most eminent and popular reporters."

The German reporters led lives that were the admiration of many of their American colleagues, for
. . . their papers were not so much interested in ordinary news, and there was no courtmartial if one of them missed a bank robbery or even a murder, provided, of course, no German was involved.  Their main business was to cover the purely German doings of the town—weddings, funerals, concerts, picnics, birthday parties, and so on.  This kept them jumping pleasantly, for there were then 30,000 of their compatriots in Baltimore, and most of the 30,000 seemed to be getting on in the world, and were full of social enterprise.  It was not sufficient for a German reporter to report their weddings as news: he also had to

dance with the bride, drink with her father, and
carry off a piece of the wedding cake, presumably for
his wife . . . When there were speeches, which was
usually, he had to make one, whether at a birthday
party, a banquet of the German Freemasons, Knights of
Pythias or Odd Fellows of the opening of a new picnic-
grounds, saloon, or Lutheran church.  Whenever re-
freshments were offered, which was always, he had to
eat and drink in a hearty manner, and he was remiss
in his duties if he failed to sneak in a nice notice
for the lady who had prepared the *Sauerbraten* or
*Haringsalat*.[19]

Whatever misgivings the German-Americans may have had
about peace arose from policies they attributed not to Germany
but to its rivals: Britain, because it was thought to be inordinately jealous of Germany's new industrial strength;
France, because it appeared to be seeking revenge for the loss
of Alsace-Lorraine; and Russia because of the sinister Pan-
Slavism of the Tsar.

The assassination of the Archduke Franz Ferdinand at Sara-
jevo on June 28, 1914, did not seem at first to be an event of
such significance as to portend the outbreak of a general war
in Europe.  But so it was to be.  In the beginning most Americans hoped that the struggle could be confined to central
Europe.  As the conflagration spread throughout the continent,
Americans watched with increasing concern and alarm.  But only
slowly did the full dimensions of the holocaust become apparent
in America.

Expressions of public opinion reflected the almost universal determination to preserve an official neutrality.  The
broad expanse of the Atlantic promised to provide a sufficient
buffer to any threatening international danger or entanglement.
President Wilson urged the country to be neutral in fact as
well as in name and "impartial in thought as well as in action."
Theodore Roosevelt was quick to lend his influence to the maintenance of a policy of neutrality, and the former president expressed his gratitude that the nation has escaped "the working
of the causes which had produced the bitter and vindicative
hatred among the great military Powers of the Old World."
Shortly thereafter, however, he repudiated his stand and swung
violently to an extremely pro-British position.  Although the
American people continued to favor an official policy of neutrality in the first years of the war, there was much confusion
about the conflicting issues.  Truth was hard to discover and
impartial judgments difficult to achieve.

It has been said that in war truth is the first casualty.
Early in the First World War, journals in Allied countries gave
wide circulation to the story that in July 1914 the Kaiser had

called his civil, military, and naval advisers together in
Potsdam for a secret conference at which it was decided to
provoke war.  There was no factual foundation for the story,
but it was widely accepted and became one of the bases for the
war guilt thesis, according to which the leaders of Germany and
Austria provoked the war as part of a plan to advance their
power by destroying their major rivals.  The Allies were seen
as wagers of a defensive war in an effort to protect themselves
and other, smaller states.  After the end of the war, historical scholarship presented insights into events and movements of
the time that made it clear that no single ruler nor government
nor people could reasonably be made to bear the preponderant
responsibility.  Ordinary Americans learned about the war
largely through mass communication media that were illequipped
to present adequately the complex issues of continental diplo-
macy and war.

German-born Americans were understandably affected by the
attachments to the land of their birth, and citizens of Irish
ancestry remembered with sharp bitterness the conflicts generated by British dominion over Ireland.  The Irish- and German-
Americans cooperated in countering those influences in the
United States that favored Great Britain.  On the opposite side,
large numbers of men and women born in Great Britain and Canada
were equally active.  They sought to stir the public into an
enthusiastic support of Great Britain and its allies, eventually culminating in military intervention.  The great masses of
native-born Americans were the target of various campaigns to
convince them of the rightness and justice of one side or the
other.  Although a great variety of opinions on the war flourished in America, it was clear from the beginning of the conflict that a large proportion of the population was sympathetic
to Great Britain and its allies.  The ties of language and
history bound Americans more closely to the British than to
other ethnic groups.  Woodrow Wilson believed, as did many
Americans, that in the last analysis American history was essentially an extension of British experience.[20]

Most American writers and journalists favored the Allies;
the channels of communication most generally available to them
inevitably influenced the manner in which they described events
and defined issues of the war to the American readers.  The
German language press in the United States in the early part of
the war had access through Germany to sources of new and diplomatic developments quite different but not necessarily either
better or worse than those available to the American press generally.  Editors of German language newspapers were convinced
that the American public was being grossly deceived by a conspiracy on the part of American editors and British propagan-
dists.  A deep-seated Anglo-phobia was widespread among German-
Americans.  There is little to suggest (as some have indeed

done) that editors had to be enticed, presumably by offers of
Berlin gold, to take the anti-British position.  It was not
necessary to persuade them, by subsidies to print, what they
were already convinced was true, or to rally them to the fatherland beset by its enemies.  Almost unanimously the German-
American press exonerated the German government of responsibility for the outbreak of war.  Only a few German Socialist or
labor newspapers, such as the *Volkszeitung* in New York and the
*Echo* in Cleveland, expressed opposing views.[21]  On all sides,
attempts at deception, plain and uncorrupted ignorance, and un-
conscious distortion intruded and confounded the already difficult task of reaching reasonable and well-founded opinions.
Three-quarters of the news dispatches filed by American correspondents in Europe had to pass through English censorship,
a fact that certainly affected American public information.
George Bernard Shaw remarked that "America, to judge by some of
its papers, is mad with British patriotism, Polish nationality,
and Belgian freedom."  The British and German governments engaged in extensive propaganda campaigns, but the contest was
ludicrously unequal.  German propaganda missions were generally
inept.  The British were, by contrast, highly effective.
     Dr. Heinrich Albert and Dr. Bernhard Dernburg were sent by
the German government to direct propaganda efforts in the
United States.  The Bavarian-born poet, Georg Sylvester Viereck,
became the leading propagandist for Germany in America.  After
the war broke out, Viereck returned to the United States and
immediately founded the staunchly pro-German weekly magazine,
*The Fatherland*.  The magazine, published in English, defended
all those who viewed the German cause sympathetically both in
the United States and elsewhere in North America.[22]  Viereck
directed the distribution of a vast quantity of books and pamphlets favorable to the Central Powers.  Under the imprimerie
of the Jackson Press, he published such books as Count Ravent-
low's *The Vampire of the Continent*, which fiercely denounced
Britain's influence abroad.  Viereck became a conspicuous symbol of the German cause, and the almost daily press attacks
made his efforts and influence seem far more significant than
they actually were.  The hatred expressed toward him, he later
wrote, did not frighten him but rather gratified him as a clear
testimony to his personal importance and professional effectiveness.[23]  Besides, to the German-born writer, propaganda wars
were not only a crucial aspect of conflict in the twentieth
century, but a "great game" for the rival professional practi-
tioners of the art of propaganda.[24]
     German-American organizations held benefit performances
and bazaars to raise money to aid the war orphans and widows in
Germany.  One of the biggest was held in Madison Square Garden
in 1916 and brought $700,000.  The National German-American Al-
liance and other organizations sought to influence public

opinion and public policy in favor of American neutrality.   In
these efforts, the Alliance made itself a very visible advocate
of policies opposed to the Allies at a time when the tide of
American public opinion was becoming more and more drawn to the
Allied cause and to intervention.   The activities of the Alliance appeared more and more treasonous, and ultimately Congress
revoked its charter.   But the efforts of many German-born Americans to gain sympathy for Germany had little effect except to
help sustain the convictions of those already favorably disposed in their own ethnic group, those Anglo-Americans who had
studied in German universities, and the Irish.

The very success that the German element had had in assimilating itself in the United States and in achieving a considerable economic and political power emboldened it to fight back
against what it regarded as British propaganda.   In the light
of what was transpiring in the country, their actions seem in-
cautious and sometimes foolish in their over-zealousness.   The
German-American Alliance in fighting for an embargo against
shipments of arms to belligerents incurred public animosity
until Congress was finally moved to revoke the organization's
charter.   Their actions and their influence were increasingly
seen as evidence of the menace they posed to the nation.   The
protestation by German-American editors and community leaders
of their loyalty to the United States and their devotion to its
enduring interests was lost in the rising tide of hostility.
The feelings of many German-Americans on the issue of national
loyalty were well illustrated by a statement by Herman Ridder,
editor of the *New Yorker Staats-Zeitung*, in his book *Hyphenations* in 1915:   "Whenever it has been a question between my own
country and that of my fathers, I have given wholehearted support to the former.   Only when it was a question of supporting
Germany or her enemies have I given rein to an unerasable affec-
tion for the Fatherland."[25]

The wartime acts of the German government compounded the
problems of the German-Americans.   The invasion of Belgium at
the opening of the conflict seriously affected American attitudes toward Germany.   In a masterful stroke of psychological
warfare, the British government induced James Bryce, a scholar
much esteemed in America, to sign the official report on alleged German atrocities in Belgium.   Stories about crucified
nuns and maimed women and children were well calculated to impress Americans with German brutality.   The alleged atrocities
gave rise to the practice of referring to Germans as the "Huns"
and "barbarians"—terms that by extension were also applied to
German-Americans.   Virtually every German-American newspaper
rejected the stories as malicious fabrications.[26]

The war brought many provocations to American interests
and well-being on the part of both groups of belligerents.
British treatment of what it regarded as contraband cargoes on

American ships was severely damaging to American interests.
British mines unlawfully sown in the North Sea resulted in the
loss of American lives and property.  One cannot easily set
these various acts on a scale in balance with the provocations
that came from the German government, such as the declaration
of unrestricted submarine warfare and the Zimmermann Affair.
Whatever an objective balancing might reveal, the fact remains
that the provocations of the Allies and Central Powers were
differently reported and assimilated in the United States.
German-Americans concentrated on a campaign to get the Congress
to declare an embargo on the export of munitions.  Mass meetings were held in major cities throughout the country.  The
efforts continued virtually up to the moment the United States
declared war.  Many other individuals and groups were also
working to keep the United States out of the hostilities.
There were pacifists like Oswald Garrison Villard and David
Starr Jordan, the distinguished scientist and president of
Stanford University, who spoke and acted on behalf of keeping
America at peace.  Senator LaFollette fought vigorously in the
Senate and throughout the country to keep America from rushing
to the aid of British imperialism and Russian autocracy, both
of which he condemned.  Ezra Pound despaired to see talented
literary friends going off to die in trenches; he saw no merit
in either side of the conflict to warrant America's joining
the conflict and sacrificing its wealth and its young men.

For the German element in the United States, the First
World War was devastating.  Wartime travail rested more heavily
upon them with each passing month, until the final blow came
with the declaration of war on April 2, 1917.  Men and women
who had lived in friendliness and mutual respect with their
neighbors were suddenly viewed with fear and suspicion.  People
whose personal integrity and decency had never been questioned
were obliged to defend their good name, even their loyalty to
their adopted country.

Various segments of the German-American population found
in the German-language press a means of communicating their
common interests and experiences in what was for them an extremely trying period.  The dailies had at least three-quarters
of a million subscribers and the weeklies reached additional
hundreds of thousands of readers.  Although the German language
press in 1914 no longer represented a predominant position in
the foreign language press, it still represented 40 percent of
the thirteen hundred newspapers and periodicals then being published in languages other than English.  German-Americans relied on the accuracy of their newspapers as an antidote to the
news presented by the general American press.  Many who had
allowed their subscriptions to lapse in the years immediately
before the war again began to subscribe.  The readers found
solace in them and spared themselves the exposure to such

epithets as "Huns" and "barbarians" frequently found in other newspapers.  The American population of German origin was nevertheless highly heterogeneous.  Many persons were assimilating into the general American population and discarding the hyphenated, German-American category, thereby joining those millions who preserved only a vague sense of special Germanic origin. Even the most assimilated, if they bore names like Schultz or Schwartz, could not always escape the consequences of being identified with Germany by Germanophobic neighbors.  Some of the newer immigrants were convinced that Germany was, as most Americans believed, primarily responsible for the outbreak of the war.  A few of the more bloodthirsty of these assumed the role of *Hunnenfresser* (hun-haters) and sought to whip up hatred for German militarism or anything German; sometimes this was done out of honest conviction, sometimes because it was profitable at the time or because it was a convenient way of establishing the genuineness of one's own patriotism to America.

German-American families were often torn apart by the issues of the war.  Hermann Hagedorn, the biographer of Theodore Roosevelt, wrote of the divisions in his own family.  Hagedorn and his brother remained in the United States when the other members of the family returned to Germany at the time of the father's retirement.  When the war broke out, communication about the war and their feelings about it became difficult. Family members on each side of the Atlantic found it difficult to understand how the family members on the other side could be so tragically deceived by the propaganda of the enemy.  From the outbreak of the War in 1914 until America's entry, Hagedorn worked diligently to convince people of German ancestry to support Theodore Roosevelt's campaign for national preparedness and to convince them that Germany was the aggressor.  "The attitude of these people, basically honest, loyal people, made me aware, for the first time, of the depth and scope of the problem that the divided hearts of the German-American presented," Hagedorn wrote.  "The great majority, I was certain, were normally for America first, last and always, having no sympathy for the German government and no more than the normal sentiment, shading off into indifference, of any naturalized American for the country of his birth."[27]

In trying to explain to their fellow citizens their feelings of loyalty to the United States, German-born citizens often used the analogy of the family: "We feel toward the land of our birth," they often explained, "as a man feels toward his parents; we feel toward the United States as a man feels toward his wife and children; it is to them that one gives his greatest love and owes his greatest obligation."  In many families, sons and daughters turned against their parents.  Parents often sought desperately to keep alive in their children some respect for German culture and some feeling of personal attachment to

the land of their ancestors despite the circumstances the War
created.  Sometimes the efforts of parents served only to widen
the differences between them and their children.  The children,
influenced by the American world about them, were torn between
loyalty to parents and hatred of their identification with a
national enemy widely portrayed as the epitome of evil.

A vast majority of the approximately three million German-
born citizens and the many millions more of second- and third-
generation German-Americans gave their allegiance to the United
States.  They served the United States during the 1914-18 war,
sometimes in very simple roles and sometimes in very distinguished capacities.  The Commanding General of the American Ex-
peditionary Force in France, General John J. Pershing, was of
German descent.

Few Americans had any notion of the personal and collective crises that the German-born among them were experiencing.
Vulnerability to emotional stress was not limited to the immigrant generation.  Whatever the degree of acculturation into
American life characteristic of members of the first, second,
or even third generation of German-Americans, the values and
sentiments attached to their national origin were in varying
measure important to their conceptions of themselves.  The sud-
den tidal wave of antipathy against Germany and Germans in the
First World War inescapably fell upon German-Americans as it
did upon Japanese-Americans in the second.  This was indeed the
intent of many of the nativists who saw the "racial flaws" of
the German character as biologically transmitted.  The wartime
hysteria brought forth a concentrated movement to eradicate
everything German from American life and culture.  It threatened German music, literature, language, and even place names
and family names.  The assaults seemed to the German-Americans
to wipe out entirely everything that generations of Germans
since 1683 had contributed to the nation.  Everything the Forty-
eighters had brought to the American people, the Sandusky *Demokrat* lamented, appeared to have been completely eradicated.

The most serious nativism that had ever been manifested in
the United States spread throughout the country.  In other wars,
national feeling had tended to unite the heterogeneous populations against the threat from abroad, and in doing so tended to
calm the currents of suspicion and antipathy directed toward
foreign-born elements in the population.  In this conflict, as
in the past, feelings of national cohesion warmed the body of
the nation, but suspicion and hostility directed against the
immigrants, especially the Germans, grew to unprecedented proportions.  In this instance, America found itself engaged in a
conflict with a country that had contributed one of the largest
contingents of foreign-born to its contemporary national population.  The hyphenated Americans—Irish-Americans, Italian-
Americans, as well as German-Americans—were seen as a menace

to national unity.  The wartime crisis shattered the old, con-
fident faith in the natural melting of many peoples into one.
In previous generations, Americans did not really demand a high
level of national solidarity or conformity; a substantial diversity among the people was in most generations taken for
granted, and ultimate absorption was expected as the inevitable
consequence of the contact of peoples.

The presidential campaign of 1916 focused much attention
upon the issue of loyalty.  Preparedness became a campaign
plank for both major political parties.  Closely allied to defense of the nation through arms was its defense through the
unity of its people.  To the extent that the foreign-born, the
hyphenated Americans, had cultural and family ties binding them
with nations overseas, the unity of national spirit and identity seemed diminished in that measure.  In the case of German-
Americans, public fear of internal aggression seemed a more
tangible threat than an invasion across the Atlantic.

The advocates of 100 percent Americanism rested upon a
cluster of interrelated assumptions; among these was the notion
that total national loyalty involved a universal conformity
that should permeate and stabilize the individual's perspectives and behavior in all important aspects of life; for beyond
the acceptance of loyalty as a passive sentiment, the proper
spirit of duty meant putting national endeavors above all
others.  The 100 percenters began with great faith in the force
of teaching and exhortation, but as the crisis deepened, the
means of persuasion became more forceful.  Such pressures were
exerted that few German societies dared to hold public meetings.
Many super patriots clamored for the suppression of all German
language newspapers.  The Congress responded to public concern
by suppressing the charter of the German American Alliance.  Efforts to eradicate the teaching of the German language in elementary and secondary schools as well as colleges and universities met with substantial success in all sections of the nation.
The Anti-Yellow Dog League was an organization of boys over ten
years of age who were recruited to detect sources of disloyalty.
Efforts were made by patrioteers to stop the use of German in
church, trains, and on the telephone.  Street assaults on people who were suspected of speaking German resulted in the abuse
of many speaking in other languages.  In Kansas, the police refused a permit for a celebration in honor of Franz Pastorius,
who had helped found Germantown, Pennsylvania, in 1683.  German
books were taken from many public libraries.  The Cincinnati
Library hid all German books and cancelled subscriptions to
German language newspapers and periodicals.  Beethoven and Bach
disappeared from concert programs.  Dr. Karl Munch, conductor
of the Boston Symphony orchestra, had to have a police guard
when he went to New York for a concert in March of 1918.  Two
weeks later he was interned for the duration of the war.

Family names were increasingly anglicized to avoid the penalty
attached to the symbol of national origin; thus, Mueller became
Miller, Schmidt became Smith, Rosenblatt became Ross.  Simi-
larly, some place names were altered in honor of a more perfect
Americanism; thus, Berlin, Iowa, was transformed into Lincoln;
East Germantown became Pershing, in honor of the most eminent
American general (ironically of German origin, *Pförsching*).
Even the national diet was affected; sauerkraut became "liberty
cabbage," and other items of diet were linguistically mangled
in the interests of cultural unity.

At the height of the hysteria, groups giving themselves
such pretentious names as "Loyalty League" and the "Security
League" were active in communities throughout the nation attempting to ferret out disloyalty and to force those suspected
of insufficient devotion to the American cause into a full compliance with what the patrioteers required of them.  Over-
zealous patriots in South Dakota raided a Mennonite community
and ran off one hundred steers and a thousand sheep, which they
subsequently sold to buy war bonds.  Vigilante groups of various kinds dragged many from their homes in the dead of night to
answer charges before self-appointed judges, jurors, and prose-
cutors.

H. L. Mencken, the bitter enemy of American provincial
narrowness, wrote in wrathful scorn of the abundant hordes of
minor league patriots:

> If the grand cordon or even the nickel-plated eagle
> of the third class were given to every patriot who
> bored a hole through the floor of his flat to get
> evidence against his neighbors, the Krausmeyers, and
> to everyone who visited the Hofbrauhaus nightly, de-
> nounced the Kaiser in searing terms, and demanded as-
> sent from Emil and Otto, the waiters, and to everyone
> who notified the catchpolls of the Department of
> Justice when the wireless plant was open in the gar-
> ret of Arion Liedertafel . . . and to all who served
> as jurors or perjurers in cases against members and
> exmembers of the I.W.W. and to the German-American
> members of the League for German Democracy, and to
> all the Irish who snitched upon the Irish—if decora-
> tions were thrown about with any such lavishness,
> then there would be no nickel left for our bathrooms.[28]

Mencken opposed American entry into the war not because of sympathy with Germany but purely because he viewed the alliance
with England as against America's interests.  There was some
suspicion that he might be a German spy and this prompted him
to write scornfully to public authorities making anonymous de-
nunciations against himself.

A war poster by Sid Greene reveals some of the ridiculousness of popular attitudes towards hyphenated Americans.

Ten Lil Hyphens sitting on a line, Uncle Sam jailed
    one and then there were nine.
Nine Lil Hyphens hiding among the freight, one dropped
    a big bomb and then there were eight.
Eight Lil Hyphens talking war and heaven, one cheered
    for the Faderland and that left seven.
Seven Lil Hyphens full of spying tricks, one had his
    nose bumped so hard that left six.
Six Lil Hyphens trying to connive, one was caught in
    the act so that left five.
Five Lil Hyphens feeling very sore, one faked his
    passport and that left four.
Four Lil Hyphens of very high degree, one joshed the
    President and that left three.
Three Lil Hyphens with very much ado, one skipped to
    Mexico and that left two.
Two Lil Hyphens fooling with a gun, the gun was
    marked USA, so that left one.
One Lil Hyphen sitting all alone, believed the German
    war news and then there was none.

The sympathies of German-Americans were overwhelmingly with Germany during the years before the American declaration of war.  American entry into the war did not suddenly cause them to change their convictions.  German-Americans supported the American war effort out of loyalty and a sense of honor. Their sons were given to fight in the American army.  They bought Liberty Bonds to support the war effort.  But loyalty apart, American involvement remained in their view a tragic blunder that the nation had been seduced into making by British propaganda and those Americans who had some political or economic advantage in promoting intervention in behalf of the Allied cause.  Among a small segment of the German-American population, a social radicalism was born of disenchantment with a system that could become thus involved in what seemed a senseless war.

Antiradical sentiments crystalized.  Attacks on radicalism were readily interwoven into anti-German hysteria.  The traditional assumption prevailed that radical dissent arises from immigrants who attempt to introduce (inappropriately) old world perspectives and ideologies into the United States.  It was easy to take the next step and see labor unrest and strikes as an obvious extension of the Kaiser's military campaigns against the United States.  Left-wing activity was often seen as pro-German manifestation.  As Wittke points out, the very rarity of overtly disloyal acts on the part of the German elements in the population seemed, paradoxically, to encourage the belief that the Germans were, with characteristic cunning, working secretly through left-wing organizations.

With the end of the war came a slow revival of German cultural activities.  Some part of what was lost in the wartime hysteria would have disappeared in time, perhaps, and the conditions of the period may only have accelerated the process. In other dimensions of cultural influence, there were losses that could never be repaired: they still remain, as casualties of war.

Community activities among the German-Americans began to revive.  Clubs and lodges that had suspended their activities began to hold meetings.  The ever-present singing societies again offered public performances.  The *Turnverein* and *Rheinischer Sängerbund* in New York, more than a century old, revived their strength.  In other cities as well, singing societies began to give public concerts and the audiences again warmed to the familiar tones of "Du, du liegst mir im Herzen" and "Muss i denn."  Interest in German music, drama, and literature revived among German-American communities, and the German language press that survived the disorganizing influence of the war period devoted itself to the promotion of such activities. The German Society of Maryland resumed its charitable work shortly after the war.

But much of the vitality that had characterized German-American cultural life was never restored.  The interest of prosperous, middle-class, city dwellers of German ancestry in German literature, which was already dwindling before the war, now largely disappeared.  Dr. George N. Schuster, former president of Hunter College of New York, wrote:

> If you step into the Milwaukee Public Library, you
> will find a good collection of German drama.  All the
> earlier plays of Hauptmann, Sudermann, and the rest
> are there.  But no titles more recent than 1914 are
> on the shelves.  The interesting fact is not so much
> that no additional books were purchased after the war
> but that nobody cared to ask the librarians to buy
> more.[29]

For years after the end of the War, most people of German descent remained shy about participating in political or cultural activities in which they would be identified as German-American.  The German language newspapers confined themselves almost exclusively to news items; even the most eminent journals, like the Cincinnati *Freie Presse* and the Cleveland *Wächter und Anzeiger*, ventured few editorial comments in the 1920s and '30s.

The American public was tired of the zealous excessiveness
that characterized the war years.  But hostility and suspicion
were not to be turned off like a spigot.  Almost two years after hostilities had ceased, the Catholic *Central-Verein* was
still pleading that other Catholics stop using such abusive
terms as "Boche" and "Hun."  Frederick Kenkel, the German
Catholic leader, expressed a general resentment of his group
against the American Catholic Church hierarchy because it had
not defended them against the excesses of anti-Germanism inside
and outside of the Church.

The National German-American Alliance was not reestab-
lished after the First World War; other organizations with different purposes took its place.  In May 1919 the Steuben Society was founded in New York with local chapters in various
communities.  Among the basic purposes for which the Society
was organized was the encouragement of men and women of German
ancestry to participate more extensively in American public affairs and to become more fully informed about them.  It sought
to keep alive "the memory of the achievements of the pioneers"
and to enlighten the American public concerning the contributions that people of German origin have made to the nation.
In 1925 two additional goals were formulated that are actually
corollaries of those previously stated: to cultivate pride
among members of the ethnic group in their ancestry so that
"they can become better citizens" and to protect people of German ancestry from misrepresentations and discrimination.

A Franz Sigel Society was organized to honor the memory
of the Civil War general and all the liberal *Einwanderer* of
1848 and to cultivate a fuller recognition of the contributions
they made to their adopted country.  In 1920 German societies
in a number of cities began again to organize "German Day"
celebrations.  In 1930 the Carl Schurz Memorial Foundation was
founded, and among the functions that it sought to perform in
the interest of the traditions of Germans in America was the
organization of public ceremonies on the anniversaries of notable events in the history of the group.

Gradually the people of German descent felt freer to hold
public celebrations.  The 150th anniversary of General Steuben's arrival in America was celebrated in 1927 in some communities.  In 1929 a centenary celebration of Carl Schurz's
birth was held in Baltimore and elsewhere.  German societies
began to take active part in such general community celebrations as those marking the 200th anniversary of the founding
of Baltimore and the 200th anniversary of the birth of George
Washington.  However, the group of German-Americans was becoming smaller and smaller; German-Americans were being transformed into Americans of German descent.

One of the most prominent figures in American intellectual
life of the postwar period was H. L. Mencken.  His grandparents

came from Germany but he had relatively little contact with
German-American community life in his native Baltimore.  He had
a strong sense of family history that included a distinguished
ancestor, Johann Burckard Mencken, who wrote a scathing trea-
tise on the intellectual quackery of men claiming erudition.
As editor of the *American Mercury* (1924-33) and as a writer and
critic, Mencken fought against what he regarded as provincial-
ism in America's intellectual life and against the infantilism,
conventionality, and banality he found in its letters.  He knew
history and had a great appreciation of continental culture and
particularly admired the achievements of German poets, musicians, and philosophers.  But he wanted above all to help
American writers achieve a new appreciation of their linguistic
and cultural individuality.  Alfred Kazin writes:

> If Mencken had never lived, it would have taken a
> whole army of assorted philosophers, monologists,
> editors, and patrons of the new writing to make up
> for him.  As it was, he not only rallied all the
> young writers together and imposed his skepticism
> upon the new generation, but also brought a new and
> uproarious gift for high comedy into a literature
> that had never been too quick to laugh . . . He was
> an irrepressible force, a stimulant, an introduction
> to wisdom.[30]

Mencken wrote a scathing description of the German element
in the United States in the 1920s.  They were without much cultural influence or political power in the postwar period.  He
concluded that there was no longer any German language newspaper or periodical of any substantial quality published in the
country.  The survival of a few excellent German bookstores was
made possible, he argued, only by the patronage of Anglo-
Americans of taste rather than by Americans of German ancestry.
    While the German-Americans were respected as law-abiding,
sober, and solid citizens in the 1920s as they had been before
the First World War, they were rarely looked up to.  Few had
shown any particular spark or spirit either in their public or
private lives.  They were obviously well represented among the
middle rungs of state and federal bureaucracies but few had
moved up into the high political levels or were contributing
significantly to national political life.  This same observation, he added, could be made of their participation in the
nation's business life.
    In their own associations and societies the rank and file
were the despair of the talented few who hoped vainly to be
able to prod them into some activities of value or consequence,
he lamented.  Leaders of the cultural and other societies were
drawn largely from among the third rate; indeed, the people of

German ancestry, he noted with disgust, "almost instinctively follow fools."

While acknowledging the contributions of the large number of people whom Albert Faust had named in his standard work on the German element, Mencken argued that proportionately to the mediocre and the foolish the virtuous were sorely underrepresented. He himself had many friends of German ancestry who were among the intellectual and artistic elite of the country; he would have liked to have people like his friends better represented than he felt they were in actuality.[31]

Mencken's bitter criticisms reflect the very general anomie among Americans of German ancestry in the 1920s; the criticisms also reflect his own pervasive class and intellectual biases.

## GERMAN-SPEAKING REFUGEES—A CHAPTER IN AMERICAN INTELLECTUAL HISTORY

Out of the Revolution that followed the defeat of the Imperial German armies in 1918 came the establishment of a liberal, democratic Republic. There was no honeymoon period for the new Weimar Republic. The internal struggle between the forces and traditions that lent strength to the new regime and those that were antithetical to it was always acute. The fact that the Weimar Republic was able to engender so much hope in Germany and gave so much substance to those hopes made its brief life span and ultimate destruction all the more tragic. The death in October 1929 of Chancellor Gustav Stresemann, who had given impetus to the rapprochement with France, was a severe blow to the political stability of the Republic. It removed the only political leader of the Weimar regime to whom any substantial charisma was attached. The end of the Republic came with the appointment of Adolf Hitler as Chancellor by the ancient warrior president, Marshall von Hindenburg, in the early months of 1933.

The Weimar era was marked by an exuberant flowering of intellectual activities. The impressive strengths of German scholarship, science, and intellectual life—and their weaknesses—were well revealed in the Republican years. The Weimar culture was, as one scholar describes it, a "precarious glory." Along with the excitement that arose from the burst of cultural creativity and imaginative experimentation in science and the arts, there was increasingly manifest a spreading fear that in the later years of the Republic became a foreboding of doom.[32] One cannot understand the magnitude of the contributions that refugees from Nazi persecution were later to make to the United States without an appreciative understanding of the vital freshness and the momentum of intellectual life that characterized

the Weimar era.  The cosmopolitanism so precious to the defenders of the Republic had to contend for survival against the
anti-Semitism and national chauvinism still flourishing in
Germany, even in the universities.  There were, moreover, cultural aristocrats never converted to the Republic, never freed
from the restraint of the traditions that tragically bound them.
The Republic failed to survive the political indifference of an
important segment of its intellectual and professional classes,
the reemergence of the power of the military and industrial
elites in political life, and the narrowness of perspectives
among the aristocratic elements.  The question of war guilt,
the Treaty of Versailles, the political isolation of Germany,
the terrible period of inflation, and finally, the depression,
which spread from the United States in 1929, all created problems that were not readily solved by a new regime with its un-
practiced democrats.  Remaining unsolved, the problems con-
spired mightily against the delicate balance of forces that
permitted the precarious survival of the Republic.  The incredible blindness and ineptness of political leaders in Western Europe in the 1920s added further distress of the internal
travail.  In the end, a master demagogue and his followers
were able to manipulate the widespread fear of Bolshevism into
such a public preoccupation as to smother the tender plant of
German democracy.

Even before Adolf Hitler actually came to power in Germany
early in 1933, the stream of German emigration was inflated by
the departure of a number of intellectuals assailed by fears of
Germany's political and economic future.  In the years after
1933 the numbers of those leaving Germany increased to significant proportions as German immigrants, both Jews and Christians,
fled to England, Switzerland, France, Turkey, and the United
States.  Among them were some of the most distinguished men in
German letters, scholarship, arts, and sciences: Albert Einstein, Paul Tillich, Walter Gropius, Bruno Walter, Thomas Mann,
Heinrich Mann, Bertholt Brecht, Ernst Cassirer, Max Reinhardt,
Arnold Schoenberg, and John von Neumann.  Among the emigres
were four distinguished scientists who had been awarded Nobel
prizes for their work in Europe: Albert Einstein, James Frank,
Otto Loewi, and Victor Hess.  Other refugee scientists won
Nobel prizes for work done in America, among them Felix Block
(1952), Otto Stern (1943), Konrad Block (1964), and Hans Bethe
(1967).  The refugees from Germany were joined by fewer but
equally distinguished refugees from Fascist Italy like G.
Borghese, Enrico Fermi, Gaetano Salvemini, and others.

Only a small proportion of the millions of people opposed
to the Nazi and Fascist regimes in Europe were able to find
asylum in countries where they could hope to remain safe and
continue their work.  Many able and distinguished men were not
able to leave.  Even world reknown was no guarantee of protec-

tion against humiliation, imprisonment, and martyrdom.  Among
the people fleeing Germany and Austria there were young and old,
poor and rich, men and women of every station in life.  It is
generally true that a migration resulting from political persecution draws less heavily from the young adult sector of a nation's population than do migrations otherwise instigated.  Yet
there were many young men who had just finished their doctoral
studies who fled.  A few came as relatively old men but were
able to lead productive lives.  Walter Friedlaender (1873-1966)
came in 1935 at the age of sixty-two to become a professor of
the Fine Arts at New York University.  Paul Frankl, who came in
1938 at age sixty, continued his studies, which culminated in
such eminent works as *The Gothic Literary Sources and Interpretations through Eight Centuries*.  The ability of scientists,
writers, and scholars to leave reflected their international
contacts with friends and colleagues in other countries who
were in a position to help them.  The chronology of events,
availability of means, and plain good fortune had much to do
with their success in fleeing Germany.  The emigre physicist,
Leo Szilard, observed that those who were successful in leaving
Germany were not necessarily more clever, but were only "one
day earlier."

The United States in the 1930s was suffering from a severe
economic depression.  Immigration was radically reduced, and in
the middle of the decade more foreign-born were leaving the
country than entering it.  The economic crisis had produced a
phenomenon that had never before appeared in the United States:
a net loss of population through international migration.  Under the circumstances it was not always easy for the refugees
to find positions.  In many instances, doctors, professors,
scientists, artists, musicians, and engineers had to find temporary employment far below their accustomed positions.  Foreign
scholars in American universities, institutes, and government
agencies are now commonplace; then they were not.  Resentment
against competition from emigres and undercurrents of anti-
Semitism restricted employment opportunities.  Nevertheless,
they generally found appropriate employment in a short time.
Various committees and organizations provided means for easing
the transition for many of them.  Most scholars and scientists
were able to remain active and productive in their fields with
little break in the tempo of their work and publication.  The
emigres were extremely diverse in their training, talents, and
personalities.  They made and are still making an immense contribution to the United States.  Many young men who arrived in
the late 1930s are still serving in American universities and
research institutes along with thousands of young Germans who
followed their paths after the Second World War in search of
greater opportunities.  Most refugee scholars and professional
men and women have become citizens and have stuck their roots

deep into American soil.  Some returned to Europe after the end
of the Hitler regime.  All of them came to the United States
with gratitude for the asylum they found, but also with both
hopes and misgivings.

Switzerland and England received thousands of emigres in
the 1930s.  Yet no country was able or willing to receive such
a large ingress as the quarter million refugees who came to the
United States between 1933 and 1944.  Erika and Klaus Mann in
*Escape to Life* conjecture that perhaps the gratifying hospital-
ity that America extended to refugees was inspired by the appreciative recognition of the contribution of the Forty-
eighters who had found sanctuary in the United States three
generations earlier.

Early in their sojourn, many emigres discovered areas of
research and inquiry between which bridges seemed to be needed
in order to establish more productive connections between American and European intellectual traditions.  Some stressed the
need for various schools or groups of scholars to learn from
each other about different approaches and methods applicable to
their disciplines.  Franz Neumann counseled his American colleagues in political science to set their empiricist perspectives in better balance by paying greater attention to historical and theoretical dimensions.  At the same time he criticized
his friends in Germany for showing such little appreciation for
the value of empirical research.[33]  Sometimes refugee scholars
shifted their interest in response to new stimuli or necessi-
ties that they encountered in their new homeland.  Kurt Lewin
established a reputation in Germany for his work in the "psychology of action," but shifted to a focus upon "group dynamics"
in the United States, where he quickly achieved eminence.  Max
Delbruck, a quantum physicist, turned to biology.  His enthusiasm convinced many young scientists that great discoveries in
biology were within reach if such rigorous quantitative methods
as physicists use were applied, for example, to virology.  His
work was a major contribution to the discovery of D.N.A., the
mode of gene replication.[34]

When Albert Einstein resigned from the Prussian Academy of
Science in 1933, he severely criticized the Academy for what he
considered to be its capitulation to Nazi doctrines.  Between
1933 and 1941, approximately one hundred refugee physicists
left Germany for the United States.  Most of them were under
forty.  Some found initial refuge in England but were able to
secure only temporary work there.  Because of its resources,
the United States afforded the greatest opportunity for scientific work as well as the possibility of permanent domicile and
citizenship.  There were problems, as there almost inevitably
are, when men and their families are uprooted from familiar
surroundings and well-formed attachments, personal and professional.  Adjustment to the asperities that went with such

transition was perhaps easier for scientists than for most
other categories of emigres.  Physicists had been particularly
active in internationalizing their field during the 1920s
through exchange of university teaching and research personnel,
international conferences, and other means.  Personal and professional contact was more highly developed than in most disciplines, and there was an extensive familiarity among physicists with the kinds of research their colleagues abroad were
doing.  Dr. Millikan of the California Institute of Technology
had been one of the leaders in bringing American scientists
into this exchange as early as the 1920s, when he was struggling to compensate for the isolation of the new California
institute.  The high level of communication among scientists
made the placement and integration of those fleeing Germany far
easier than was true of most refugee groups.

   The contribution of German emigre scientists to American
science was immense.  As Robert Oppenheimer has observed concerning the development of physics in America, the impact could
not have been so substantial had not there already been a sound
development of the discipline to build upon.[35]

   The influence of German psychology, as it was introduced
to the United States by immigrant scholars, created a considerable tempest because of basic differences between the American
and German traditions in the field.  A generation earlier such
controversies would have been unthinkable because in large
measure American psychology was a reflection of German psychology.  Students and scholars then looked to Germany as the center of activity in the field.  The behaviorists (under John B.
Watson), the functionalists, and Pavlovians had helped to create new traditions in America through experimental research
that relied substantially upon comparative animal research but
which specifically denied the scientific validity of introspec-
tive evidence.  American psychology had developed distinctive
paths of its own; German psychologists, especially the Gestaltists were regarded as alien in interest and approach.

   The three leaders of the Gestalt school, Max Wertheimer,
Wolfgang Köhler, and Kurt Kaffka, came to the United States.
Eventually through their influence Gestalt psychology gained
acceptance as an American school of thought.[36]  The Vienna
school, led by Karl Bühler, also exerted a major influence in
the field.  It cannot perhaps be proved that American psychology would not have reached its present stage of development
without the influence of the emigres, but it can be safely as-
serted that the German ingredient served as a leavening agent
and restored to American psychology the knowledge of its philosophical past.

   Throughout the interwar period, but especially in the
1930s, thousands of highly trained German and Austrian architects, artists, art historians, and publishers came to the

United States.  Their contributions to the development of these
fields in America was monumental.

The ferment existing in some sectors of American architecture during this period served to create a milieu highly receptive to the influence of European architects.  Former teachers at the Bauhaus, including Ludwig Mies van der Rohe, Walter
Gropius, and Marcel Breuer, are certainly to be counted among
those who most profoundly affected the development of architecture in America.  Their work in the new environment evoked an
appreciative response, and they prospered.  Their enthusiasm
for innovation and experimentation was given scope by the open-
ness with which Americans considered their ideas and by their
willingness to take risks.[37]  Historians of modern architecture
have pondered not only the influence of emigre architects—individually and collectively—but also the influence of the
various dimensions of the American milieu upon each emigre
architect.  Thus, for example, the question has been posed:
Would Breuer have moved, as he did in the United States, toward
his distinctive architectural forms had he remained in Europe?
What can be concluded with certainty is that emigre architects
found a stimulating environmental milieu in the United States
and accordingly responded in their teaching and work in ways
that enriched and accelerated the development of architecture
in America.

In the 1930s, the United States experienced a unique period of efflorescence in the critical and historical study of
art.  The decade following the end of World War One was marked
by the accelerated maturation of scholarship in the field of
art.  By the mid-1930s the United States was becoming one of
the most notable centers of such studies.  An amazing number of
Germans, especially German Jews, emigrated to the United States
and exercised their talents to bring American scholarship to a
level comparable to that on the continent.  In the early depression years many European scholars had to take simple jobs
in order to earn their livelihood.  But there was a need for
the trained scholar in the expanding fields of teaching in art
history, museum and gallery curatorial work, as well as art
publications.  The contributions of the many distinguished men
in the field, men like Marcel Röthlisberger, Walter Horn, and
above all Panofsky, are richly diverse.  In the 1960s and 1970s
the building of many new university campuses, museums, and
galleries has reflected a greater public knowledge and appreciation of art than has ever before existed in the United States.
The students of the great emigre scholars of the 1930s are
maturing into positions of leadership in their various specialties.  They represent a great testimony to the influence
that has endured far beyond the lifetime[38] of the foreign-
born scholars and teachers.

There were emigres like Theodor Adorno and Klaus Mann whose attachments to Europe were such that they could not remain in the United States when a democratic regime had been established in Germany after the Nazis' fall from power.  There were obligations that also pulled them back.  For all the gratitude they felt and expressed for America, there were aspects of life in the land of their exile that distressed them and that made their attachments to Europe all the more precious. In Adorno's view, the educated European, the *gebildete Mensch* (cultivated man), stood in sharp contrast to the expert technician he thought he discovered in the American social scientist; the latter was in general less sophisticated philosophically, less historically grounded, less able to contribute to the development of theory.  Even more distressing to Adorno were those emigres who in their passion to assimilate became more American than the Americans.  Like others, he was gratified by the greater willingness of Americans to accept innovation and by their generosity in giving help.  In 1949, he returned to Germany greatly concerned by the lack of discrimination he believed to be characteristic of quantitative thinking in American social science.  This concern did not, he repeatedly stressed, alter his gratitude for the intellectual dimensions of his experience in America.

The emigres who came in the 1930s in the full bloom of their careers have largely passed from the academic scene, although their influence remains strong.  Younger refugees like Reinhard Bendix in sociology, Gustave von Grunebaum in near Eastern studies, and countless others made their mark on the academic world in the 1950s and 1960s.  The younger academicians from Germany presently found in large numbers in almost every American university came after the war in search of academic opportunities.  A large proportion of them were able to emigrate only because of the financial support they received with their appointment as Fulbright scholars.

It would be misleading to leave the impression that all of the people who fled Nazi tyranny were scientists, artists, and scholars.  An extraordinarily high proportion were, but a great many were not.  Among the refugees there were artisans, businessmen, doctors, lawyers, and mechanics.  For these people, finding employment was often difficult.  Language handicaps had to be met.  Doctors had to pass state medical examinations in order to practice.  Lawyers skilled in German law faced long preparation in order to pass the American bar examinations. Many professional men had to take very simple employment in their first years; there were judges who for a time became busboys and dishwashers; there were factory owners who first found employment as mechanics or gardeners.  For the skilled technicians, the chances of a smooth transition to the same kind of job as they had held before were relatively good.  Maurice

Davie in his *Refugees in America* makes the observation that
fortunately the refugees exhibited good humor and an amazing
willingness to work at any job available for the time being,
no matter how menial, in the expectation that better opportunities would arise.[39]

A postscript should be added to this chapter to give at
least some attention to German-American letters, a subject that
deserves serious consideration for its own sake in any discussion of the intellectual and cultural history of German communities in the United States.  German emigre writers had a
stimulating effect upon German-American literature in the period from the mid-1930s through the war years.  Refugee writers,
however, remained largely distinct from the mainstream of German literati in America.  Some final comments should be made
here about the whole evolution of German-American literature
and some of the influences that gave it shape.

German-American literature still suffered from a narrowness of interest that arose from the tendency of immigrants to
see their emigration from the homeland as the most significant
experience of their lives.  German-American literature of the
period of the First World War and the 1920s was largely non-
political.  In the early part of this period they had to avoid
writing about the greatly disturbing dilemmas which the war
created for them.  Writers in the 1920s began to find new
things to write about in the complex urban life around them.
A new sense of discipline was reflected in their writing, and
the dilettantism that so widely characterized earlier writers
began to fade.[40]  German-American readers became more discrim-
inating: poetry was no longer defined as anything that rhymed.

The appearance of major German writers in the United
States as political refugees during the Nazi period brought re-
newed interest in political themes.  One cannot consider temporary refugees like Thomas Mann, Berthold Brecht, Franz Werfel,
Lion Feuchtwanger, and others as German-American writers.  However, in the period from the end of the Second World War to the
present, a number of German-American writers of considerable
merit have appeared.

The refugees compared with the great waves of immigration
of the past represented a small group.  They were well distributed throughout the country and were quickly absorbed into the
general population.

## THE FAILURE OF NAZI PROPAGANDISTS IN AMERICA

As individuals, people of German ancestry were doubtless
as politically active in the inter-war period as other elements
in the population of their city or region; they participated in
the electoral campaigns of the various parties largely as indi-

viduals rather than as members of an ethnically identifiable
group.  The experiences of the war years had made most voters
of German background reluctant to expose themselves in any way
by appearing to respond as a group to current political issues.
German-American political organizations that had once been active were quiescent in the 1920s and 1930s.  Only a few of the
liberal or "progressive" organizations remained politically
active: the Roland German-American Democratic Society, the
*Deutsch-Amerikanische Reform Bund* (which supported Robert La
Follette for the presidency in 1924), and the *Deutsch-Ameri-
kanischer Bürgerbund* of Milwaukee.  The liberal organizations
worked in cooperation with labor organizations and were sympathetic to the interests of the political emigres from Nazi
Germany.  To the left of the liberal factions were the various
elements of the German-American labor movement that remained
strong in the large cities where German workers had maintained
organizations since the 1870s.  A number of socialist organizations among the German-Americans took early notice of the
rising tide of National Socialism in Germany and opposed it
strenuously.  Organizations related to German-American socialist groups also were part of an anti-Nazi front, including the
*Freidenkerbund*, the *Naturfreunde*, and the *Arbeiter Sängerbund*.

The middle class German language newspapers remained ada-
mant in their reluctance to become involved in controversial
issues, however.  When the Nazi movement won control of Germany,
few of the editors of these newspapers showed any inclination
to support them.  Not many of the editors were stirred to con-
demn Nazism, for it was a painful matter; and they hoped that
if they could simply avoid it, it would eventually disappear.
Some editors argued that the issues were, indeed, greatly over-
stressed by the American press and that neither the domestic
nor the puny export brand of Nazism had much impact upon the
Germans in America who read their newspapers.

Shortly after the formation of the Nazi Party in Germany
(the *Nationalsocialistische Deutsche Arbeiterpartei* or N.S.D.
A.P.), a small and militant offshoot appeared in the United
States.  A group of recent immigrants and their sympathizers
founded an organization called *Teutonia* on October 12, 1924.[41]
The leader of *Teutonia* was Fritz Gissibl (born in Nürnberg in
in 1903) who had arrived in the United States in 1923 and had
immediately become active.  The organization announced that its
goals were to oppose Communism and to arouse the national consciousness of Germans in North America.  But *Teutonia* never
prospered.  Small groups appeared in Chicago, New York, Rochester, Philadelphia, Detroit, and Milwaukee.  In 1932, the last
year of its existence, the Chicago organization had a total
membership of fifty.

In 1932, the N.S.D.A.P. had gained sufficient power in
Germany to encourage Nazi leaders to organize sympathetic

movements outside of the country.  The party established some
small Nazi cells in American communities in which only the
*Reichsdeutsche*, German citizens, were eligible for membership.
An affiliate organization called "The Friends of the Hitler
Movement" was founded to proselytize among American citizens
of German ancestry.  Shortly thereafter, when the N.S.D.A.P.
came to power in Germany, the American government became ex-
ceedingly sensitive to the existence of a branch of the Party
in which citizens of Germany resident in the United States were
enrolled.  Because of American diplomatic pressures, Rudolf
Hess, who was in charge of the foreign activities of the Nazi
Party, took action to dissolve the organization in the United
States.  Almost immediately, however, a new organization, or
*Bund*, was formed under the leadership of Heinz Spanknöbel,
who had previously directed the Nazi Party's American "branch."
The new *Bund* was called "The Friends of the New Germany."  The
change was simply a tactical maneuvre; it did not reflect any
disposition to alter the goals or the methods of German agents
involved in the organization.  Besides being ineffective, the
movement was badly shaken by a bitter personal struggle between
Gissibl and Spanknöbel.  The German government had reason for
dismay in that the internal struggle made the organization all
the more visible to the watchful eyes of the American government.

Spanknöbel became increasingly aggressive.  He attempted
to intimidate the German language press.  He presented a file
of clippings from the *New Yorker Staatszeitung* to its publishers, Bernard and Victor Ridder, with a protest against what he
charged was pro-Jewish and anti-Nazi propaganda.  He demanded
that they cease publishing articles harmful to the Nazi cause
and that in the future they publish more articles favoring to
Hitler.  Victor Ridder ordered Spanknöbel out of his office.

In the fall of 1933, the United German Societies in New
York, embracing more than seventy societies, were planning for
the two-hundred-and-fiftieth anniversary of German settlement
in America.  Spanknöbel and his supporters used strong-arm
tactics to gain entrance to the sessions.  They made every
possible effort to bully representatives of the various societies into compliance by threatening that their parents or
other relatives remaining in Germany would suffer for their
opposition.  It was not long before such conduct created a
storm of protest among German societies and in the German-
American communities.  In early October, Congressman Samuel
Dickstein of New York, chairman of the Committee on Immigration
and Naturalization, announced that his Committee would immediately begin an inquiry into Nazi activities in the United
States.  Spanknöbel was charged by the Attorney General with
acting as a foreign agent without registering as such with the
Department of State.[42]  A warrant was issued for his arrest
and deportation along with more than thirty others.

Spanknöbel disappeared before he could be sentenced or deported. Later he reappeared as a general in the N.S.D.A.P's elite corps, the SS (*Schutzstaffel*). In October 1933, a directive was issued by the *Auslands-Organization* of the N.S.D.A.P. that the leadership of the *Bund* (or New Germany) should be placed in the hands of American citizens.

The Friends of the New Germany increased its membership between October 1933 and March 1934 from four hundred to four thousand members according to Reinhold Walter, one of its contemporary leaders. Of these, Walter estimated that only fifty or sixty members in that period were American citizens.[43] Despite its emphasis on broadened representation for German-Americans, the *Reichsdeutsche* remained the dominant element in both the leadership and the general membership of the *Bund*.

The organization published numerous pamphlets and newspapers that were distributed to members and to many German-Americans. These party organs had the avowed purpose of telling the "truth" about Hitler and the Third Reich as well as of explaining the National Socialist principles and world view. The publishers hoped by this means to renew the German-Americans' ethnic pride and consciousness of national unity. They also hoped that with such renewal, the German-Americans might be enlisted in the struggle against the "enemies" of the Third Reich: the Jews, Bolsheviks, liberals, and, later, the English.

The Friends of the New Germany was clearly imitative of the N.S.D.A.P., both ideologically and tactically. Its leaders hoped that the resemblance could somehow be disguised and that they could achieve an acceptable image in the eyes of the American people. Although there was widespread concern among Americans over the internal threat posed by the *Bund*, it was apparent even to the most casual observer that the movement was dependent for its existence upon support from the Third Reich.[44]

On January 1, 1936, when Fritz Kuhn assumed the leadership of the Friends of the New Germany, the name of the organization was changed to the America-German Peoples Society (*Amerika-Deutscher Volksbund*), or simply the German-American Bund. In March a national convention of the *Bund* held in Buffalo named Kuhn *Führer* of the Bund. The change in name was made to symbolize a (pretended) shift in interest and orientation of the organization away from political action to cultural activity. The use of the swastika, which had aroused so much antagonism in America, and the militant tactics introduced from Germany were to be abandoned. The German Foreign Ministry was hopeful that the new leader could, by the change in focus of activities, prevent further erosion of relationships between the two countries.

Fritz Kuhn was not American-born. Like a number of other Nazi leaders in America, he was born in Bavaria, in 1896. Kuhn

served in the German army during the war and later received a
degree in chemistry at the University of Munich.  He was active
against the Communist movement in Bavaria and joined the National Socialist group in 1921.  In 1924 he emigrated to Mexico
and four years later moved to Detroit where he found a position
as a chemical engineer with the Ford Motor Company.  Sometime
in 1933 or 1934, Kuhn became an American citizen.  He was active in Detroit's Nazi circle and was rewarded with the position of *Gauleiter* for the Middle West in 1935.

At the same time, other fascist imitators like the Silver
Shirts and the Black Legion were busily engaged in attempts to
organize automobile workers with a view to their own purposes.
Such efforts met with powerful opposition from Walter Reuther
and the C.I.O.

In assuming leadership of the German American Bund in
1936, Kuhn's intentions were to pursue the traditional political goals of the Nazi movement in America despite any professions of reorientation of the organization's goals.  The
hopes that the German Foreign Office had placed upon the change
of leadership of the Bund soon eroded into bitter disappoint-
ment.  Like his predecessors, Fritz Kuhn became active in domestic politics despite warnings from Berlin.  The swastika became
the symbol of the new Bund and the old tactics remained un-
changed.  The tall, burly, square-jawed Kuhn was a forceful
platform speaker and worked hard at the role of America's *Führer*.  For all his posing, however, he was not such a devoted
ideologue or self-sacrificing leader as his followers believed.
He was a jazz enthusiast and many of the bush-league *Führer's*
free hours were spent escorting girlfriends on tours of the
New York night clubs.  Ultimately his interest in accumulating
membership fees and selling Nazi uniforms tempted him beyond
his capacity to resist, and his position of leadership was
totally destroyed.

One of the spectacular events in the history of the Bund
was the celebration organized in Madison Square Garden in 1936,
attended by more than twenty thousand Bundists, the interested,
and the curious.  Avery Brundage, chairman of the American
Olympic Committee, was the chief attraction, addressing the
crowd on the subject of the Olympic Games in Germany.[45]

The Bund, in imitation of the large-scale public extrava-
ganzas of the N.S.D.A.P., held its largest celebration in Madison Square Garden on February 20, 1939.  It proved to be both
its most successful and its most disastrous event.  The New
York newspapers headlined the meeting of twenty-two thousand
Nazis, describing the presence of three thousand Bund members,
dressed in the notorious brown uniforms of the movement.  The
speeches extolled Hitler and Father Coughlin and denounced
President Roosevelt and members of his cabinet.  The public re-
action to profascist activities in the United States reached
high tide.

In late 1939, Fritz Kuhn was accused and found guilty of misappropriating funds belonging to the Bund.  He was sent to prison and ultimately deported to Germany.  The efforts of Bund newspapers to make Kuhn an innocent victim of official efforts to persecute him failed.  Fritz Kuhn was not a martyr, but an embezzler.  Although several unofficial leaders took over the direction of the Bund, it quickly faded as the events of the times swept the nations closer to military confrontation.  The German-American Bund was completely dead after Pearl Harbor.

In February 1939, Fortune Magazine estimated the Bund's membership at 4,000.  This was close to the estimate of Reinhold Freytag, who held the chief American desk of the German Foreign Ministry.  Congressman Samuel Dickstein, who led the early investigations of the Nazi movement in the United States, warned colleagues in Congress that 450,000 Bundists were operating in the country.  Fritz Kuhn on one occasion bragged that the membership was 230,000.  Later he estimated the numbers more modestly to be a little over 8,000, which was still 1500 larger than the figure reached by the F.B.I.[46]

The Bund drew most of its members not from the native-born German-American sector of the population, but largely from that of the residents who had emigrated from Weimar Germany in the 1920s.  Some had become citizens of the United States.  The insignificant proportion of native-born German-Americans who actually joined the Bund were young men and women who were alienated by the economic and political crises of the Depression years.  It is estimated that 50 percent of the membership was concentrated in New York City and its surrounding urban areas.  Cities like St. Louis and Milwaukee, which were traditional centers of German-American life, lent the Bund little support.  In 1938, the German Consul General in San Francisco estimated that there were hardly 100 members in his consular district.[47]  Kuhn testified that 40 percent of the membership of the Bund was not even of German ethnic origin but drawn from right-wing elements in the general American population.

Thus, despite all the sound and fury of its brief history, the *Bund* had little success.  The N.S.D.A.P. had anticipated far greater results of influence on German-Americans and of promoting the interests of the Reich.  Relatively few German-Americans, even of the hundreds of thousands of immigrants from Germany in the 1920s, showed interest in the Nazi movement or in the Germany of Adolf Hitler.  Almost all German-Americans were opposed to and profoundly embarrassed by the regime.

The files of the German Foreign Ministry attest to the bitterness that members of the Ministry felt as a result of the lack of response to German propaganda.  The antagonism engendered in America by anti-Semitism and the bullying tactics of the Bundists proved to be a source of serious ignominy for the

Foreign Ministry rather than bringing it any advantage.  The
historian, Joachim Remak, expresses the conclusion that the
Bund was indeed a serious impediment to the efforts of the
Third Reich, which sought to achieve more satisfactory relations with the United States and to prevent the erosion of
isolationist sentiments.  Instead, the Bund provided those
who were hostile to the Third Reich with the best possible
instruments for use in arousing the American public to the
danger Nazi Germany represented to the world.[48]

The most talented and successful propagandist working on
behalf of the Third Reich was Georg Sylvester Viereck, who had
served Germany effectively as a propagandist during the First
World War.  The German-born writer was effective in stimulating
and coordinating the various expressions of antiwar sentiment
and profascist sympathies among rightist Americans.

Georg Sylvester Viereck's literary talents were doubtless-
ly modest; in any case he never attained the place in American
belles lettres to which he had once aspired.  When Hitler came
to power in Germany in 1933, Viereck presented himself to the
German Consul General in New York and to the German Ambassador
in Washington.  To these officials and to others in Germany
with whom he was in correspondence he announced his willingness
again to act as an adviser and agent in propaganda work in the
United States.  His offer was accepted.  Although for appear-
ances he was on the payroll of the *Münchner Neueste Nachrichten*
as a foreign correspondent, he received large sums from the
German Foreign Ministry for his propagandist activities.  The
post-propagandist thought he discovered in Hitler a unique
human phenomenon—a man of many dimensions: part mystic, part
realist, part Mohammed, part Napoleon, a statesman, and military genius.  He confessed also to being attracted by Hitler's
"magnetic blue eyes."[49]

Viereck served as liaison between the Foreign Ministry in
Germany and various individuals and groups in the United States
who were sympathetic to Nazism and Fascism.  As a liaison per-
son among a number of people notorious for their activities,
Viereck again became, as he had in the period of the First
World War, the target of bitter attack by American newspapers.

A number of books were published by Viereck's Flanders
Press for the German Foreign Ministry.  He distributed a large
number of pamphlets and antiwar advertisements.  The latter he
published under the name of bogus organizations such as "We,
the Mothers," and "Mothers of America."  He served as editor-
in-chief of a weekly journal called *Facts in Review*, which was
distributed by the German Library of Information in New York.
Viereck was instrumental in securing the publication and wide
distribution of a large number of antiwar, anti-British, anti-
Roosevelt, anti-Semitic materials.  Throughout the late 1930s
he remained in close collaboration with a number of American

public officials, especially with Senator Ernest Lundeen of
Minnesota and Senator Rush Holt of West Virginia.  He also
worked with a number of Congressmen and other national figures
with whom he shared certain common interests, especially antiwar sentiments.  Viereck wrote or edited extensive materials
for Senator Lundeen, which the latter delivered on the floor
of the Senate.  These became part of the Congressional Record.
Viereck was able to secure their publication and, through the
Senator's franking privilege, their distribution at the expense
of the American government.

After the entry of the United States into the Second World
War, Viereck, leaders of the German American Bund, and a number
of native American profascists were made defendants in a noteworthy sedition case.  Among the most notorious was Lawrence
Dennis, author of *The Coming American Fascism*, who was one of
the earliest followers of Hitler in the United States.  By the
mid-1930s he had established contact with many German officials.
William Dudley Pelley was also one of the first native Fascists
to announce his support of Hitler.  He formed a group of activ-
ists called the Silver Shirts.  George Deatherage, leader of
the Knights of the White Camelia, attempted to unite the various organizations of the extreme right into a federative organization and ultimately into a Fascist Party.

These pro-Nazi and pro-Fascist efforts among members of
the American right-wing extremists ceased almost completely
with the American entry into the war.

## SOCIAL CHANGE AND THE GERMAN-AMERICAN CHURCHES

The extent of assimilation into the culture of the Ameri-
can-Germans and Scandinavians in the Midwest during and after
the First World War is revealed by the fact that during this
period the English language began to be consistently used in
church services and in all aspects of religious life.  The most
rapid phase of the language transition occurred in the twenty-
five year period from 1915 to 1940.  It is interesting to note
that the statistical curves of language transition in the German and Norwegian Lutheran churches show a close similarity.[50]
When German Lutheran schools ceased to teach German in the
1920s and succeeding decades, an important institutional support to the use of German in the church was removed.

In the nineteenth century most German-Lutherans held fast
to the conviction that an organic relationship existed between
the language of Martin Luther (German) and Lutheran beliefs and
that the fate of each in America was inextricably bound with
the others.  German-born Lutherans brought with them a deep
love of Luther's rich German translation of the Bible, and the
strength of this attachment bound language and religion all the

more firmly together.  The Lutheran churches that were established in the United States during the nineteenth century had
to make some accommodation to American society simply because
it differed significantly from that of Germany.   The changes
were not so much in theological principles or in liturgy but
rather in cultural elements imbedded in both language and religious traditions.   Immigrant families were loathe to abandon
their religious practices or "our language and our ways."   The
German language not only represented a carrier of cultural and
religious elements but acted as a shield to protect them from
inundation by the Anglo-American world about them.

Changes in the American environment and in the nature of
the church congregations necessarily brought an acceleration
in the pressures for accommodation.   But the transformation
took several generations to complete, as it had in the case of
the earlier Lutheran churches established in the American
colonial period.   By the beginning of the twentieth century,
the annual cohorts of German immigrants that had previously
been so substantial began to diminish significantly.   This
demographic fact brought important changes to the character of
Lutheran congregations.   The twentieth century transformation
of Middle Western Lutheran churches was a phenomenon of the
second and third generation offspring of German and Scandinavian immigrants.   A generation born in Germany that preserved
strong cultural attachments to it was replaced by one with
less binding ties and less command of the German language.   The
second and third generation German-Americans who became more
dominant each year in the membership rolls of Lutheran congregations were progressively more insistent upon concessions to
their needs, tastes, and convenience.   What was in some measure
an inter-generational conflict died down as the older generation died out.   Immigrant recruits to the dwindling army of
defenders of older linguistic and cultural traditions in the
church became too few to offer much resistance, and the balance
of internal power shifted gradually in congregations and in
synods.   The "language problem," which many Missouri Synod Lutherans in the early twentieth century complained about, was
the young peoples' preference for English, in addition to
which, they lamented, "impetuous efforts" were constantly being
made in individual congregations to replace the German language.   Many seminarians held the conviction that the transition to English should be and could be rapid.[51]

There were innumerable but often insignificant signs of
the acculturation of German-Lutherans and their church.   Decisions were made that, taken singly, seemed undramatic and insignificant but nevertheless contributed to the momentum for
acculturation, for thus does acculturation occur.

Seminaries reflected the cultural changes taking place in
Lutheran congregations and exerted an influence upon them.   One

of the first evidences of change in the seminaries was the
Americanization of leisure time activities among the seminarians and the introduction of American sports.  The use of English appeared early in extracurricular activities and in such
enterprises as student publications.  Seminaries began to
publish catalog materials and reports to church authorities in
English as well as in German.  Concessions were made to student demands for English as well as German devotions.  Courses
given in English were added gradually to the curricula of seminaries.  In the academic year 1910-11 students in doctrinal
theology were given lectures in English at the Concordia, the
seminary of the Missouri Synod.  By 1930 more classes were
taught in English than in German; the First World War had done
much to accelerate the shift.  By 1940 all the courses were
taught in English with the exception of one elective course
taught in German.[52]   The shift in language use was accompanied
by less noticeable changes in cultural interests and traditions.

Most German-American congregations began the process of
language change with an innocent concession to the young people
and others in the congregation who knew little or no German.
English services were provided first one Sunday a month and,
as demand grew, two and three.  Then German services were retained one Sunday a month for the comfort of the diminishing
group of older members who often knew English but still found
special gratification in German church services.  In the later
stages of transition, the lack of available ministers fluent
in German hastened the shift.  By 1950 the transition was complete in almost all Lutheran congregations in the United States
except in a few of the "German Districts" of the churches.  In
Manitoba, Saskatchewan, and Alberta the transition was much
less advanced.  No mention is made in the 1971 edition of Missouri Synod's *Statistical Yearbook* of church services given in
languages other than English.  This does not, of course, mean
that the German language is not still used in ministers' pas-
toral work today.

A Lutheran minister recently observed to the author that
despite the almost complete Americanization of his denomination,
a new convert who was not of German-American background was
amazed in his study of Lutheran doctrine and practice at the
residue of German culture imbedded in contemporary Lutheranism.

Perhaps the most distinctive and stable subcultural groups
in America are the German-American sectarian communities still
found in various regions of the continent.  Some of these communities have existed for several generations in this country
and others were established in the earliest days of colonial
Pennsylvania.  They represent an unusual hybridization of old
Rhenish-German and American cultures.  They are set apart from
fresh cultural influences from Germany because their religious
counterparts are no longer found in Germany and remain apart

from the larger cultural communities that surround them in contemporary Canada and the United States.

German sectarian groups have been the most successful of all groups attempting to establish utopian communities in the United States.  A century after the Hutterites arrived in the United States, they represented the largest family-type communal society in the Western World.  One hundred and seventy colonies are scattered throughout the area of South Dakota, North Dakota, Montana, and the prairie provinces of Canada.  No Hutterite communities survive in the areas of Moravia and the Austrian Tyrol where their sect was founded centuries ago.  Their German speech and distinctive dress symbolize and reenforce the social distances maintained between the Hutterites and people neighboring on their communal settlements.[53]

The Hutterite communities are characterized by the absence of disparities of wealth; there are no very rich and no very poor members.  They have adapted to the physical conditions of their environment.  A rigid, traditional ideology and social organization have served to sustain their stability.  They believe that the Divine order governs both material and social relationships of mankind throughout the span of their lives.  They accept the fact that man suffers and endures hardship as part of life, and their acceptance and faith fortify them in meeting travail.  The Hutterites accept the capacity of man to think and act wrongly and sinfully, and for that reason they insist upon the daily search for repentance.  They seek surrender of self to God and His purpose, and receptivity to His will.  Constant religious instruction keeps their social system integrated.  Child-rearing and socialization are highly successful in preparing for communal life.  They are effectively organized to provide for continuity.

Hutterites believe they are honoring God by living in warm communality; they are devout in their pacificism and in their application of religious beliefs to their ways of living.

Withal, they have remained extraordinarily receptive to scientific and technological development where it is relevant to their agricultural economy.  The acceptance of innovation is selective, managed, and made to serve the traditional goals of communal life.  Innovations are evaluated as to their possible effect upon the community and the extent to which they can be assimilated into existing values and behavior.  Technological change is not a value in itself.  The Hutterite leadership is utilitarian and rationalistic in its decision-making on matters arising from changes in its expanding technology.

A remarkable quality of Hutterite life is the extent to which strong incentives for individual achievement have been directed toward the good of the whole group.  Their communal life clearly indicates how the individual's desire to achieve, to do important things well, can be separated from individualism.

The urge to create and produce is directed not to fulfilling the individual's personal aspirations as something separate or above group welfare.[54]

The Hutterites enjoy a higher than normal life expectancy. High fertility demands the sufficient accumulation of capital to acquire new land—sometimes to the concern of the neighboring *Welt-Leut*, the worldly people. They are prepared for persecution from those around them, and the memory of their martyrs remains. Their first confrontation with military conscription in the United States occurred in the First World War. The law made no provision for those refusing military service on grounds of religious principles. The Hutterite colonies suffered humiliation and abuse from neighbors. Some Hutterites died in military stockades from maltreatment. This led to a mass movement to Canada. Since the Second World War, young Hutterite men in the United States have been drafted as conscientious objectors and assigned to work in national parks and forests.

To the Hutterite, the word of God is embedded in the German language. English language schools teach facts (many of them seem of little use); the communal German school teaches children how to live. The schools are different, but both are seen as necessary.[55] This division of function and balance may help to prevent excessive disruption and defection.

Approximately fifty thousand Amish live in sixty settlements in North America. Each Amish settlement has its own special character, its own way of making decisions and solving problems. The unity once maintained through face-to-face contact and personal relationships is no longer possible.

Many have predicted the absorption of the Amish into the larger society. The question as to whether the Amish can, indeed, survive as a separate community remains unanswered. It may well be a naive question, as Hostetler suggests, for we may also ask whether any particular social system will endure as such; we may speculate as to the conditions that would permit any human society a future.

There are among the Amish people undeniable tendencies toward secularization. There are also trends toward sacralization, by which things are assigned new and more sacred meaning. There is a drift of the Old Order Amish to affiliation with the Beachy Amish group. The Old Order congregations tend to be more conservative in their observation of traditional practices. There is a persistent tendency among them to seek the reconstruction of traditional community life through migration to new areas less densely settled. Whey they migrate, they take their social institutions with them, but the geographical change allows them to reformulate the structure of community organization.

Conflicts in recent years between Amish and surrounding people have arisen over compulsory education.  In some areas friction has also developed over state laws requiring the horse-drawn vehicles of the Amish to have lights front and back as well as flashing red lights and turn signals, which many of them find abhorrent.

The New Order Amish farmers have moved toward greater agricultural specialization and commercialization.  At the same time their conception of the Amish community (*Gemeinschaft*) is gradually altering from the traditionally sharp differential between Amish and the worldly people.  The Amish communities are likely to endure as long as the children of Amish families find, in the midst of a severely contrasting world, that their needs can be met or their lives can be satisfying in their separate enclaves.[56]

## NOTES

[1]George E. Concloyannis, "German-American Prose Fiction from 1850 to 1918," unpublished Ph.D. dissertation, Columbia University, 1953.  See also Robert E. Ward's *Handbook of German-American Literature from its Beginning to the Present* (Chicago: American Library Association, 1973).

[2]Hermann Hagedorn, *The Hyphenated Family, An American Saga* (New York: Macmillan, 1960) 78-79.

[3]See Robert E. Ward, "Deutsches Bühnenwesen in Amerika," *German-American Studies* V (1972) 54.

[4]Henry A. Pochmann, *German Culture in America, Philosophical and Literary Influences 1600-1900* (Madison: University of Wisconsin Press, 1957) 357.

[5]Frederick C. Luebke, "The German-American Alliance in Nebraska, 1910-1917," *Nebraska History* IL (Summer, 1968) 165.

[6]See John A. Hawgood, *The Tragedy of the German-Americans, The Germans in the United States of America During the Nineteenth Century and After* (New York and London: G. P. Putnam's, 1940) 45-53.

[7]See Frederick C. Luebke, *Immigrants and Politics, The Germans of Nebraska, 1880-1900* (Lincoln: University of Nebraska Press, 1969).

[8]Wells, *op. cit.*, 157.

[9]Elwyn B. Robinson, *History of North Dakota* (Lincoln: University of Nebraska Press, 1966) 258-259.

[10]H. L. Mencken, *Happy Days, 1880-1892* (New York: Alfred A. Knopf, 1940) 170.

[11]Patrick Donnelly, "The Milwaukee Public Schools" in *Columbian History of Education in Wisconsin*, ed. by John W. Stearns (Milwaukee, 1893) 458-459.

[12]Cunz, *op. cit.*, 335.

[13] William I. Thomas and Florian Znaniecki, *The Polish Peasant in Europe and America* (New York: Dover) vol. II, 1533.

[14] Wells, *op. cit.*, 149.

[15] Roger Wyman, "Wisconsin Ethnic Groups and the Election of 1890," *Wisconsin Magazine of History* IL (Summer 1968) 277.

[16] *Ibid.*, 290.

[17] Luebke, German-American Alliance, *op. cit.*, 165 ff.

[18] Wittke, German-Language Press, *op. cit.*, 238-239.

[19] H. L. Mencken, *Newspaper Days*, 1899-1905 (New York: Alfred A. Knopf, 1941) 252-253.

[20] John Blum, *Woodrow Wilson and the Politics of Morality* (Boston: Little, Brown, 1956) 95.

[21] Wittke, German-Language Press, *op. cit.*, 239.

[22] O. John Rogge, *The Official German Report* (New York and London: Thomas Yoseloff, 1961) 137.

[23] Georg Sylvester Viereck, *My Flesh and Blood* (New York: Horace Liveright, 1931) 203.

[24] Georg Sylvester Viereck, *Spreading Germs of Hate* (New York: Horace Liveright, 1930), see especially chapter 6.

[25] Herman Ridder, *Hyphenations* (New York: M. Schmetterling, 1915).

[26] Wittke, German-Language Press, *op. cit.*, 241.

[27] Hagedorn, *op. cit.*, 235.

[28] Cited in Richard O'Connor, *The German-American* (Boston and Toronto: Little, Brown, 1968) 415.

[29] George N. Schuster, "Those of German Descent," *Common Ground* (Winter 1943).

[30] Quoted from Alfred Kazin, *On Native Grounds, An Interpretation of Modern American Prose Literature* (New York: Reynal & Hitchcock, 1942) 198 ff.

[31] H. L. Mencken, "Die Deutschamerikaner," *Die Neue Rundschau* XXXLX (November 1928) 486-495.

[32] Peter Gay, "Weimar Culture: The Outsider as Insider," in Donald Fleming and Bernard Baily, *The Intellectual Migration, Europe and America, 1930-1960* (Cambridge: Harvard University Press, 1969) 12.

[33] H. Stuart Hughes, "Franz Neumann, Between Marxism and Democracy," in *ibid.*, 460.

[34] Donald Fleming, "Emigre Physicists and the Biological Revolution," in *ibid.*, 163.

[35] See Charles Weiner, "A New Site for the Seminar: The Refugee and American Physics in the Thirties," in *ibid.*

[36] J. M. Mandler and G. Mandler, "The Diaspora of Experimental Psychology: The Gestaltists and Others," in *ibid.*

[37] William H. Jordy, "The Aftermath of the Bauhaus in America," in *ibid.*

[38] Colin Eisler, "Kunstgeschichte American Style: A Study in Migration," in *ibid.*

[39] See Maurice R. Davie, *Refugees in America* (New York: Harper & Row, 1947).

[40]See Linus Spuler, "Von deutschamerikanischer Dichtung,"
*German-American Studies*, vol. I, no. 1 (1969).  For
*Emigraten-Literatur* or *Exil-Literatur*, the mass of
German-language literature by emigrees, see Robert E.
Cazden, *German Exile Literature in America 1933-1950*
(Chicago: American Library Association, 1970).

[41]Klaus Kipphan, *Deutsche Propaganda in den Vereinigten Staaten,
1933-1941*, Beiheft zum Jahrbuch für Amerikastudien
(Heidelberg: Universitätsverlag, 1971) 56-57.  Gissibl
later returned to the Third Reich to serve as a captain
in the Elite Guard.

[42]Rogge, *op. cit.*, 21.

[43]Kipphan, *op. cit.*, 62.

[44]*Ibid.*, 66.

[45]Rogge, *op. cit.*, 33.

[46]Kipphan, *op. cit.*, 82.

[47]*Ibid.*, 82.

[48]Joachim Remak, "Friends of the New Germany: The Bund and
German-American Relations," *The Journal of Modern History*,
vol. XXIX, no. 1 (March 1957) 38-41.

[49]Rogge, *op. cit.*, 50.

[50]John E. Hofman, "The Language Transition in Some Lutheran
Denominations," Joshua A. Fishman, ed., *Readings in the
Sociology of Language* (The Hague: Mouton, 1968) 621.

[51]Carl S. Meyer, *Log Cabin to Luther Tower: Concordia Seminary
. . . 1839-1964* (St. Louis: Concordia, 1965) 136-137.

[52]Hofman, *op. cit.*, 627.

[53]John A. Hostetler and Gertrude Enders Huntington, *The Hutterites in North America* (New York: Holt, Rinehart and
Winston, 1967) 1-4.

[54]John W. Bennett, *Hutterite Brethren: The Agricultural Economy
and Social Organization of a Communal People* (Stanford,
Ca.: Stanford University Press, 1967) 160.

[55]Hostetler and Huntington, *op. cit.*, 98 ff.

[56]John A. Hostetler, *Amish Society*, rev. ed. (Baltimore: John
Hopkins, 1968) 325 ff.

# CONCLUSION

## THE GERMAN-AMERICANS AND AMERICAN CULTURAL DIVERSITY

The thousands of German immigrants who enter the United States each year scatter widely throughout the country but are particularly concentrated in urban areas.  In a number of cities, large and small, they form concentrations substantial enough to permit the survival of at least part of the institutions and organizations established generations ago to serve much larger constituencies.  A glance at the social columns of the regional German language newspapers reveals the continued existence of various singing groups, a *Damenchor Liederkranz* or *Männerchor*, and such musical clubs as a *Deutscher Musikverein*, as well as performing groups of instrumentalists. Metropolitan areas and their surrounding suburbs in many instances still sustain benevolent societies of various kinds an *Unterstützungsverein* or *Arbeiter Krankenkasse*.  Only a fragment remains of the once powerful political-gymnastic organization of the *Turnvereine* found in almost all German-American communities in the nineteenth and early twentieth centuries. But on a Thursday evening in San Francisco or Milwaukee one can still "turnen" with other members of the local *Turnvereine*. Provincial loyalties among the German-born prompt some of them to seek social relationships in such regional societies as the *Schwaben Verein* for the Swabians or the *Bayern Bund* for the Bavarians.  In some communities *Schulvereine*, or school societies, provide German language courses, usually for three hours on Saturday, largely for the children of immigrant parents. More general associations, like the *Hermanns Söhne*, still function as social organizations in communities in various parts of the country.  In areas where more than a few societies and clubs exist, an association of German-American societies is often organized to coordinate the activities of the German-American population.  In some places in the United States, the German-born and their families can, if they choose, rely largely upon such organizations for their social relationships and leisure time activities.  But the German language church, the

German language schools system, the German labor associations,
the political organizations, and the myriad numbers of large
and active *Vereine* that once served as intermediating structures between the individual German-American and what seemed
to him the complex, anonymous society around him—these no
longer survive except in a few spots especially favorable for
their existence.

Any extensive contact of the first generation with the
numerous elements of German ancestry (of the third or fourth
generation) in any community is not readily achieved.  The
German-American community in its historical, corporate sense
no longer exists except in a few special areas of the country.
Nevertheless, some measure of contact still occurs through the
churches and voluntary associations.  In Lutheran churches with
German traditions, most of the membership is likely to be, as
in the past, predominantly German in origin even though the
churches have in the past generation sought to overcome any
ethnic exclusiveness in church membership.  Because of the
relatively high degree of stability in ethnic membership of
Lutheran churches, they provide an institutional context for
the meeting of church-oriented Lutheran immigrants with the
descendants of earlier immigrants.  In general, however, the
absence of strong sentiments of shared interests and experiences between newcomers and the mass of Americans of German
ancestry often inhibits any sustained relationship.  Such national associations as the Steuben Society are today much more
concerned with cultivating knowledge and appreciation of German contributions to America than they are in preserving any
kind of collective ethnic entity or in nurturing their distinctive cultural traditions.

The Steuben Society, as a voluntary association of a certain segment of the American citizenry that is "wholly or in
part of Germanic extraction," remains dedicated to effective
political action on behalf of good government through lobbying
and other means at the national, state, and local level.  It
has challenged what it regards as the tendency of earlier generations of German-Americans to shun participation in public
affairs.  The Steuben Society is organized in local units and
in state, county, and regional councils throughout the country;
but the membership is particularly concentrated in New York and
New Jersey.  The members continue to work to advance the general awareness among all segments of the population of the accomplishments of their German-American ancestors.  The Society's *Steuben News* of May 1973 called attention to the proposal
of Congressman John R. Rarick, Democrat of Louisiana, to give
"over-due recognition" to General von Steuben by the erection
of a national monument in his honor; it is a proposal, it was
noted, that merits "the support not only of all good Steuben-
ites and their Units, but of the entire German American

Community throughout our great Nation." The Society claims to
be politically independent. It has developed a set of political platforms relating to national and state political issues.
Its "Briefs" present formal statements of policy on a wide
range of topics of contemporary interest to its membership:
pollution, fiscal responsibility, social security reform, drug
control, capital punishment, mass transit, and others. Through
its National Committee on Public Affairs, the Steuben Society
has exerted a significant influence in political life, particularly in regions where its membership is largely concentrated,
through systematic and energetic lobbying in Washington and
Albany. The Society seeks to gain honorable recognition for
distinguished German-Americans of all political persuasions who
have exerted a significant influence upon American life. But
the Society's political positions reflect the more conservative
political traditions of some elements of the German-American
population rather than the more liberal and radical traditions
of the Forty-eighters and the German-American leaders in labor
legislation and labor organization in the last decades of the
nineteenth century.

The German American National Congress (Deutschamerikanischer National Kongres or D.A.N.K.) with headquarters in Chicago, like the Steuben Society, takes political positions in
state and national politics. It is credited with exerting considerable influence among some segments of the German-Americans
subscribing to *Der Deutschamerikaner*, its official organ. Actually there is little verification by careful scholars of
broad popular support of such organizations or indeed of any
tendency among contemporary Americans of German ancestry to expect or seek representation of their political interests
through ethnically based organizations.

There are a number of regional historical associations
that have sections devoted to the study of local German settlements and their influence. They serve to encourage and direct interest in both broad and specialized aspects of the
historical experience of the group in America. They serve also
to provide invaluable aid to the numerous scholars in the
United States whose research interests relate to such matters.
In geographical areas where German ethnic influence has longest
and firmest traditions, one would expect to find the best organized voluntary associations. Among such organizations are
the Society for the History of the Germans in Maryland, which
publishes *The Report*, a journal relating to history of the
Germans in Maryland and surrounding areas. The German Society
of Pennsylvania reflects the interest of various distinctive
elements in the region of diverse German backgrounds and origins. The Society for German-American Studies publishes a
journal, *German-American Studies*, which, in its careful scholarship on German-American literature, gives evidence of an

enduring and authentic interest in German-American poets, prose
writers, dramatists, and journalists of the past and present.

Among the most venerable of these societies is the Pennsylvania German Society, which, among its various activities, published sixty-three volumes of its *Proceedings* between 1890 and
1966.   The articles published over the period of almost seven
decades reflect, in substantial measure, the range and inten-
sity of the interest of its members in such aspects of the
group's history and culture as biographies and geneologies,
the influence of Pennsylvania Germans individually and collectively upon local, regional and national life; the nature and
circumstances of emigration from the Palatinate; vital records
of births, baptisms, confirmations, marriages and deaths; military accounts and records of service; social conditions and
home life; and language, literature, and folk culture.   People
of widely varying professional interests and occupational backgrounds have been associated with the Society, and contributors
to the *Proceedings* have included many distinguished scholars
as well as local historians and antiquarians.   The Pennsylvania
German Folklore Society was organized in 1935; and while sharing many of the fields of interest of the older group, it
focused more especially upon folk art and music, architecture,
language studies and dialect literature, and the various arts
and crafts of the Pennsylvania Germans including the practical
crafts of iron work, wagon making, tool and implement making,
gun manufacturing, coppersmithy, and others.   In 1966 the two
organizations combined to form the Pennsylvania German Society
with headquarters at Breinigsville, Pennsylvania.   The Society
produces a new series of *Publications* edited by Pastor Frederick Weiser, a descendant of Conrad Weiser, and a periodical,
*Der Reggeboge* (The Rainbow).   While members share a strong interest in Pennsylvania German history and culture in general,
their individual spheres of activity and special interest within this broad category differ widely.   Membership provides the
means of discovering others with whom one shares particular
personal and hobby or research interests.   Membership also af-
fords, as the April 1973 issue of *Der Reggeboge* explains, the
"privilege of . . . using the headquarter's facilities and be
classed with an elite society interested in the ways of our
successful Pennsylvania Dutch forebears."

Among the most remarkable and certainly among the most
vigorous groups are the American Historical Society of Germans
from Russia (AHSGR), and the North Dakota Historical Society
of Germans from Russia.   These societies draw their membership
from the Middle West and West where Russian-German settlements
were most strongly developed in the nineteenth and early
twentieth centuries.   The preimmigration experiences of the
German colonists in Russia in preserving the language and culture of *"Unser Leute"* (our people) bred a particularly strong

sense of identity and led to the accumulation of substantial
knowledge about culture and language maintenance.  The AHSGR
is primarily concerned with the history of the colonies in
Russia and the Russian-German settlement and dispersion in
America.  Much attention is given in the annual membership
meetings and in their publications to the history of their
intricately interrelated families.  Seminars are held in practical geneology, and well-trained scholars and specialists of
Russian-German origin have provided excellent instruction and
guidance for those who wish to trace their families back to the
Russian colonies and ultimately back to the province of origin
in Germany.  Both organizations maintain a close relationship
with their Russian-German counterpart in Stuttgart, the *Landsmannschaft der Deutschen aus Russland*.  While they have largely
assimilated into American society, the descendants of German
colonists in Russia are maintaining a strong sense of family
and group identity.  Their earlier experience as a minority in
Russia and their concentrated settlement in particular areas
in the United States have facilitated that retention.

For most Americans of German ancestry, the connections
with a German past are more tenuous and less important.  But
the meaning attached to ethnic origins among the present generation is not easy to describe or assess and indeed may well
have dimensions that scholars of immigration history and ethnicity have not suspected.

What is the substance of the memories and attachments that
are associated with one's self-identification as an "American
of German origin?"  There may be many constituent parts of it:
the memory of the distinctive German character of grandparents;
Christmas songs and the warmth of the traditional way the family celebrates Christmas; the lingering taste for German baking
and cooking; the bonds with a church (Lutheran, Mennonite, and
others) with some residue of German traditions; some values
that seem to have been ingrained into family life by German
forebears; visits and correspondence with relatives remaining
in Germany; the German *Bibel* and Prayer Book that are more than
heirlooms; remembered German words like *Gemütlichkeit*, or evoc-
ative phrases like *um Gottes Willen*, or half-remembered German
songs and nursery rhymes that are still part of family communication; the volumes of Schiller and Goethe brought from Germany;
the ornate baptismal certificates in *fraktur*; the knowledge
that in some way or other, the chain of generations links one
to antecedents in Germany; or perhaps only a vaguer sense of
family origins, loyalty, or curiosity.  For some there are many
of these, for others few, for still others none.

German immigration flowed without interruption over a
longer period of time than that from any country except Great
Britain.  The influx of people from Germany over the course of
generations was the largest and most diverse of the immigrant

groups coming from continental Europe. The fragmented state
system of pre-Bismarckian Germany was characterized by a great
variability in political institutions and traditions; German
*Kleinstätterei* gives testimony not only to political diversity
but to social, economic, and cultural diversity of the German
people during most of the period of almost three centuries of
emigration to North America. The main flow of *Auswanderung*
changed its course from time to time, first draining population
from one geographical area or segment of German society and
then shifting its course to drain another. In the last three
decades of the nineteenth century, a whole network of tribu-
taries fed into the mainstream simultaneously; this made the
flow of emigrants more representative of the total German population both regionally and socially than it had ever been
before. The existence of major temporal shifts in the dimensions and demographic selectivity of the *Auswanderung* has made
it useful to describe the generalized patterns of the migratory
movements: the early colonial settlements of Rhenish Quakers,
Mennonites, and Pietists; the eighteenth century Lutheran and
Reformed settlements of farmers and artisans from the Rhineland; the westward-bound *Dreissiger* of the 1830s and 1840s; the
communalistic settlements of Zoar, Teutonia, and other religious and secular groups in the fourth and fifth decades of the
nineteenth century; the swelling influx of the late 1840s and
late antebellum period, particularly the liberal refugees from
the aftermath of the Revolution of 1848, including German-
Christians, freethinkers, and Jews; the Saxon Lutherans who
fled the attempts at state control of religious life; the German Lutherans, Mennonites, and Catholics from the autonomous
German colonies in Russia; the large influx of farmers, workers,
artisans, and professional people from all sections of Germany
in the late nineteenth century; and the political and religious
refugees from Hitlerian Germany. Other less easily characterized German groups entered as well. Each of those described
was characterized by noteworthy variations, but nonetheless
the description of the generalized patterns provided in this
survey illustrates the diversity of German *Einwanderung* to
America.

The forces that impelled individuals and families to leave
the homeland and the forces that attracted them to North America varied greatly from period to period and from social group
to social group as the diversity of groups clearly reveals.

The immigration was diverse not only in its continental
origins but also in its patterns of settlement in America.
Movements occurring over so long a period of time and embracing
social groups so heterogeneous were bound to show great variability in the place and circumstances of settlement. The newcomers scattered widely over the American landscape, although
areas of particular concentration were formed in various major

geographical regions of the country and in some instances persisted for several generations.

German America was in a state of continual change that was
perhaps inevitable in a social environment so predominantly
Anglo-American in character.  The Pennsylvania Germans established their own separate and distinct American identity.
Their society was and remains neither German nor Anglo-American,
but a combination of both with distinctive elements arising directly from neither but rather from their own peculiar experience in America.  If some groups of German origin have been the
most resistant to absorption, the vast majority of them have
been among the most rapidly acculturating of immigrant populations.  German-born residents acculturated relatively quickly.
The acculturation of people within any group of German newcomers was apt to vary significantly from individual to individual according to the interplay of a number of social and
personal factors.  The differences reflect the contrasting cultural elements that they brought with them, the social character of the regions and classes from which they were selectively
drawn, as well as the time and circumstances of their introduction into American society.  The general experience of the
various national groups coming in varying numbers and at different times has been vastly different.  Particularly in the
beginning of the large scale immigration of each group, the
immigrant generation has sought to perpetuate those values,
exercise those preferences, and preserve those ways that seemed
most important to them.  Also there were always the external
influences in the decisions the individual immigrant had to
make in his accommodation to American life concerning what was
useful or not useful, appropriate or inappropriate, good or bad,
under the altering circumstances of his life.

German America existed in large enough scale and in populations concentrated sufficiently to permit the exercise of
some choice in the matter of preserving a measure of old-world
cultural life and institutions in the new world.  The church,
the German language schools, the German language press and literature, the benevolent societies, the *Vereine*, the beer gardens, ties of family and friendship, and the shared memories
and attachments to the old country permitted a community life
among many foreign-born that preserved much of the culture that
they most prized; this allowed their accommodation to American
life to proceed with less personal travail than might otherwise
have been true.  The German-born and their children lived in a
cultural world that was in reality a shifting hybridization of
German and Anglo-American cultural elements.  But the pace of
change varied greatly from time to time and from place to place
and according to individual preferences.  Sometimes German immigrants lived much of their lives in their new homeland in a
cultural environment that was largely transitional; sometimes

circumstances or their own choice brought a more rapid and radical accommodation. Where the cultural intrusions of the Anglo-American world were powerful, the gap in values and perspectives between the first generation and their children was likely to be sharp and bring differences painful to both. Where change was less rapid the accommodation of the younger generation to American ways was likely to be less perceptible and less productive of inter-personal strife. In the normal course of events, the immigrant generation was replaced by their children's generation whose ties to the old world were weaker and whose contacts with American society more extensive than those of their parents. Only in communities where the degree of social solidarity was exceptional and the traditional European institutions largely intact could the erosion of old world culture be halted. This occurred rarely. Almost inexorably, German-American families experienced the first difficulties of initial accommodation to American communities, then acculturation, and finally assimilation. Sometimes the process occurred in a single generation; sometimes it took three or more generations. Assimilation removed people of German ancestry from significant participation in German-American community life. But what was subtracted was replaced by immigrants fresh from Germany. The net balance of loss and gain was important to the continuity of the German-American community.

The broad social consequences of German immigration to the historical evolution of the national community are difficult to define and measure. One of the most common ways of demonstrating the substantial quality of contributions made by national groups is to parade the names of the great and influential men of that nationality in America. Filiopiety dictates the recording of presidents (Eisenhower was of German and Hoover of German-Swiss origin), generals and admirals (Nimitz, Arnold, Eichelberger, Eisenhower, and others), statesmen (Schurz and Kissinger), writers and artists (Dreiser, Wolfe, Damrosch), cartoonists of genius (Thomas Nast and Charles Schulz), scientists and professors (Einstein, Steinmetz, von Braun), folk heroes and great athletes (Babe Ruth, Bob Meusel, Honus Wagner, and Lou Gehrig) and—to show objectivity—some particularly notorious criminals of that nationality (perhaps John Dillinger). American theologians like Paul Tillich and Reinhold Niebuhr have exerted an influence upon their contemporaries as significant as that of the foremost European theologians like Emil Brunner and Karl Barth. The other theologians like Walter Rauschenbusch and E. Richard Niebuhr have also been distinguished.

It was once said that people of German origin were less interested in politics and played a lesser role than other major ethnic groups in the highest levels of government. In any case, this is no longer true. The distinguished men and women

of German origin in all of the fields named are abundant and
their influence individually and collectively is immensely important in American history.  It is far more difficult, however,
to assess the consequence to American social history of the
presence of millions of ordinary persons of German (or any
other) ancestry.  The collective significance of these more
numerous groups may well outweigh that of the eminent men.  The
impact of German influence in the country generally and in regions of concentrated settlement, such as Wisconsin or Pennsylvania, cannot be adequately represented by an examination of
the lives and influence of its most eminent men alone.  Social
and cultural history has been impoverished by the failure thus
far characterizing the efforts of historians and social scientists to record and analyze what happens when culturally different people come into intimate contact and, in interaction
over a substantial period of time, come to form a single cultural community different from its constituent groups.

Although the instruments are not yet available for the
kind of cultural and social history that would reveal the
principal dimensions of immigrant influence on host societies,
they will certainly be developed in time.  When they do develop and when they are directed to the systematic analysis of
the influence of immigrants on the evolution of American society, it is likely that the impact of the diverse streams of
immigrants from Germany will emerge as one of the major influences in American social history.

# INDEX

# DATE DUE

| | | |
|---|---|---|
| ~~APR 1 '76~~ | | |
| MAR 2 '77 | | |
| ~~OC 29 '81~~ | | |
| ~~SE 26 '83~~ | | |
| | | |
| OCT 11 '90  OCT 12 '90 | | |
| MAR 28 '96 | | |
| RT'D  APR 0 4 '96 | | |
| | | |
| NOV 1 0 2004 | | |
| | | |
| | | |
| | | |
| | | |
| | | |

187

Pastorius, Franz Daniel
  commemoration of arrival,
    143
  as leader in Germantown,
    10-13
Penn, William, 10, 11, 12, 16
Pennsylvania:
  in American Revolution, 36 ff
  arrival of Anabaptists in,
    20-21
  early settlement of Germans
    in, 10-15, 29
  Economy Settlement, 52
  ethnic diversity in, 20
  German enlistment in Civil
    War, 88-89
Pennsylvania Dutch (see Pennsylvania Germans)
Pennsylvania Germans, 110-119
  area of concentrated settle-
    ment, 111
  attachment to land, 31
  early settlement in, 12 ff,
    29
  education of, 113
  family life, 31
  folk art and music, 73, 116,
    118
  homes and barns, 32, 111
  language and literature,
    114, 115, 116
  religious life among, 35, 36
  Benjamin Rush's comments
    on, 30
  spread out from Pennsyl-
    vania, 24
Pennsylvanish (as German dialect), 35, 112-114, 115-117
Peoria (Illinois), 124
Pershing, General John J., 142
Pestalozzi, Heinrich, 85
Philadelphia, 11, 25, 37, 62,
  122-124, 126-127
Place names, German, 48, 142
Pochmann, Henry A., 124
Political party affiliations,
  125
Precht, Viktor, writer, 124
Presbyterians, 57, 142

Professional journals in Ger-
  man, 100-101
Prohibition, 127-129
Prussia
  conditions in, 77
  Lutheran dissenters from, 58
Pulitzer, Joseph, 82

Quakers, German, 10-13, 16,
  36-37

Raine, Friedrich, Baltimore
  editor, 64
Rapp, Johan Georg, 52
Rauschenbusch, Walter, 178
Reading (Pennsylvania), 64,
  124
Reformed Church, 110, 114
  in American Revolution, 36
  in early colonies, 22
  leadership of Michael
    Schlatter, 22
  relations with Lutherans, 58
Reichert, Richard Hess, 118
Reizel, Robert, writer, 122
*Republik der Arbeiter, Die*,
  working class journal, 83,
  85
Revolution of 1848, 77 ff
Ridder, Bernard, 158
Ridder, Herman, 139
Ridder, Victor, 158
Rochester, 157
Röbling, John A., 99
Roosevelt, Theodore, 141
Rosencrans, General William,
  89
Röthlisberger, Marcel, 154
Rush, Benjamin, 29 ff
Russian Germans:
  colonies in Russia, 92
  ethnic cohesiveness, 174-175
  settlement in America, 93
Rütlinger, J. J.:
  on social characteristics of
    Americans, 72, 76
  treatment of Indians, 76, 77
Ruttlinghausen, William, 12